UNITY, PLURALITY AND POLITICS

ESSAYS IN HONOUR OF F.M. BARNARD

F.M. BARNARD
Photographed by Erik Singer

unity
plurality
&
politics

ESSAYS IN HONOUR OF F.M. BARNARD

EDITED BY

J.M. PORTER AND RICHARD VERNON

ST. MARTIN'S PRESS
New York

Scholarly & Reference Division,
St. Martin's Press, Inc., 175 Fifth Avenue, New York, NY 10010
First published in the United States of America in 1986
Printed in Great Britain

Library of Congress Cataloging in Publication Data
Main entry under title:

Unity, plurality, and politics.

    Bibliography: p.
    Includes index.
    1. Political science—Addresses, essays, lectures.
2. Political sociology—Addresses, essays, lectures.
3. Barnard, F.M. (Frederick M.) I. Barnard, F.M.
(Frederick M.) II. Porter, J.M. (Jene M.), 1937–
III. Vernon, Richard, 1945–
JA71.U55   1986   306′.2   85-26262
ISBN 0-312-83331-8

CONTENTS

PREFACE

Nations have a unity often described as 'cultural'; and within them there are divergences some of which are termed 'political'. But culture and politics do not, therefore, comprise two wholly distinct zones or orders of experience, the one marked by unity, the other by plurality. For in political experience what is diversely viewed may be unity itself: that is, rivalry may concern the themes or the symbols or the history in which identity may be found, though what is found there is not always the same, nor necessarily self-consistent. Similarly, just as plurality within nations may not be absolute, the plurality of nations is not wholly unqualified. For the diverse local ways of living and understanding termed 'cultures' may share a common human experience. It is differently mediated, as it were, in each national experience, just as national identity is itself subject to discrepant political interpretations.

The above thoughts are meant to resemble — at least approximately — Herder's. The relevance of noting them here is that F.M. Barnard has taken Herder's thoughts not as a subject of mere historical curiosity — nor as mere dogma — but as the source of questions which demand attention. For some, the history of ideas has at best only an oblique relation to contemporary concerns: it is one of the strengths of F.M. Barnard's writings, however, that they insist on the interdependence of the historical and the contemporary. Intellectual history, political sociology and political philosophy may be present in varying proportions in his writings, but are never wholly detachable from one another. We may thus ascribe to him something which Hanna Spencer, in her contribution below, attributes to Heine: 'an uncanny sensitivity to the portents of ideas'.

That ideas have consequences is implied, above all, by the central political concerns of F.M. Barnard's writings. His concern has not been to advance one kind of politics or another; he has sought to rediscover what necessarily forms the context of political life. And politics, however its ends are conceived, is scarcely sustainable in a context in which all human actions are held to be reducible to, and thus explainable by, causes independent of the actor's purported reasons, will or intentions. Hence it has been a continuing task to explore the relation between reason and action, will and action, culture and politics; here, too, what F.M. Barnard has written has been consistently informed by an acute sense of the relevance of one realm for another.

We have tried to capture something of this sense in planning this volume. We solicited contributions from scholars familiar with F.M. Barnard's work, drawing their attention to the theme noted above, but imposing no limitations on topics or styles of enquiry. The results, unsurprisingly, cover a good deal of ground. But whether the essays have taken as their overt theme that of history, or myth, or *patria*, or political will, or community, they shed light upon the terms through which societies experience and interpret their own unity, and also come to terms with, or else suppress, their own plurality. They do not suggest any single answer. They do, however, attest to the importance of the question which F.M. Barnard has tried to keep before us; and they may remind us that — as he has always insisted — what constitutes politics is itself a question, and not someone's answer to it.

1 HEINE'S 'VARIOUS CONCEPTS OF HISTORY'

Hanna Spencer

The following, in translation,[1] are reflections by Heinrich Heine which were found among his literary remains:

The Book of History is given various interpretations. Among them two completely opposing views are prominent. There are those who see in everything on earth only a cheerless cycle. In the lives of nations, as in the lives of individuals, just as in organic nature generally, they perceive a perpetual cycle of growing, blooming, fading and dying: spring, summer, autumn, winter. "There is nothing new under the sun" is their slogan. And even this is nothing new, having been mournfully proclaimed by the King of the Orient two thousand years ago. They shrug their shoulders over our civilization, which will give way to barbarism again anyhow. They shake their heads at our struggles for liberation, which will merely produce new tyrants. They smile at the aspirations of political enthusiasts who would strive to make this a better and happier world, because the fervor will cool in the end without having borne any fruit. In the little chronicle of hopes and fears, of afflictions and mishaps, pains and pleasures, of mistakes and disappointments which make up the life of the individual, in this human story they also see the history of mankind.

In Germany especially, the sages of the Historic School and the poets of Goethe's age of art lean toward this view. With this attitude the latter like to glamorize their own emotional indifference to all the political concerns of their fatherland. A well known Government in North Germany particularly welcomes this point of view, practically offering travel grants on the strength of it, so that a person may cultivate these soothing, fatalistic thoughts among the elegiac ruins of Italy and then, together with preachers of Christian servility, dampen the three-day-fever of the people with cool journalistic compresses . . .[2]

In contrast to this ill-fated fatalistic outlook there is a brighter one, one closer to the idea of a providence, according to which all things of this world are maturing toward a beautiful state of perfection and great heroes and heroic eras are merely stages and steps on the way to a higher, more godlike human condition. Man's moral and political struggles will

1

eventually result in perfect peace and brotherhood, and eternal bliss. The Golden Age, so they say, lies not behind us but before us; we were not driven from paradise with a flaming sword but must conquer it with a flaming heart – with love. The fruit of knowledge gives us not death but eternal life.

Disciples of this view have long used "civilization" as their motto. In Germany, the School of Humanitas, above all, was dedicated to it. How unequivocally the so-called Philosophic School tends in that direction is commonly known. It gave impetus to enquiries into political questions and culminates in the vision of an ideal state, based entirely on reason, which ultimately shall make mankind noble and happy. There is, I suppose, no need to name the enthusiastic champions of this view. In any event, their high aspirations are more pleasing than the petty convolutions of lowly creepers:[3] and if one day we fight against them, then with the most precious sword of honour, while the most congenial means of despatching the creeping knave is the knout.[4]

Neither of these two positions is really in accord with our most instinctive feelings about life. On the one hand we don't want to be enthusiastic in vain and stake our all on the useless and futile; on the other hand we also want the present to retain its own worth and not be regarded merely as a means toward a future end. Indeed, we feel ourselves to be more important than mere means to an end. At any rate, it seems to me that ends and means are simply conventional concepts which man has philosophised into nature and into history, concepts of which the Creator knew nothing. For each thing created is an end in itself, each event issues from its own cause, and everything exists and happens for its own sake, like the universe itself.

Life is neither an end nor a means: life is a right. Life wants to assert this right against the rigidity of death, against the past, and this assertion is Revolution. The elegiac indifference of historians and poets must not be allowed to paralyse us in this undertaking. The fantasies of utopian dreamers must not mislead us into forfeiting the present. The right most urgently to be fought for is the right to live. 'Le pain est le droit du peuple' said Saint-Just, and these are the greatest words spoken in the entire Revolution.

This mini-essay was published by A. Strodtmann, the first Heine biographer and editor of his collected works, in 1869 – 13 years after Heine's death – in the volume *Letzte Gedichte und Gedanken von Heinrich Heine* (Heine's Last Poems and Thoughts). The title *Verschiedenartige Geschichtsauffassung* (Various Concepts of History) was probably Strodtmann's. Far from representing Heine's final position, the passage was probably written in the early 1830s, when Heine, too, was in his thirties. He was already well known. Not, however, as the poet of *Buch der Lieder* (Book of Songs) on which his reputation was to be solidly based throughout the nineteenth century. *Buch der Lieder* had appeared in 1827 but without creating much interest: it was only a decade later that its popularity began to soar. Eventually, this collection of bitter-sweet songs of unrequited love was to achieve an unprecedented circulation in German speaking countries (second only to the Bible!), becoming perhaps the most widely known book of poetry anywhere. In the early 1830s, Heine was famous — and notorious — mainly as the author of *Reisebilder* (Travel Sketches). Beginning with the amusing, though still relatively harmless *Harzreise* (Journey through the Harz Mountains) and ending with the hilariously provocative Italian Sketches, these feuilletonistic essays created a sensation among German readers and established his reputation as a social and political humourist and iconoclast. Even then he was surrounded by a controversy which was to continue, in one form or another, well into the twentieth century. In some quarters, it has barely abated even today.[5] His readers were challenged and delighted by his whimsical observations, his scintillating style, his penetrating insights, his satirical irreverence and, above all, his humour. He had a rare talent for giving fresh, unexpected significance to a familiar object or situation through a flash of wit. It was this ability to simultaneously amuse, illumine and expose which turned his essays into journeys of discovery. But what charmed some readers, shocked and infuriated others. The fourth (and last) volume of *Reisebilder* was banned in Prussia immediately upon publication.

There is, however, nothing particularly shocking — not at a first glance, at any rate — in this little essay that here, as far as I know, makes its debut in English. Nor does it exhibit any of Heine's humour or proverbial irony. The topic of emancipation, of political engagement, of what he usually calls *Enthusiasmus*, is one of the few about which he rarely joked.

The piece speaks for itself. As a matter of fact, Heine invariably speaks best for himself: Heine quotations are usually the most telling - quite aside from most amusing — passages in commentaries on him. He was a supreme master of German prose, one who has been credited with having had a liberating influence on the German literary language, making it more concrete, more lively, more flexible, more reflecting the casual flow of the spoken word. That he should have regenerated and enriched the German language is all the more remarkable since he lived for the last 25 years of his life — that is to say, during the better part of his writing career — in Paris, exiled into a foreign language.

The seemingly effortless ease of Heine's style is very deceptive, as the translator quickly learns. This apparently casual language is, in fact, deliberate and dense. Not only does Heine exploit the subtle nuance of every word, he often brings out the literal, concrete image contained in an expression and then plays with it in subsequent formulations, thus reinforcing the uncovered meaning. His sentences, therefore, are triply bound: syntactically, semantically and metaphorically. In translation, something has to give; the more faithfully one reproduces Heine's intention, the more stilted the effect. And so, what in the original sounds fresh and lively, may turn out laboured or mannered. Explanatory comments on Heine's terse or veiled references occasionally need to be complemented by observations on his writing technique. He is a calculating writer, intent on blurring the line between medium and message, skilled at taking the reader where he want him. What he says is rarely separable from the way in which he says it. Manipulation? Of course. But what may be reprehensible in a social scientist may also be the hallmark of a successful poet. No wonder Plato wanted poets banned from his Republic!

With his very first word Heine introduces a pregnant metaphor: '*Das Buch der Geschichte findet mannigfache Auslegungen.*' Not simply 'history', but 'the book of history'. A book is a man-made product and its interpretations may be varied and subjective. So it seems a sensible term to lead into a discussion of divergent ways of reading history. Or should it be writ large? Do we sense the possibility of an allusion to a less modest sort of book, perhaps in analogy to the book of books, *biblia*? This would place history in both realms, the human and the divine. Augustinus had done just that in describing history as ordained by God but also the result of human actions; Heine 'merely' uses a metaphor. A metaphor may evoke and suggest without having to prove anything.

'There is nothing new under the sun.' The notion of the circular movement of history is itself a recurring idea, as Heine reminds us, using King Solomon of the Old Testament (chapter 1, verse 9) as his authority. Concepts of an eternal cycle date back to Poseidonios and Pythagoras and, more recently, the 'law of cycles' had been of interest to Giambattista Vico. Heine's work contains references to it elsewhere, most explicitly in a note to *Reise von München nach Genua* (Journey from Munich to Genoa).[6] But this segment was not included in the manuscript which went to the printer. Evidently, while Heine was intrigued and perhaps strangely haunted by the idea of eternal repetition, he was unwilling to accept it. In the passage before us, he makes this rejection rather obvious — well before explicitly stating and explaining it — by a description of this world view that is anything but objective. In fact, he makes the cyclical view seem intrinsically bleak and cheerless — *'gar fatal fatalistisch'* he calls it — almost making us forget that this need not be necessarily so. It it interesting to call to mind, for instance, how differently Nietzsche, a generation later, was to deal with the same notion. A great admirer of Heine, Nietzsche 'borrowed' a surprising number of his major tenets and ideas from his work. For Nietzsche, however, eternal recurrence (*Ewige Wiederkehr des Gleichen*) represents the highest form of affirmation, a joyous 'yes' to life.[7]

Presently the reader is to get an inkling of the cause — though not the reason — for Heine's dislike of the cyclical concept of history: he identifies those whom he associates with this view in Germany. Heine was given to judging ideas by their practical implications and consequences. When he alluded to the *Weltweisen* — the wise men of the historic school — he had a clear idea of what they stood for. Founded by Gustav Hugo (who was a professor at Göttingen University and happened to be Dean of Law and thus Heine's chief examiner when he graduated), and most prominently represented by Karl von Savigny (who was a professor in Berlin while Heine studied there), the historic school was a trend in jurisprudence according to which law is based exclusively on tradition: the history of law is all that matters, overriding any concerns for justice, fair play and reasonableness. Its proponents saw their main task in the search for primary, unwritten sources as the wellspring of what is right. The examination of national, 'organic' authenticity became an end in itself, with each historic fragment considered to be of equal value with the rest. Almost by definition, adherents of this school of thought were against change and found eighteenth-century ideas of progressive reform unacceptable. Heine considered the *Côde Napoléon* to be a model of rational legislation, a product of the Revolution, of the struggle for human rights; whereas the historic school epitomised the antithesis of emancipation, equality and social justice. Savigny, in fact, pleaded successfully for the cancellation of a provision under the Napoleonic code that had been introduced in Prussia, which had granted the Jews the right to citizenship and would have allowed them to hold public positions. Even more specifically: the anti-Semitic Savigny was instrumental in preventing the academic appointment of Eduard Gans. Not to mention the fact that Heine's own hopes for public office had been in vain. It seems a long way from the consideration of the theory of cycles to such experiential evidence, but it was typical of Heine to make these connections. Never taking a phenomenon for granted or seeing it in isolation, he was convinced that 'facts are merely the results of ideas', and he had an uncanny sensitivity to the portents of ideas.

Secondly — so to speak in the same breath — Heine points to 'poets of Goethe's age of art' (*Kunstperiode*) as prone to resort to the cyclical nature of the world as an excuse for their political apathy. The use of the plural may be charged to poetic licence, for Heine's quarrel in this matter was mainly with Goethe. Goethe had recently died but his presence in the minds of Germans continued to be felt. This was especially true for Heine who, throughout his life, never lost sight of his eminent precursor and antipode. His internal dialogue and reckoning with Goethe — more often implied than articulated — is a theme that pervaded his entire work and was actually closely linked to his self-understanding as a writer. At all times he saw in Goethe a supreme, peerless genius. He felt akin to him in his emancipation from religious dogmatism and in his 'Hellenic' embrace of life. But he accused him of *Indifferentismus*, an ivory-towered detachment which he found all the more objectionable since Goethe's voice had been so potentially powerful in Germany. In his words: *'Die Tat ist das Kind des Wortes, und die Goetheschen schönen Worte sind kinderlos.'*[8] (The deed is the child of the word, and Goethe's beautiful words are childless.) On the other hand, by scolding him for his indifference with regard to 'the political concerns of the fatherland', Heine did, by inference, stake out a place for himself as a writer who responded to the concerns of his own time. He saw himself as a torch bearer in the cause of liberation, the representative poet of his age as Goethe had been of his. To be sure, a decade later, when he wished to emphasise his own role as an autonomous artist, albeit still a politically responsive one, he treated Goethe as a model and an ally.

The next target in the context of our passage is the historian Leopold von Ranke whose prolonged study in Italy (1827-32) was supported by the Prussian government. Puns on Ranke's name — puns which by their very nature strike modern readers as tasteless, especially when the obligatory footnote removes the challenge of having to decode them — were intended to identify the recipient of the subsidy without naming him; while the barb at *Prediger christlicher Unterwürfigkeit* (preachers of Christian servility) drew attention to Ranke's friendship with the theologian Schleiermacher. From 1832 onward, Ranke was editor of *Historisch-politische Zeitschrift*. Subsidised by the Prussian authorities, this 'historic-political journal' sought to combat any liberalising movements that may have been stirring in Germany in the wake of the Paris

Revolution of 27-30 July 1830. Hence the 'cool journalistic compresses' that were to bring down the 'three-day-fever of the people' (*'um durch kühle Journalaufschläge das dreitägige Freiheitsfieber des Volkes zu dämpfen'*). Heine had been greatly affected by this event, which he considered to be of epochal significance. He exuberantly welcomed it as the fulfillment of the liberal's ultimate dream: an elected king, victory of the 'little people' - at least that is what he thought then − radical change without terror or bloodshed. His move to Paris followed a year later.

Bias against the cyclical theory and disparaging comments about those who would invite an escape into the past now give way to the other, 'brighter' view. The juxtaposition of contrasting positions in order to emphasise one or the other or both − was one of Heine's favourite, very effective practices. He now pulls out all the stops in extolling those who believe in historic progression and progress. He even gives this world view a certain religious aura by linking it to the 'idea of providence' and then, characteristically, he enriches and reinforces the invoked notion by speaking of a 'paradise' to be conquered by love, and of 'disciples' of civilization. He is careful not to call it a new religion; once again, the evocative metaphor does the work instead, more or less subliminally. As for the thus heightened significance of 'civilization', the author hopes of course that the reader remembers the shrug of contempt with which those others, a page earlier, had dismissed it. A 'school' of *humanitas* (*Humanitätsschule*) − from his beloved Herder and Lessing to Kant and perhaps including some contemporaries like Moses Moser and Eduard Gans − is obviously invented to provide (or complete) the antithetical companion-piece and foil for the 'historic school', once again calling to mind and bringing into focus the contrasting tendencies of both schools of thought.

On the other hand, the 'so-called philosophic school' did exist. The unnamed mentor who postulated the forward movement of history toward a spiritual utopia was, of course, Hegel. When Heine came to Berlin in 1821 to study there, Hegelian philosophy dominated the university. Heine took lectures from him, met him in person, and was a close friend of such devoted Hegel students as Moses Moser and Eduard Gans. A remark in his *Briefe aus Berlin* (Letters from Berlin)[9] ridiculed the atmosphere that was steeped in Hegelian talk and thought, while striking to the core of his own subsequent criticism of Hegel (and, incidentally, anticipating Marx, who was to become his friend 22 years later): *'Wie das unter den Linden wogt! Wie mancher läuft da herum, der noch nicht weiss, wo er heut zu Mittag essen kann! Haben Sie die*

Idee eines Mittagessens begriffen, mein Lieber? Wer diese begriffen hat, der begreift auch das ganze Treiben der Menschen.' (What a hustle and bustle under the linden! Many a one is running around who does not know yet where he can get his noon meal. Have you grasped the idea of a noon meal, my friend? Whosoever comprehends it, comprehends all human activity.) Unfortunately, the English version fails to capture the subtler nuances of the above quotation, although the passage seems straightforward enough. There is no English equivalent for the simple, basic solidity of a German *Mittagessen* – neither 'dinner' nor 'lunch' will do, sounding either too grand or too casual. Conversely, there are overtones in *begreifen* – overtones that have to do with the utter abstractness of *Begriff* – that neither 'grasp' nor 'comprehend' quite capture; and so the irony which results from the blending of *Mittagessen* with *begreifen*, taking aim at Hegel's abstract idealism, is partly lost. Not to mention the loss of Heine's light, idiomatic touch.

Many other Hegel references by the student Heine were flippantly ironic and poked fun at the master's grey eminence. Still, Hegel's influence on him was profound and lasting, even though, as an older Heine admitted, he understood him better in retrospect. In the mid-1830s, Hegelian together with Saint-Simonian influences were reflected in Heine's version of the progressive emergence of the human spirit and man's aspirations, contained in his brilliant essays, *Die Geschichte der Religion und Philosophie in Deutschland* (History of Religion and Philosophy in Germany) and *Die Romantische Schule* (The Romantic School). There, he was to re-interpret and re-evaluate European intellectual history by recording the development of western thought from pre-biblical times onward as a movement of progressive secularisation. Moreover, the search for emancipatory elements in art, philosophy and literature, and the consideration of their effect on socio-political realities, constituted the dominant theme in his reports about the Paris scene. Still later – specifically from 1848 onward – when he was very ill, and disillusioned about the turn of public events, when he witnessed what he perceived to be the consequences of Young Hegelian thinking, resulting not in mature and noble acts of emancipation but in bloody excesses and mob rule, he repudiated Hegel together with his disciples. Heine's position with regard to Hegel is complex as well as controversial. So much depends on the timing of the remarks one chooses to quote. Suffice it to say, his view of Hegel changed with his own changing circumstances and outlook, just as his attitude to Goethe changed. In fact, there is an inverse relationship between his positive and negative evaluation of Goethe and Hegel; which is not altogether surprising since both men came to epitomise certain traits in his self-image.

But let us return to the passage under discussion and to the early 1830s when it was written, when Heine was in his prime, and when in France the Bourbon Charles X had just been replaced, without violence, by the 'Citizen-King' Louis Philippe of Orleans. Having proclaimed the superiority of the optimistic vision of a movement toward a better future and having seemingly given it his spirited endorsement, Heine drops the puzzling hint — initially puzzling at any rate — that he anticipated a conflict with the 'enthusiastic champions' of this view, *'die begeisterten Kämpen dieser Ansicht'*, whom, he says, he need not name. Does he refer to the eighteenth-century rationalists — notably Lessing — who believed that enlightened education alone would bring about advancement toward a more perfect society? Most certainly he meant Hegel's idealism in the realm of speculative philosophy. Hegel had taught him that facts are the results of ideas, yet he condemned the political activists who would change the status quo. This is where Heine's critique of the master set in.

Heine has been credited with having been one of the first to recognise, in the notoriously impenetrable web of Hegel's prose, the radical implications of his thought. He perceived him to be fundamentally radical, at the time when Hegel appeared to be a servile upholder of Prussian authoritarianism. Tongue in cheek, a reminiscing older Heine claimed that Hegel quite deliberately took care not to let fall a single clear unambiguous word, for fear of being understood. With one clever stroke of his pen he thus managed to point to the philosopher's difficult rhetoric, his radicalism and his deference to the Prussian establishment.

After obviously exploiting the gloomy aspects of the notion of cycles in order to make the vision of a progressive movement of history appear all the more appealing and radiant, the author begins the concluding paragraph with the surprising admission that he rejects both views: *'Beide Ansichten... wollen nicht recht mit unseren lebendigsten Lebensgefühlen übereinklingen.'* Our innermost instinct, our 'gut feeling' — the use of the plural allows the possibility that he speaks not only of himself, in the editorial 'we', but of human experience in general — refuses to accept either concept; both kinds of historic design, cyclical and teleological, ultimately diminish the importance of the living self, the here and now. Characteristically, he judged the interpretations of history that he had outlined not by any objective criterion but only on the basis of their impact. Perceiving this effect to be debilitating, he rejects altogether the notion of history having an intrinsic significance, suggesting that meaning exists only in the eyes of the beholder, that pattern or purpose was merely 'philosophised' (*hineingegrübelt*) into history by man. With this, the reflection comes a full circle, leading us, at least by implication, back to the beginning of our passage and to the notion of a man-made 'book of history' that one may interpret as one feels inclined. Life itself, so his feelings and his sense of importance tell him (and he again speaks in the plural), is of overriding importance and value.

This outspoken pronouncement, which to modern ears has a distinctly existentialist ring, surely was bold and unique for the time in which Heine lived; yet it was by no means cynical or nihilistic. On the contrary: his respect for life as the highest good led Heine to call for political engagement, to welcome political *Enthusiasmus* – Fred Barnard might term it 'political will' – in the struggle to achieve the good life for everyone. Heine calls it 'revolution'.

Why was this intriguing little essay, which clearly is too carefully crafted to be considered merely as a casually jotted aside, not printed in Heine's lifetime? Perhaps the stark, existentialist statement would not have passed the censor. Or did Heine himself have doubts? For all his forceful eloquence, did he fail to convince himself? For presumably not long after composing these lines, his energy and attention were taken up with the writing of the momentous twin essays referred to above, *Die Geschichte der Religion und Philosophie in Deutschland* and *Die Romantische Schule*, where he traced western thought in a bold line that was definitely shown to be progressing, leading to the emancipation from Judeo-Christian dogma through German philosophy. This intellectual liberation would surely – Heine was convinced of this at the time – bring about socio-political liberation as well. Heinrich Heine, like Hegel, was certain of the inevitability of the dialectic process; yet he recognised the need for personal involvement in its realisation. Believing in the power of the idea and, consequently, of the written word, he looked on his writing as his active contribution to the 'liberation of mankind'.

Notes

1. I am indebted to my colleague A.R. Anderson for helping me with this translation.

2. The omitted sentence would be pointless in English because it turns mainly on puns on 'Ranke', exploiting the meanings of the words *Ranke* and *Ränke*: climbing, creeping plants, and intrigues. The sentence reads: '*Immerhin, wer nicht*

durch freie Geisteskraft emporspriessen kann, der mag am Boden ranken; jener Regierung aber wird die Zukunft lehren, wie weit man kommt mit Ranken und Ränken.' Hans Kaufmann (ed.), *Heinrich Heine, Werke und Briefe*, Aufbau Verlag, Berlin, 1961-64, vol. 5, p. 378.

3. See note 2 above.

4. The German '*mit der wahlverwandten Knute*' carries connotations that cannot be captured in English, e.g. allusions to the Prussian use of the knout and Ranke's 'elective affinity' with the Prussian police state. That is to say, Heine accuses Ranke of endorsing a servile attitude.

5. To wit: In the 1970s demonstrating students in Düsseldorf carried Heine's name on their banners. They still sport T-shirts with the imprint *Heinrich Heine Universität* to assert their choice of name for their *alma mater* in spite of the refusal of the powers that be to name the institution after the city's famous son. Without wishing to comment on the merit of their cause: what other nineteenth-century author can make a similar claim to 'relevancy'?

6. *Heinrich Heine, Werke*, vol. 3, p. 620.

7. Karl Schlechta (ed.), *Friedrich Nietzsche, Werke und Briefe* (Munich, 1966), vol. 2, p. 1128 (Ecce Homo). For a list of apparent parallels or coincidences, see my article 'Heine and Nietzsche' in *Heine Jahrbuch* XI (Hoffmann und Campe, Hamburg, 1972).

8. *Heinrich Heine, Werke*, vol. 5, p. 50. Heine's ambivalent relationship with Goethe has been the topic of much discussion among, and analysis by, Germanists. I dealt with it in the essay '*Heines Spiel mit Goethes Erbmantel*' in *Dichter, Denker, Journalist* (Peter Lang Verlag, Bern, 1977), pp. 37-51.

9. *Heinrich Heine, Werke*, vol. 3, p. 306.

2 UNITY AND DIVERSITY IN POLITICS: CASSIRER'S MYTHIC MODE REVISITED*

Willard A. Mullins

This essay explores certain links between myth, unity and diversity in politics as understood by the philosopher Ernst Cassirer. He treats this theme explicitly only in his more political writings — mainly in his last major book, *The Myth of the State*,[1] and, less directly, in such works as *The Question of Jean-Jacques Rousseau*[2] and *Rousseau, Kant and Goethe*.[3] A full understanding of Cassirer's views on this and related political themes, however, cannot be gained from his more political writings alone. For these are enhanced and completed by his reflections on the philosophy of human culture — particularly in *The Philosophy of Symbolic Forms*,[4] *Language and Myth*[5] and *An Essay on Man*.[6]

Accordingly, it is my aim not only to show the coherence of Cassirer's thought in this more comprehensive and integrated sense, but to examine, as well, certain tensions that arise between his more strictly political observations and his general philosophical position. In both connections I consider the place of myth in a politics that meets the demands of both unity and diversity, and this issue is addressed systematically in the concluding section.

In treating the theme of myth, unity and diversity in politics, I seek to interweave several threads of Cassirer's thought: how an individualistic and diverse social-political formation comes to transcend the original condition of tribal solidarity, the dialectic of person, world and community that accompanies this process, the Nazi movement and the reversion to tribalism, and the significance of culture — particularly of myth and reason -- in these developments. Because Cassirer considers the emergent articulation of human consciousness to be at the dynamic centre of advances in social and political heterogeneity, his theory of the growth of individualism and social complexity is also a phenomenology of the human spirit.[7] The section headings indicate this connection.

Culture, Myth and Human Development

Cassirer regards the symbolic forms — myth and language, religion, art, history and science — as a record of human spiritual growth. 'Human culture taken as a whole', he says, 'may be described as the process of man's progressive self-liberation.'[8] For it is by his construction of symbols that he escapes the immediacy of biological need and practical necessity to make a world that is his own.[9] By symbols man articulates external reality and gains distance from it, achieves awareness and control of his manifold powers, and develops the capacity for moral judgement and ethical choice. And it is by symbols that he becomes a social and political animal.

The various symbolic forms, Cassirer holds, function not as copies of, or attempts to copy, the 'real' world, but as the organs by which experience and knowledge of the world are possible.[10] The forms of perception are not acted upon by 'external' reality but give us experience that is already organised: 'Man lives with *objects* only in so far as he lives with these *forms* . . . .'[11] Cassirer says:

> Man is surrounded by a reality that he did not make, that he has to accept as an ultimate fact. But it is for him to interpret reality, to make it coherent, understandable, intelligible — and this task is performed in different ways in the various human activities, in religion and art, in science and philosophy. In all of them man proves to be not only the passive recipient of an external world; he is creative and active.[12]

In considering the relations of the symbolic forms within the whole fabric of culture, Cassirer assumes their 'functional unity'.[13] He says, 'each of these is a particular way of seeing, and carries within itself its particular and proper source of light.'[14] Each follows a characteristic principle and has its distinctive assignment in the overall development of the human spirit. Hence, Cassirer concludes, 'this multiplicity and disparateness does not denote discord or disharmony. All these functions complete and complement one another.'[15]

Cassirer, it follows, does not regard myth as a 'distortion' of 'reality' or as a 'disease of language': it is not the result of linguistic confusion and the misinterpretation of names originally given to natural phenomena; nor is it a consequence of the self-deceiving nature of language.[16] Similarly, Cassirer rejects all interpretations of myth as having a fanciful or allegorical basis: it is not an 'invention' devised to 'explain' historical persons or events or the phenomena of physical nature, for this presupposes a psychological 'distance' from objects the basis of which rests in mythical conception itself.[17]

Myth must be understood in its own terms. It is a structure of consciousness that makes possible a certain kind of human sensibility; and,
being the original such form, it is the matrix for the subsequent development of other forms.

Its objectivity — and from the critical standpoint this is true of all
cultural objectivity — must be defined not thing-wise but function-
ally: this objectivity lies neither in a metaphysical nor in an empirical-
psychological 'reality' which stands *behind* it, but in what myth itself
is and achieves, in the manner and form of *objectivization* which it
accomplishes. It is objective insofar as it is recognized as one of the
determining factors by which consciousness frees itself from passive
captivity in sensory impression and creates a world of its own in
accordance with a spiritual principle.[18]

The question, therefore, arises: What are the norms immanent in
myth itself, and how, in its formulation and development, is there 'that
progressive differentiation of "subject" and "object", "I" and "world",
through which consciousness issues from its stupor, its captivity in mere
existence, in sensory impression and affectivity, and becomes a spiritual
consciousness?'[19] How, in other words, does myth assist the progressive
emergence of man and the realisation of his humanity?

Man, Myth and Magic: The Consubstantial World

It is distinctive of Cassirer's approach to myth that he does not treat it
exclusively, or even primarily, according to the meaning of the Greek
mythos — as a system of tales or narratives about nature, gods or heroes.
Myth as narrative requires a perceptual and linguistic sophistication that
is achieved only after a long cultural struggle. In many societies, Cassirer
insists, such stories do not exist, yet the actions of the natives betray a
mythical outlook. And, in societies where myth does appear as narrative, it is a concomitant of, and cannot properly be understood apart
from, the psycho-motor basis in which it is rooted. Archaic man is not
a 'primitive philosopher' who practices his mythico-religious rites in a
contemplative or analytical spirit, but is emotionally immersed in his
activity; and his first expression is not in language but in 'the motor
manifestation of psychic life' known as ritual.[20] It is Cassirer's view,
therefore, that we must begin the study of myth as a dynamic phenomenon and treat the mythic material in its 'immediate qualitativeness'.[21]

In Cassirer's phenomenology of knowledge, myth is the spontaneous, expressive mode by which man first discerns qualities in the 'other' as bearing significance, and, in that process, becomes dimly aware of a tension between himself and an outer world.[22] As yet objects are not perceived as having a determinate and stable existence within a logical web of relations to other objects, or even as identities separate from the subject conceived as an independent 'I'. Their nature is what Cassirer calls 'physiognomic' — pertaining to their outward character as they immediately and emotionally concern the still undifferentiated subject.

In the sensuously immediate, consubstantial world of mythic expression there is no distinction between wish and fulfillment, appearance and reality, image and thing, a sign and something signified. There is, strictly speaking, no symbolisation, for the symbol is not known as symbol; it is perceived as being identical with the object and as possessing all its qualities.[23] Those who live in myth do not know the mythic images as images.[24] In accord with its physiognomic character, myth

> moves on a single plane of being, which is wholly adequate to it. Here there is neither kernel or shell; here there is no substance, no permanent and enduring something which underlies the changing, ephemeral appearances, the mere 'accidents.' The mythical consciousness does not deduce essence from appearance, it possesses — it has — the essence in the appearance . . . Here the phenomenon as it is given in any moment never has a character of mere representation, it is one of authentic presence . . .[25]

Hence, the 'meaning' of ritual actions must be understood as inhering in the acts as such which are intrinsically potent and refer to nothing beyond themselves. 'It is no mere play that the dancer in a mythical drama is enacting; the dancer *is* the god, he *becomes* the god. What happens in these rites . . . is no mere imitative portrayal of an event but is the event itself; it is . . . a real and thoroughly effective action.'[26]

The world of myth, Cassirer says, has an order, but one so conceived that things 'are differentiated without being separated from one another'.[27] Reality is fluid, plastic, ever-capable of changing into something else. This chameleon, dream-like world of the moment is far from the settled and predictable universe conceived scientifically.

> Mythical metamorphosis is bound by no logical law of identity, nor does it find a limit in any fixed constancy of classes . . . Here, on the contrary, all the boundary lines drawn by our empirical concepts of

genera and species keep shifting and vanishing. Not only does one and the same being perpetually take new forms; at one and the same moment of its existence it also contains and combines within itself an abundance of different and even mutually opposed forms of being.[28]

Keeping in mind this immanent quality of mythic perception, the kinship between myth and magic is understandable. In word magic, the name does not 'stand for' the person or the thing, but carries all the powers of the object in it; to invoke the name is, therefore, to make the object present, to participate in its power, and perhaps to control it.[29] In image magic, what happens to the image happens to the thing or person of which the image is not merely a likeness, but with which it is an identity.[30] And in certain cases of what Sir James Frazer called 'contagious magic', it is believed that to possess any part of the body of another – one's pared nails or cut-off hair, for example – is to have control over one's entire body, for, in the mythico-magical context, the part carries within it all the powers and attributes of the whole. 'The mere fact that it . . . has been connected with the whole, no matter how casually, is enough to lend it the full significance and power of that greater unity.'[31]

Mythico-magical consciousness follows what Cassirer calls 'the law of the leveling and extinction of specific differences'.[32] Its constructions bring together diverse phenomena – what from the perspective of a logical-theoretical consciousness would be unrelated or even contradictory elements – and concentrates them into a single point. 'Whereas the members of a synthetic combination effected by theoretical thinking are preserved as independent elements within this very combination, whereas theoretical thinking keeps them distinct even while bringing them into relation with one another, mythical thinking causes those things which are related to one another, which are united as though by a magical bond, to merge into *one* undifferentiated form.'[33]

Only in the very loosest sense, therefore, may the ways of magical practice be regarded as means or techniques, for they operate in a continuous world where neither the self is distinguished from its objects and the desire from its fulfillment, nor are the causal links between wish and aim considered. At the root of the magical outlook is a belief that 'an immediate power inheres in the wish itself . . . Here are needed no middle links which lead from the beginning to the end of the process of causality in a definitely ordered sequence; in the beginning, in the mere act of will, consciousness immediately apprehends the end, the result and product of the willing, and links the two together'.[34] In this 'desire'[35] to control the world by magic, Cassirer says, the idea of an objective world and the human capacity to control it is awakened, but still man is not free.[36] Paradoxically, the apparent power and omnipotence of the self as conceived mythically is quite other than it might seem. Lacking distance from other persons and things, one is bound to them by magical connections every bit as much as they are tied to oneself: the world lacks 'outwardness' and independence from the self, and the self lacks 'inwardness' and disengagement from the world.[37]

> The enhanced feeling of self which seems to express itself in the magical world view indicates actually that at this stage there is as yet no true self. Through the magical omnipotence of the will the I seeks to seize upon all things and bend them to its purpose; but precisely in this attempt it shows itself still totally dominated, totally 'possessed,' by things . . . The soul itself appears as a demonic power which acts upon man's body from outside and possesses it – and hence possesses the man himself with all his vital functions.[38]

The Emergence of the Individual: Separation from the Other

In Cassirer's view, the development of individual self-awareness and of the self as an independent, creative agent, requires the general development of culture. This entails the increasingly complex and variable mediations between man and the world, and, ultimately, the conscious recognition and employment of this process. It means the acceptance of constraints on the powers and scope of the self and the attribution of limits to the forces and objects of the external world, as well as the conception of links between self and other.

> All cultural work, be it technical or purely intellectual, proceeds by the gradual shift from the direct relation between man and his environment to an indirect relation. In the beginning, sensual impulse is followed immediately by its gratification; but gradually more and more mediating terms intervene between the will and its object. It is as though the will, in order to gain its end, had to move away from the goal instead of toward it; instead of a simple reaction, almost in the nature of a reflex, to bring the object into reach, it requires a differentiation of behavior, covering a wider class of objects, so that finally the sum total of all these acts, by the use of various 'means,' may realize the desired end.[39]

Yet, the self only gradually and indirectly becomes aware of this cultural process and its distinctive features. This it does by spontaneously creating objects and conceptions which become, in turn, the cultural lenses by which the subjective self is perceived.

Within the mythic mode, the self creates products and images which, once fashioned, seem wholly objective, and whose connection with the self is therefore initially obscured; 'all spontaneity is felt as receptivity, all creativity as being, and every product of subjectivity as so much substantiality'.[40] Tools and implements, for example, are seen as being the result of non-human activity, as the gift of a god or totem animal, and a tool or weapon is conceived magically as possessing powers in itself which remove it from human control.[41] But, by a reflective reversal, these same objectifications make it possible for man to eventually apprehend the world as differentiated, and himself as a unified personality distinct from the world.

Cassirer holds that all cultural work is connected with the emergence of the individual, but this process may be amply illustrated by reference to several of its key elements — the fashioning of tools, the evolution of religious consciousness, and the formation of communities. All of these originate within the mythic outlook and yet, paradoxically, enable man to surpass it.

Man does not first differentiate himself from nature by mental reflection or simple empirical observation: his meeting with things is through desire and activity.[42] Man's actions in the world are enormously enhanced by the use of tools. At the outset, tools are simply the undeliberate extension of bodily actions and powers exerted on the world — 'the natural articulation of the human body'.[43] Once created, however, they provide an external counterpart by which man comes to understand the structure and workings of his physical self; in the reflection of the mediating tools he has fashioned, he begins to understand his bodily nature. This 'organ projection' and reflexive understanding, moreover, are significant beyond the perception of a merely physical self: it is also the first step in man's awareness of his spiritual being, of his 'inwardness' and independence from the outer world, for he glimpses in what he has authored a record of his own mental powers.[44] 'The larger the circle becomes which the self fills with its activity, the more clearly the character of objective reality and also the significance and function of the I are manifested.'[45]

This development interpenetrates with, and is for a time governed by, man's mythico-religious conception of the gods. Hence there occurs a concurrent series of objectifications which are now primarily mental rather than material, and which mainly affect man's image of self as a spiritual being. From this emerges, eventually, the conception of the self as a unified, ethical personality, a soul as well as a body.

The first impressions of the world, Cassirer says, are unformed feelings of special intensity which set certain areas of experience apart from the ordinary and mundane. They concern not objects as such, but the intuition of significance, power, or holiness — undifferentiated, fluid, and ubiquitous — which momentarily rests, in a concentrated and compelling way, in some person or thing.[46] This involves what may broadly be termed a religious sensibility, for it separates the sacred from the profane, and it subtly shades off into the next and more distinct form of religious consciousness which Cassirer, adopting a phrase from Usener, calls that of the momentary Gods'. Here the gods are still anonymous and understood primarily as force or power, but have an individual and personal character.

> When, on the one hand, the entire self is given up to a single impression, is 'possessed' by it and, on the other hand, there is the utmost tension between the subject and its object, the outer world; when external reality . . . overcomes a man in sheer immediacy, with emotions of fear or hope, terror or wish fulfillment: then the spark jumps somehow across, the tension finds release, as the subjective excitement becomes objectified, and confronts the mind as a god or a daemon.[47]

This conception of a god of power and personal significance, Cassirer says, is a first and crucial step in man's emerging self-awareness and individuality, for man's successive conceptions of god are the basis for his developing self-concept.

The divine world, then, is originally composed of those 'momentary gods' or 'nature demons' connected with particularly intense, yet transitory, personal impressions. But as man relates to nature by action and creation, not simply by emotion, a new form of god arises alongside the old. These 'special gods', or 'occupational gods', govern man's various activities, thus giving them objectivity and definition; and they also, in accordance with the process of reflection and reversal, give man an image by which he comes to understand himself spiritually — an intuition of 'his own will and accomplishment'.[48]

In the development of the 'special gods' man comes to comprehend various particular spheres of his creative activity, but in the subsequent appearance of 'personal gods' — gods with a name and character — there arises in man the notion of a unified personality encompassing diverse creative powers.

The appearance of the personal gods, Cassirer says, marks a new relationship between the individual and the group. In the previous modes of religious consciousness the gods are of the clan or tribe as a whole, not of the person, and this fact is tied to the lack of a clear distinction between the community and the individual. Now, however, the individual gains 'a personal stamp, a personal face' within the group.[49] Add to this that the personal gods, where they continue also to be the gods of a group, are no longer confined to a narrow cult or locale. They are more universal, again freeing the individual from the stifling identity with tribe or clan. The Homeric personal gods, for example, are 'the first national gods of the Greeks . . . Thus personal consciousness and national consciousness are achieved in one and the same fundamental act of religious formation.'[50]

From the idea of a personal god there issues, at last, a notion having the highest significance for man's self-understanding — the idea of the 'supreme creator god' conceived in Judeo-Christianity.

In him all the diversity of action seems, as it were, concentrated in a single summit: the mythical-religious consciousness is now oriented not toward an aggregate, an infinite number of particular creative powers, but toward the pure act of creation itself, which like the creator is apprehended as one. And this new intuition drives the religious consciousness toward the idea of a unitary *subject* of creation.[51]

Man, therefore, discovers in the generative power and unity of the one god the metaphor for his own unity, subjectivity and power. This, as we will see, contains far reaching ethical implications.

Individual and Community: The Bond With the Other

Finally, there is a third distinctive way in which man differentiates and structures the universal life feeling in which myth originates, thus fostering the development of individual subjectivity, self-awareness and freedom. This is the process of class formation or the awareness of community whereby one sympathetically relates to kindred others and reflexively comes to know oneself more intimately.

Initially this occurs within a narrow community such as a family, clan or tribe, and later within a broader grouping such as a people or a nation. At every stage, however, the mythico-religious consciousness again plays an important role, for each of these communities is associated with a divinity which provides coherence and unity for the group. These gods do not merely reflect the existing condition of the objective social structure, but are, indeed, the vehicles by which the community is brought into being. Cassirer quotes with approval Schelling's observation in his *Philosophie der Mythologie* that a nation is not bound together by agriculture or trade, by common customs, or by legislation or political authority alone: for it is through the mythico-religious conceptions that these factors and the very idea of the nation itself are first conceived.[52] Cassirer concludes:

> the mythical-religious consciousness does not simply *follow* from the empirical content of the social form, but is rather one of the most important *factors* of the feeling of community and social life. Myth itself is one of those spiritual syntheses through which a bond between 'I' and 'thou' is made possible, through which a definite unity and definite contrast, a relation of kinship and a relation of tension, are created between the individual and the community.[53]

This mythic process, Cassirer notes, is buttressed by language, and in a passage that points up not only the importance of language but the relative importance of community in man's overall development Cassirer says. 'Indeed, it is the Word . . . that really reveals to man that world which is closer to him than any world of natural objects and touches his weal and woe more directly than physical nature. For it is language that makes his existence in a *community* possible; and only in society, in relation to a "Thee," can this subjectivity assert itself as a "Me".'[54]

In the awareness of community, Cassirer says, the world is differentiated, not according to a 'separating vision' as in the discrimination of 'corporeal phenomena', but by an 'identifying vision' that relates an individual to other 'living subjects'.[55] One finds a counterpart in other egos and thereby becomes aware of one's own.[56]

> Here the I is oriented not immediately toward the outside world but rather toward a personal existence and life that are similar to it in kind. Subjectivity has as its correlate not some outward thing but rather a 'thou' or 'he,' from which on the one hand it distinguishes itself, but with which on the other hand it groups itself. This thou or he forms the true antithesis which the I requires in order to find and define itself.[57]

The I discovers itself only within a relation of intentionality directed 'toward other centers of life' and in the awareness that it shares with other living beings a common world.[58]

The relationship of I and thou, it should be emphasised, is not, for Cassirer, one of sameness even though it implies unity. Cassirer states that the 'personal' sphere, unlike the 'material' sphere, is not easily homogenised conceptually, and that its relations tend always, by 'origin and essence', toward groupings that are heterogeneous. Hence, the I never simply mirrors the thou:

> the 'second' is not a mere repetition of the first, but is qualitatively 'other.' True, the 'I' and the 'thou' can fuse into the community of the 'we' — but this form of union is quite different from a collectivization of things. As early a writer as Jacob Grimm stressed the difference between objective plural concepts and personal plural concepts; he pointed out that whereas the objective plural can be defined as a sum of similar elements, 'men' for example as 'man and man,' the 'we' can by no means be represented as a sum of this sort, since it must be construed not as 'I and I,' but rather as 'I and thou' or 'I and he.'[59]

In Cassirer s view, it seems, the community, even at the most primitive levels, is to some rudimentary degree diverse and highly articulated, for the specialisation of functions requires it. Although the social order at this early stage is rigid and restricts the scope of individual action and responsibility, there is some differentiation of individuals, classes and orders: 'it is impossible to conceive of any community, however primitive, as a mere collectivity in which there is only an intuition of the being and action of the whole but no consciousness of the action of the parts.'[60]

From the start, it appears, the inherently qualitative basis of the community vision directs it toward a richly articulated, diverse structure which is its proper and normal form. Community is not incompatible with, and, indeed, from the beginning contains the seeds of, a more individualistic, more diverse and freer social order.

The Ethical Individual

The fullest liberation of man and most complete realisation of the ethical individual do not come primarily within the mythic outlook, but arise from a successful struggle against the mythic mode itself. This occurs as man is freed from the immediacy and immanence of mythic life and learns to govern his conduct by freely chosen principles that transcend his present condition. In this way is the spirit released from the chains of the sensuous present and allowed to strive for ethical improvement in accord with the demands of a projected ideal.

A crucial juncture in this odyssey of the human spirit is the form of religious consciousness put forth in the prophetic books of the Old Testament and subsequently developed in Christian thought. Here, religion takes a decisive turn away from its mythical beginnings. The divine no longer inheres in mere images nor can it be understood, as in the polytheistic world, in an immediate, sensuous way. The realm of nature, instead of being infused with divine presences, now points to the divine as something beyond. Instead of collapsing the symbol and the signified as in mythical consciousness, the world is now seen as 'the speech of God',[61] which is not to be conflated with God himself. God, and His pledge to those who follow his moral law, must be conceived as something absent and are intelligible only as a hope and a promise.

> The entire ethical-religious pathos of the Prophets is concentrated in this one point. It rests on the power and certainty of the religious will that lives in the Prophets — of a will which drives them beyond all intuition of the given, the merely existent. This existence must vanish if the new world, the world of the Messianic future is to arise. The Prophetic world is visible only in the religious idea and can be encompassed in no mere image which is oriented solely toward the sensuous present and remains confined within it.[62]

What does not belong to the spiritual-ethical relationship between man and God loses its religious importance, hence the outer world of nature is devalued in favour of the inner world of the moral subject: 'this alone makes possible the new deepening of pure religious subjectivity which can no longer be expressed in any material image'.[63]

Cassirer emphasises that this new form of religion heightens human freedom by offering to man an ethical idea which is obeyed, not out of compulsion, but by attraction. He chooses, by his own free will, to be bound by a transcendent ideal and thus actually breaks through the bonds of traditional, static, religion and an oppressive, taboo-governed society. 'There arises a new dynamic form of religion that opens a fresh perspective of moral and religious life. In such a dynamic religion the individual powers have won the preponderance over the mere powers of stabilization.'[64]

This ascent of man to ethical subjectivity, however, is not solely the product of prophetic, monotheistic, religion and Cassirer finds additional sources for it, mainly in Greek thought. In the tragedies of Aeschylus man is presented as an independent ethical agent who is responsible for moral choice,[65] but perhaps the most important watershed in Greek ethical thought comes with the speculations of Socrates and Plato. In the mythical-magical view, the self and the world have no separate, independent status: the self attempts to control the external world by the practice of magic, but, concurrently, it is never free of invasion and control by outside forces. One may be possessed by soul demons of either a beneficial or malignant sort, but one is not free to choose for oneself a moral disposition. With the Socratic doctrine of *eudaemonia*, however, this changes:

> the soul ceases to be a mere natural potency and apprehends itself as an ethical subject. Only now is man free from fear of the unknown, from the fear of demons, because he no longer feels that his self, his innermost being, is dominated by a dark mythical power but knows himself capable of molding this self from clear insight, through a principle of knowledge and will.[66]

There are, Cassirer says, important differences between Greek thought and the Judeo-Christian tradition — mainly in so far as the former views the ethical law as something inherent in the universe eternally, to be discovered by rational, dialectical inquiry, whereas the latter conceives of the moral law as coming from a personal law-giver who wills it, proclaims it, and demands obedience to it.[67] Yet there is also a crucial similarity between the two ethical outlooks: a transcendent moral principle is established after which the ethical subject strives, and which carries him beyond the confines of present existence. Here the philosophical and religious ethical streams meet. 'When Plato teaches that the idea of the good is "beyond being" and accordingly compares it with the sun, which the human eye cannot view directly but can contemplate only in its reflection in the water, he has provided the language of religion with a typical and enduring means of expression.'[68]

In the idea of a responsible subject who freely strives for a value that is beyond the sensuous present, we find what is, in Cassirer's view, the core of all truly ethical life and the factor in it that surmounts all traditional, group-bound morality. Hence Cassirer writes:

the best and, in a sense, the classical definition of [ethical freedom] has been given by Kant. As Kant pointed out in his *Critique of Practical Reason,* freedom is not an exemption from binding rules; it is, on the contrary, a rule which the moral will gives to itself. It means 'autonomy,' that is to say, it means self-control and individual responsibility. As Kant says, freedom is not *gegeben,* but *aufgegeben.* It is not a gift but a task, and perhaps the hardest task that we can impose upon ourselves.[69]

Again, echoing this Kantian notion, Cassirer says: 'It follows from the very nature and character of ethical thought that it can never condescend to accept "the given." The ethical world is never given; it is forever in the making.'[70]

One can, therefore, understand why, in the matter of ethics and ethical freedom, Cassirer favours Plato over Hegel. Tradition is blind to the choice of this ethical principle or that, and is bound merely to accept what is given. This is morality only by unquestioning routine and social pressure — a morality unfitted for free men.[71] One can perceive, as well, why in the question of ethics Cassirer sees Kant, not Hegel, as the heir of Plato. For Kant, unlike Hegel, never forswears the 'dualism between *Sein* and *Sollen*' — between the world as it exists and the world as it should be — nor does he reject the notion of the will of a moral subject as the foundation of moral action.[72] In Hegel's system of politics, therefore, the failures of the state are not susceptible to correction by individual moral choice or by appeal to an alternative philosophical or political system.[73]

Totalitarianism: the Reversion to Tribal Consciousness

In *The Myth of the State* Cassirer addresses the nature and antecedents of the totalitarian state, particularly as it developed under the National Socialist regime of Adolph Hitler. Cassirer's critique of Nazism stresses the capacity of its leaders to create a mythically based politics which massified the German populace and fostered their acquiescence in whatever momentary policies and actions the party and its leader pursued.

Cassirer discusses how various features of myth and magic were employed to seduce and control the German nation — to compel not only approved outward behaviour as in traditional autocracies, but to shape the very structure of thought and belief. As in primitive groups, the leader comes to embody the collective wish, and he is presumed to possess the strong magic by which that desire may be fulfilled. The leader thus replaces all other articulations and mediations by which a diverse society is bound together and conducts its relations. All 'social bonds – law, justice, and constitutions – are declared to be without any value'.[74] There is a widespread use of magical language which 'does not describe things or relations of things; it tries to produce effects and to change the course of nature'.[75] There is the use of political rituals which prevent every independent social or political activity and circumscribe individual freedom, which make every feature of life public, and subordinate individual responsibility to the responsibility of the group.[76] There is generally, as in myth, the substitution of emotion and desire for ethical and rational judgement, the sacrifice of criteria and standards to impulse and action.

Cassirer notes, however, that the reversion to mythic consciousness in 'a great civilised nation' required something that is not present in primitive society – the application of technique to the construction and dissemination of culture. The totalitarian leader combines the ancient function of *homo magus* with the more recent one of *homo faber*, and non-rational myth is produced – as myth in its spontaneous traditional form never was – according to plan.[77] 'The twentieth century developed a *technique* of mythical thought which had no equal in previous history.'[78] Implicit in Cassirer's position, though he does not develop the point, is that ancient myth combines so well with modern technology because both are bereft of a transcendental value and are, therefore, subject to no external principle.[79]

This reversion to mythical consciousness, it has been noted, entails not only the demise of a diverse and richly structured political, social and cultural order, but, in addition, the collapse of individual ethical freedom and moral responsibility. Both of these are at risk in the Nazi policy of *Gleichschaltung* – political co-ordination and the bringing into line or elimination of opponents. And because the Nazis aimed for political control of all social and cultural elements, and aspired to mobilise the entire nation as a uniform political grouping, the notion of *Gleichschaltung* applied to any real or alleged opposition to Nazi policy whatsoever, and, indeed, to any independent institution or principle.

On this matter of the homogeneous nation Cassirer notes, with implicit agreement, that Hegel, despite his political realism and traditionalist historicism which left him no appeal from the present, would have opposed the Nazi outlook. Hegel affirmed the value of a nation's inner spirit articulated in its social, political and cultural life, and held that the cultural forms – the realm of art, religion and philosophy – while they are to be nurtured by the state, are not the instruments of the state for political purposes, and are not at the behest of a political party or political leader.[80] Hegel's views, it follows, are therefore incompatible with the Nazi notion of *Gleichschaltung*. In order to subsist, Cassirer says, the totalitarian state must

> eliminate all other forms of social and cultural life and efface all distinctions. According to Hegel such an elimination can never lead to a true, organic unity. Its result would only be that 'abstract' unity which he incessantly denounced. A real unity does not erase or obliterate the differences; it must protect and preserve them. Though Hegel was strongly opposed to the ideals of the French Revolution he was convinced, nevertheless, that to abolish all distinctions in the social and political body, under the pretense of strengthening the power and unity of the state, would mean the very end of freedom.[81]

The Nazi ideal of *Gleichschaltung* is similar to the very earliest, relatively undifferentiated, stage of tribal consciousness, and is not merely to be equated with those richly articulated political communities having a significant mythical component.

This same point may be inferred from Cassirer's discussion of the Romantics which shows, once again by implication, his own position. On the one hand, the Romantics revere the mythic past for its own sake, and they do not aspire to a principle beyond what is given historically in order that they might improve politics and society. In this way they are quite apart from the thinkers of the Enlightenment who did not treat history as an end in itself but regarded it as something one studies only as a basis for achieving a better human future.[82] Yet the Romantics, such as Friedrich Schlegel, show a genuine respect for human diversity and cultural freedom. They are fascinated with myth and its deeper, often cryptic, meanings; their aim, nevertheless, is not 'to politicize but to "poeticize" the world,' and while they wished 'to maintain the peculiarity of the German character . . . they never meant to . . . impose it upon other peoples.'[83] The apotheosis of this attitude may be found in Herder who, Cassirer says,

> possessed the keenest sense and the deepest understanding of *individuality*. That individualism became one of the outstanding and most characteristic features of the romantic movement. The romanticists never could sacrifice the particular and specific forms of cultural life, poetry, art, religion, and history, to the 'totalitarian' state. They

had a deep respect for all the innumerable, subtle differences that characterize the life of individuals and nations. To feel and to enjoy these differences, to sympathize with all forms of national life, was to them the real scope and the greatest charm of historical knowledge. The nationalism of the romantics was, therefore, no mere particularism. It was the very contrary. It was not only compatible with a real universalism but presupposed it. To Herder every nation was only an individual voice in a universal, all-embracing harmony.[84]

In Cassirer's view, like that of Herder, the notion of individual freedom is inseparable from that of political, social and cultural diversity, and the existence of the one presupposes the presence of the other. Yet the Kantian notion of the ethical subject is a leading theme in Cassirer's philosophy of man, and his devotion to this conception continues to be foremost in his analysis of the Hitlerian state. Here, again, moreover, we may measure Cassirer's views by his commentary on the theories of others.

He criticises Oswald Spengler's *Decline of the West* for its pessimism and fatalism, and for its abandonment of the western cultural tradition which Spengler pronounces dead and incapable of revival. This presumption to divine the course of human affairs and to accept one's fate without protest or the attempt to surmount one's condition, Cassirer says, is one of the oldest themes of myth, and it is incompatible with the notion of ethical freedom and personal responsibility. Spengler, Cassirer notes, was a conservative, not a fascist, but his conclusions were helpful to the Nazi movement which was eager to abandon speculation about external principles of truth and morality, and to get on with the technique of transforming the world according to its immediate desires.[85]

Cassirer's views on Martin Heidegger's existentialist philosophy are similarly critical of the departure from the western tradition of transcendent ethical principles. Heidegger speaks of the *Geworfenheit* – the 'being thrown' – of man who is cast into the stream of time. To discover principles which surpass one's historical condition is impossible, Heidegger contends, and we cannot, therefore, change the course of historical existence; we can only, perhaps, interpret our historical condition.[86] Cassirer does not claim that Heidegger's philosophy had a direct bearing on the development of National Socialist doctrine. 'But the new philosophy did enfeeble and slowly undermine the forces that could have resisted the modern political myths. A . . . theory that sees in the *Geworfenheit* of man one of his principal characters [has] given up all hopes of an active share in the construction and reconstruction of man's cultural life.'[87]

Indeed, the theme of *The Myth of the State* is that western political thought reveals an abiding tension between mythical and rational conceptions, and that whereas philosophy may temporarily subdue and contain the mythical forces, it is itself always in danger of being overthrown. Unless the 'intellectual, ethical and artistic forces' of civilisation are vigorous and strong, mythical consciousness, which lurks always in the lower stratum of the cultural order, will arise again to predominance and will again create chaos.[88] As one writer has noted, there is, in all this, Cassirer's own mythic creation – of 'a shining plumed knight of scholarship perennially doing battle with dark, satanic myth'.[89] Cassirer might well have acknowledged this point, for he connects his notion of the cultural combat between myth and reason with a Babylonian legend about the struggle to conquer myth and bring order out of chaos.[90] In *The Myth of the State*, Cassirer's deepest hope is for the heroic triumph of a rational politics over the cthonian politics of unreason: 'For there is a logic of the social world just as there is a logic of the physical world. There are certain laws that cannot be violated with impunity. . . . We must learn how to obey the laws of the social world before we can undertake to rule it.'[91]

Conclusion: Myth, Unity and Diversity in Politics

We have seen how, in Casirer's view, mythico-magical thought is the original mode by which man addresses the world and his place within it. Myth in its earliest stages is, therefore, a form of sensibility, although a plastic one in which things appear and disappear, change their natures, and possess no independent, stable existence. Yet it is within the mythic outlook and a mythically rooted primitive religion that man first achieves knowledge of the objective world and of himself as an independent being – a being not only separate from nature, but one also related in an I-Thou bond with other beings in a structured community. It has been shown, moreover, that Cassirer holds man's highest moral achievement to be the discovery and refinement of ethical subjectivity, a feat that was made possible with the consciousness of, and willing commitment to, an external principle that frees human consciousness from the sensuous present. And, finally, it has been shown how Cassirer relates the rise of fascist totalitarianism in Germany to the resurgence of the most primitive mythic stage and the concomitant decline of pluralism and individual ethical responsibility.

In this final part of Cassirer's analysis he gives a particularly harsh assessment of myth's political role, and appears to conclude that mythic consciousness is antithetical to a humane, pluralistic and ethically responsible society. It is to a discussion of this apparent conclusion that we now turn, asking both how it stands within the whole of Cassirer's thought, and, concurrently, whether it adequately accounts for the relationship of myth, the individual and community in modern politics.

It is Cassirer's view, it may be recalled, that myth makes possible a relationship between the individual and the community which is at once one of unity and contrast, of kinship and tension — and which alone gives self-identity a distinctively human content. Recall, as well, that Cassirer admires Herder and many of the Romantics who saw no incompatibility between mythically rooted national communities on the one hand, and the heterogeneous, individualistic articulation of these communities on the other. And Cassirer agrees with Hegel that a genuine community is not merely a crowd, but a synthesis among richly structured and diverse elements, leaving always a space for individual freedom. Cassirer would insist, of course, that the individual moral will must always be free to judge inherited social standards, but his view suggests, as well, that without the nourishment and support of the community the moral individual would be ultimately impossible.

There is abundant testimony in Cassirer's work, then, to myth as a continuing and constructive element in human culture — including culture's scientific-rational component and its social-ethical component as well. Mythic perception, Cassirer says, is not 'absolutely extinguished, however much it is crowded out and modified by other modes of seeing'.[92] It remains an integral part of the world of ordinary experience, and is a necessary stage in the formation of objective understanding.[93] Moreover, there is one area where myth is not merely a necessary step on the way to scientific understanding, as in the case of object-perception. There is a realm of knowledge where the immediate, direct, mythical intuition of the other stands on its own and is capable of no further intellectual refinement or cultural mediation. This is in the 'thou' form of perception where 'the reality . . . of other subjects is opened up to us. This knowledge of the other psyche seems to form a natural and self-evident part of our total knowledge of experience . . .'[94]

It does not seem far fetched to infer that, for Cassirer, myth is the continuing ground of both scientific reason which requires the original data given by mythic perception, and ethical reason with seems impossible without the knowledge of characteristics that both mark off our humanity and relate it to the humanity of other subjects. Without a mythic basis reason would have neither anchor nor substance. In the ethical sphere, therefore, we come to view more clearly the link between the ethical subject who wills his own moral principle, and the community within which he comes to understand and will it. The perception of other subjects, that self-sufficient stratum of basic perceptions which may be treated theoretically but may not be further refined from their original axiomatic nature, is tied, inexorably and perpetually, to the community vision with which it is concurrent. Here, it appears, the unity of community and the diversity of moral subjects are interpenetrating dimensions of a continuous process.

It is not a far step to view myth as the horizon within which a rational and humane politics may be pursued — the underlying conviction of understanding, identity and belonging which provides a context for moral and political debate. Cassirer himself has remarked that the leaders of the Weimar Republic had too much faith in the centrality of economics and economic solutions to the German crisis, and that they, therefore, missed seeing the importance of the political myths and the danger they posed in the hands of the fascists. 'The opponents of National Socialism had lost their cause even before the battle began.'[95]

This is part of the point to be made, but it is not the whole point. The Nazis came to power, it may be argued, because they ruthlessly exploited the German desire, perhaps even a universal human desire, for identity and community — and this had been denied the Germans not only by the economic ravages and social and political instability following World War I, but by the widespread *Kulturpessimismus* and breakdown of unifying German cultural ideals generally. Both Walter Laqueur and Peter Gay, for example, describe the desire for unity and wholeness that characterised Germany before and during the Weimar period, and the lack of emotional commitment to the Republic by either the population at large or by the intellectuals, the *Vernunftrepublikaner*, whose commitment to parliamentary democracy was based on a rational judgement that it was merely the least of contending evils.[96] There was no myth to sustain the continuation of sharp debate without political breakdown as there was in England or France. Laqueur says: 'In no other country were the internal conflicts more bitter, the distance between the various factions greater than in Germany. If from time to time the battle was suspended, it was not because all passion was spent, but because the two sides were no longer speaking the same language.'[97]

Not only is a unifying myth necessary to a viable democratic politics, but, it may be added, rational-technical devices do not, of themselves, make such a politics possible. It has been noted, for example, that both 'the Austrian Constitution of 1920 and Germany's Weimar Constitution were models of technical excellence and rational construction', yet both were 'short lived'.[98] Our first conceptions, Cassirer has said, are rooted in what emotionally concerns us about the world, not in distanced observation or objective contemplation, and politics seems forever to retain some of this element. It is always concerned with what ultimately engages our interest and our passion. A politics that is indifferent to this will lose, and a social science that disregards it will be incomplete. It is with this in mind that Cassirer's remark concerning the 'logic of the social world' should be understood. The laws of society, Cassirer has made clear, are quite unlike the laws of the natural world; and its perceptual foundations remain more intimately tied to myth than do the facts of nature.

It may be objected to this that myth does not function always to unite a political society – that it sometimes acts, as in the case of the Nazi racial myths, to divide populations into irreconcilable groups. Cassirer himself emphasises this feature of myth under National Socialism: 'In the mythical pandemonium we always find maleficent spirits that are opposed to the beneficent spirits. There is always a secret or open revolt of Satan against God. In the German pandemonium this role was assigned to the Jew.'[99] In answer it may be said that there is nothing to guarantee the uniform function of myth. Its normal social function is to unify, but in certain contexts it may divide; and, although myth's usual function is to support an existing order by linking it to the mythical beginnings, it may be used, as it was in Homeric Greece with the myth of Dionysius and as it has been in this century with the myths of National Socialism, to challenge existing society.

In addressing this issue we should bear in mind that reason does not function uniformly either and that it can also have negative social-political consequences as writers from Rousseau to Nietzsche have so persuasively shown. There are dangers in high civilisation, and the excessively articulated, rationalised and individualised world may bring in its wake a disintegration of life and alienation of the individual. It is not without sympathy that Cassirer notes Rousseau's life-long affection for his 'Swiss homeland' where, Rousseau felt, 'he had still possessed life as a true entity, as an unbroken whole', and observes, as well, the oppression and dehumanisation Rousseau felt in the face of the highly rationalised and civilised Parisian society.[100] In *The Myth of the State*, moreover, Cassirer suggests that there is a universal human resistance to the articulated world. The myth of Dionysius challenged the ancient Greek civilisation's Apollonian values of logical symmetry and balance, and rejected the rationally elaborated social order of classes and individuals:

> What appears here is a fundamental feeling of mankind, a feeling that is common to the most primitive rites and to the most sublime spiritualized mystic religions. It is the deep desire of the individual to be freed from the fetters of his individuality, to immerse itself in the stream of universal life, to lose its identity, to be absorbed in the whole of nature . . .[101]

Cassirer goes on to note that the Dionysian cult was itself tamed — was systematised and regularised — by the Orphic theologians, and was thus brought into a balance that met the human desire for unity and community while, at the same time, tempering the Dionysian myth's violent and destructive potential.[102]

This suggestion of a fruitful and necessary balance between the mythical and rational elements of political culture is, I believe, a persuasive one. Here, neither myth nor reason is the overweening mode of consciousness and neither uproots and destroys the other. Both the diversity toward which reason is basically inclined and the unity which is connected more intimately with mythic consciousness are concomitants of a healthy political order.

Such a view avoids the overly optimistic assumption of Cassirer prior to 1945 which regards the forms of culture as comprising a functional unity where the 'multiplicity does not denote discord or disharmony',[103] for such dissonance does from time to time occur. Yet it allows us Cassirer's insight that each cultural mode makes a unique contribution to human sensibility, and that these modes may balance and complement one another. It also avoids Cassirer's caricatured and unduly pessimistic treatment of myth in *The Myth of the State*. Yet it allows us to acknowledge not only the dangers of myth, but of reason as well, under certain cultural conditions — particularly, it seems, conditions within which modern politics takes place. Finally, this notion of a balance between myth and reason, unity and diversity, accords with the overall tendency of Cassirer's position, for the antidote to his occasional one-sidedness may be found elsewhere in his own writings.

Notes

*My thanks to the Faculty of Graduate Studies and Research, Carleton

University, for financial support in preparing this essay, and to The Warburg Institute, University of London, for both the use of their facilities
and the gracious assistance of staff.

1. (New Haven, Yale University Press, 1946). Several essays related to the
development of this work as well as essays generally concerned with myth and
symbol, may be found in Cassirer, *Symbol, Myth, and Culture: Essays and Lectures of Ernst Cassirer, 1935-1945*, ed. Donald Phillip Verene (New Haven, Yale
University Press, 1979), pp. 219-67.
2. Peter Gay (ed. and trans.) (Bloomington, Indiana University Press, 1954).
Based mainly on Cassirer's essay, 'Das Problem Jean Jacques Rousseau' in *Archiv
für Geschichte der Philosophie*, vol. 41 (1932), pp. 177-213, 479-513.
3. James Gutmann, Paul Oscar Kristeller and John Herman Randall, Jr. (trans.),
Rousseau, Kant and Goethe (Princeton, New Jersey, Princeton University Press,
1963).
4. Ralph Manheim (trans.): Volume I, *Language*; Volume II, *Mythical Thought*;
Volume III, *The Phenomenology of Knowledge* (Yale University Press, 1957).
Originally published as *Die Sprache* (1923), *Das Mythische Denken* (1925) and
Phänomenologie der Erkenntniss (1929) (Bruno Cassirer Verlag, Berlin).
5. Susanne K. Langer (trans.) (New York, Harper and Brothers, 1946). Originally *Sprache and Mythos: Ein Beitrag zum Problem der Götternamen* (Leipzig,
B.G. Teubner, 1925). This was vol. VI in a series of studies by the Warburg Library,
then located in Hamburg.
6. *An Introduction to a Philosophy of Human Culture* (New Haven, Yale University Press paperback, 1962). Originally published in 1944.
7. For differences and similarities between Cassirer's phenomenology and that
of Hegel, and a comment on Cassirer's debt to Hegel as well as to Kant, see Donald
Phillip Verene, 'Kant, Hegel, and Cassirer: The Origins of the Philosophy of Symbolic Forms' in *Journal of the History of Ideas*, vol. 30, no. 1 (Jan.-Dec. 1969),
pp. 33-46.
8. *Essay on Man*, p. 228.
9. Ibid., p. 41.
10. See *Language and Myth*, Ch. 1, 'The Place of Language and Myth in the
Pattern of Human Culture'.
11. Ibid., p. 10.
12. 'Language and Art II' in *Symbol, Myth, and Culture*, pp. 166-95, at p. 195.
13. In his last major work, *The Myth of the State*, Cassirer erodes the force of
this principle. The importance of this is discussed in the concluding section.
14. *Language and Myth*, p. 11.
15. *Essay on Man*, p. 228.
16. *Language and Myth*, pp. 3-6 and *Essay on Man*, p. 109.
17. *Philosophy of Symbolic Forms*, vol. III, pp. 61-2.
18. Ibid., vol. II, p. 14.
19. Ibid., p. 13.
20. See *Essay on Man*, p. 79 and *Myth of the State*, Ch. 3, 'Myth and the
Psychology of Emotions', esp. pp. 23-4 and 28.
21. *Essay on Man*, p. 79.
22. See *Philosophy of Symbolic Forms*, vol. III, esp. Ch. 2, 'The Phenomenon
of Expression as the Basic Factor in the Perceptive Consciousness'.
23. Ibid., vol. II, p. 36.
24. *Myth of the State*, p. 47.
25. *Philosophy of Symbolic Forms*, vol. III, p. 67-8.
26. Ibid., vol. II, p. 39. See also, ibid., p. 238.

27. Ibid., vol. III, p. 61.

28. Ibid.

29. See *Language and Myth*, Ch. 4, 'Word Magic', and *Philosophy of Symbolic Forms*, vol. II, p. 40.

30. *Philosophy of Symbolic Forms*, vol. III, pp. 42-3.

31. *Language and Myth*, p. 92. See also *Philosophy of Symbolic Forms*, vol. II, p. 159.

32. *Language and Myth*, pp. 91-2.

33. *Philosophy of Symbolic Forms*, vol. III, p. 181.

34. Ibid., vol. II, p. 212.

35. Cassirer says 'The first energy by which man places himself as an independent being in opposition to things is that of desire.' Ibid., p. 157.

36. Ibid.

37. Ibid., pp. 158 and 212-14.

38. Ibid., p. 158.

39. *Language and Myth*, p. 59.

40. Ibid., p. 62.

41. Ibid., pp. 59-60.

42. Ibid., pp. 37-9.

43. *Philosophy of Symbolic Forms*, vol. II, p. 215-16.

44. Ibid.

45. Ibid., p. 200.

46. See *Language and Myth*, p. 62.

47. Ibid., p. 33.

48. *Philosophy of Symbolic Forms*, vol. II, pp. 203-4.

49. Ibid., p. 199.

50. Ibid.

51. Ibid., p. 206. See also *Language and Myth*, p. 83.

52. *Philosophy of Symbolic Forms*, vol. II, p. 177.

53. Ibid.

54. *Language and Myth*, p. 61.

55. *Philosophy of Symbolic Forms*, vol. III, p. 86.

56. Ibid., pp. 88-9.

57. Ibid., vol. II, p. 175.

58. Ibid., vol. III, p. 89.

59. Ibid., vol. I, p. 246. See also *Essay on Man*, p. 223: 'Man's social consciousness depends upon a double act, of identification and discrimination. Man cannot find himself, he cannot become aware of his individuality, save through the medium of social life.'

60. *Philosophy of Symbolic Forms*, vol. II, p. 185.

61. Ibid., p. 253.

62. Ibid., p. 240.

63. Ibid., p. 241.

64. *Essay on Man*, p. 225. See also ibid., pp. 104-8.

65. *Philosophy of Symbolic Forms*, vol. II, p. 198.

66. Ibid., p. 172. See also *Myth of the State*, pp. 75-6.

67. *Myth of the State*, p. 92.

68. *Philosophy of Symbolic Forms*, vol. II, p. 252.

69. 'The Technique of Our Modern Political Myths' in *Symbol, Myth, and Culture*, pp. 242-67 at p. 257.

70. *Essay on Man*, p. 61.

71. See *Myth of the State*, p. 73.

72. 'Hegel's Theory of the State' in *Symbol, Myth, and Culture*, pp. 108-20 at p. 112.

73. Ibid., p. 119. See also *Myth of the State*, pp. 275, 295. Elsewhere, however, Cassirer notes also an ethically dynamic implication to Hegel's thought. Like Kant's 'critical idealism', Hegel's 'absolute idealism' does not view mind as merely submitting to an 'outward fate': human self-realisation is an active process toward ever greater consciousness, freedom, and responsibility. 'Critical Idealism as a Philosophy of Culture' in *Symbol, Myth, and Culture*, pp. 64-91 at pp. 89-90.

74. *Myth of the State*, p. 280.

75. Ibid., pp. 282-4.

76. Ibid., pp. 284-5.

77. Ibid., pp. 277, 280-2. See also 'The Technique of Our Modern Political Myths', pp. 252-3.

78. 'The Technique of Our Modern Political Myths', p. 253.

79. This point is made by Donald Phillip Verene, 'Technology and Myth: A Hegelian View of Contemporary Culture', *Proceedings of the XVth World Congress of Philosophy*, 17-22 Sept. 1973, Varna (Bulgaria), published, Sophia, 1974, pp. 297-9. See also Verene, 'Cassirer's Philosophy of Culture', *International Philosophical Quarterly*, vol. 12, no. 2 (June, 1982), pp. 133-44, and his reference on p. 141, to an article which applies Cassirer's insight to the politics of Ronald Reagan, Michael J. Arlen, 'The Governor's Brief Brush with Logic', *The New Yorker*, 31 March 1980, pp. 112-14. I further develop this theme of immanentism in an essay entitled 'Myth, Technology, and Totalitarianism: Reflections on Ernst Cassirer's *Myth of the State*.'

80. *Myth of the State*, pp. 274-5.

81. Ibid., pp. 275-6.

82. Ibid., p. 181.

83. Ibid., p. 184.

84. Ibid., pp. 184-5.

85. Ibid., pp. 287-9. See also Cassirer, 'Philosophy and Politics', *Symbol, Myth, and Culture*, pp. 219-32, esp. pp. 226-9.

86. *Myth of the State*, pp. 292-3.

87. Ibid., p. 293. See also 'Philosophy and Politics', p. 229. For Heidegger's critique of Cassirer's account of myth, see 'Review of Ernst Cassirer's *Mythical Thought*' in *The Piety of Thinking: Essays by Martin Heidegger*, James G. Hart and John C. Maraldo (trans.) (Bloomington and London, Indiana University Press, 1976), pp. 32-45. On the differences between Cassirer and Heidegger see the account of their meeting at Davos, Switzerland in 1929: Carl H. Hamburg, 'A Cassirer-Heidegger Seminar', *Philosophy and Phenomenological Research*, vol. 25 (1964-65), pp. 208-22.

88. *Myth of the State*, p. 298.

89. Lee C. McDonald, 'Myth, Politics and Political Science', *The Western Political Quarterly*, vol. 22, no. 1 (March, 1969), pp. 141-50 at p. 149 f.n.

90. *Myth of the State*, pp. 297-8.

91. Ibid., p. 295.

92. *Philosophy of Symbolic Forms*, vol. III, pp. 78-9.

93. Ibid., vol. II, pp. 14-15, and vol. III, pp. 79, 81.

94. Ibid., vol. III, p. 79.

95. 'Judaism and the Modern Political Myths' in *Symbol, Myth, and Culture*, pp. 233-41, at p. 236.

96. Walter Laqueur, *Weimar: A Cultural History 1918-1933* (New York, G.P. Putnam's Sons, 1974; Pedigree Books edition, 1980); Peter Gay, *Weimar Culture: The Insider as Outsider* (New York, Harper and Row, 1968).

97. Laqueur, *Weimar*, p. 41.

98. Donald Phillip Verene, 'Cassirer's View of Myth and Symbol', *The Monist*, vol. 50 (1966), pp. 553-64, at p. 560, referring to the argument of Gregor Sebba,

'Symbol and Myth in Modern Rationalistic Societies', Altizer, Beardslee and Young (eds.), *Truth, Myth and Symbol* (Englewood Cliffs, New Jersey, Prentice-Hall, Inc., 1962), pp. 141-68.

99. 'Judaism and the Modern Political Myths', pp. 238-9.
100. *The Question of Jean-Jacques Rousseau*, pp. 40-3.
101. *The Myth of the State*, p. 41.
102. Ibid., pp. 41-3.
103. *Essay on Man*, p. 228.

3 THE FATHERLAND IN MACHIAVELLI

Anthony Parel

The idea of fatherland (*patria*) in Machiavelli raises a number of points that are significant for a discussion of the theme of 'unity, plurality and politics'. The first of these points concerns the relationship of the citizen to the state, and the second concerns the relationship of one fatherland to another, and to the international community taken as a whole. Machiavelli had definite views on these issues; and an understanding of them helps gain a clearer appreciation of his political theory. In what follows the various meanings attached to Machiavelli's idea of the fatherland are first identified, followed by a discussion of their significance. Three distinct meanings of fatherland can be identified in Machiavelli: the politico-cultural, the theological and the moral; each will be dealt with in turn.

Fatherland in the Politico-cultural Sense

Fatherland in the politico-cultural sense normally refers to the politically-organised territory to which one feels emotionally attached. The basis of this attachment may be the fact that one is born there, or it may be the love that one feels for the political regime existing there, or the language and culture peculiar to it, or a combination of all these. Even though Machiavelli sometimes uses such terms as *citta* (city) and *nazione* to refer to such political entities, they do not have the emotional significance that the term fatherland has.[1] The fatherland is the object of one's 'labours' and 'love'. Thus, he says in the Preface to the First Book of the *Discourses* that 'in all ancient kingdoms and republics, kings, generals, citizens, lawgivers and others laboured for their fatherland'.[2] 'Love' of the fatherland was more powerful than any other consideration in the early republican Romans.[3] Moses, Cyrus, Romulus and Theseus were said to nobilitate their respective fatherlands.[4] To Oliverotto, the tyrant of Fermo, and to Nabis, the tyrant of Sparta, Fermo and Sparta were respectively their fatherlands.[5] These and similar uses of the term by Machiavelli indicate that the fatherland stood for any politically-organised territory. The fatherland is distinct from the regime that operates it; monarchy or republic or tyranny could exist in one's fatherland, and one could feel attached to each of these because of the fatherland. For Machiavelli love of the fatherland was more fundamental than love of the regime. It was love of the fatherland rather than any moral virtue that made one a good citizen.[6]

However that may be, fatherland in the politico-cultural sense did present some problems. This was particularly true of the Italians of Machiavelli's days, including Machiavelli himself. There was, for example, the difficulty of identifying which territory constituted one's fatherland. Even Moses faced such a difficulty, for it was not clear which fatherland he nobilitated, Egypt where he was born, or Israel which he founded but in whose territory he did not set foot. In the case of Machiavelli there was a conflict between Florence and Italy, for he spoke of both of them as his fatherland.

In *The Prince* and in the *Art of War*, for example, he spoke of Italy as a political unity, and he seemed to identify himself with it.[7] In *The Prince*, Italy is referred to as 'this fatherland' (*questa patria*) and Lorenzo di Medici of Florence is exhorted 'to nobilitate' it.[8] Contrasted with the barbarians — the French, the Spaniards, the Swiss and the Germans — Italians constituted a distinct group and Italy was their fatherland. But to Lorenzo di Medici Italy was very much like what Israel was to Moses: a fatherland only in hope, not in fact. Just as Moses had not taken possession of Israel, so Lorenzo had not actually established Italy as the fatherland of Italians.

The famous last chapter of *The Prince* does give some hints of the tension between Italian patriotism and the other patriotisms of the Italians. The hint is apt to escape notice in the fine rhetoric that Machiavelli uses in the last chapter of *The Prince*. He takes the trouble of reminding Lorenzo that intra-Italian 'jealousies' ought not to deter him from the enterprise of nobilitating the fatherland. He assures Lorenzo that he would be received with 'love' by all the 'provinces' (*provincie*) of Italy; that 'the thirst for revenge' against the foreigners and the 'loyalty' and 'devotion' (*pieta*) which these 'provinces' feel for Italy will make them rally under him. No 'doors' will be closed to him, no 'people' will deny him obedience. Machiavelli would not have raised these issues of jealousy, loyalty, obedience, love and opposition, unless he was aware of their existence. He raises them precisely because they were obstacles to be overcome.

Nor can I express with what love he (the liberator of Italy) will be received in all those provinces that have suffered through these foreign floods; with what thirst for revenge, with what obstinate loyalty, with what devotion (*pieta*), with what tears! What doors will be closed to him? What peoples will deny him obedience? What jealousy could oppose him? What Italian would deny him obedience?[9]

If *The Prince* only hints about the existence of the conflicts between intra-Italian patriotisms and Italian patriotism, his other writings definitely make the hints explicit. His voluminous writings as secretary to the government of Florence were all written from the Florentine perspective, often against other Italian fatherlands, like Pisa or Siena or Venice. The most significant of such writings is perhaps that dealing with the revival of the Florentine militia. The object of the Florentine militia was the defence and expansion of Florence against other Italian states; they were not meant to defend Italy against foreigners. In these documents Machiavelli appears as a harsh Florentine imperialist who wanted the submission of neighbouring states such as Pisa to Florence.[10]

Apart from the chancery writings, there are three of his later writings that bear unmistakable signs of Florentine patriotism: *A Discourse on Remodelling the Government of Florence, The History of Florence*, and *The Discourse or Dialogue on Our Language*.

A Discourse on Remodelling the Government of Florence was commissioned by Leo X and Cardinal Guiliano Medici, the future Clement VII. The Commission was occasioned by the death of Lorenzo di Medici (1519) to whom, as everyone knows, *The Prince* was dedicated, and who had been exhorted by Machiavelli, only a few years previously, to liberate the Italian fatherland. If Machiavelli had a consistent idea of where Florentine patriotism stood in relation to Italian patriotism, one would expect to find some trace of it in this *Discourse*. Yet we find no such trace. On the contrary, the work is dedicated to the glorification of Florence, with no mention of Italy at all. As in *The Prince*, here, too, there is a fervent patriotic exhortation, but the patriotism in question is Florentine, not Italian.

The 'greatest honour possible' that men can receive, Machiavelli reminds Leo, is that given to them by their fatherland. and the 'greatest good' that men can do is that which they do for their fatherland. On the basis of this principle, Leo is exhorted to reform Florence, the fatherland, and thereby attain glory and immortality. If he serves his fatherland in this way, Machiavelli reminds him, he would achieve an even greater glory than that achieved by either Plato or Aristotle. And no greater gift can the heavens give to any man than the opportunity to benefit his fatherland.[11]

The *History of Florence*, a work commissioned by Clement VII, celebrates Florence as the fatherland.[12] It makes no effort to reconcile the conflict between Florence and Italy.

However, it is in the *Discourse or Dialogue on Our Language* that we see the full depth of his Florentine patriotism. This is a highly polemical work: the topic of controversy is the origin of the Italian language, whether it originated in the Tuscan dialect or in a combination of all the dialects of Italy. And Machiavelli's chief adversary is none other than Dante himself, who defended the Anti-Tuscan side. In his *De vulgari eloquentia* (1305), Dante had asserted that Italian was a composite of all the 14 dialects of Italy, and that it did not arise from any one dialect, not even Tuscan.[13]

Machiavelli picked up Dante's challenge. He pointed out 'irrefutably', as one commentator puts it, the close concordance of standard Italian with Tuscan 'not only in vocabulary, but also in phonetic and morphological structure.'[14] We are not concerned here to judge who was correct, Dante or Machiavelli. We are concerned to point out that for Machiavelli the defence of the Tuscan side was a patriotic act, and the denial of the Tuscan origin of Italian was an unpatriotic, a 'parricidal' act, as he put it. Dante had called all the dialects of Italy (*linguae patriae*, fatherland languages) the common source of Italian. But for Machiavelli the contributions of these languages, which he refers to as foreign languages,[15] is merely subsidiary to those made by Tuscan, the *lingua patria* of Florence. Words and idioms 'proper to those fatherlands' (*termini proprii patrii*[16]), are mere additions to the basic Italian language, which is Tuscan. The analogy which he uses to convey the relationship of other dialects to Tuscan is itself significant. He compares the relationship of the non-Tuscan dialects to Tuscan to that of the Roman soldiers to the foreigners in the Roman legion. The Roman legion contained more foreigners than Romans. Though the Roman soldiers were a numerical minority, the legion as a whole was a Roman institution. Similarly, though the speakers of Tuscan were fewer than the speakers of the other *linguae patriae*, it was, nevertheless, Tuscan that gave the Italian language its form and its structure. 'The truth of this can be seen today', writes Machiavelli, 'when there are many Ferrarese, Neapolitans, Vicentines and Venetians who all write well and have qualities needed for a writer.' This could not have happened but for the Florentine literature. 'For aiming to reach this height, but being hindered by their *lingua patria*, they needed someone who by his example could teach them how to forget the original barbarism (*naturale barbaria*) in which their *patria lingua* steeped them.[17] Just as Machiavelli saw Italy as a fatherland *if it was led by a Florentine prince*, so he was prepared to see Italian as 'our language' *if it was recognised as the outgrowth of Tuscan*. In the *Discourse* on the language the phrase 'our language' is used; but its meaning remains ambiguous. Does it refer to Italian or to Tuscan? The same phrase 'our language', (*nostra lingua*), occurs also in *The Prince*; however, here he clearly identifies it with Tuscan.[18]

His criticism of Dante was that he was a political turncoat, and that he took the anti-Tuscan line out of spite for his banishment from Florence. Dante 'showed himself at every point to have excelled in genius, learning and judgement, except when he spoke of his fatherland, which he attacked with every sort of injury in a way unworthy of humanity and philosophic teaching.'[19] His banishment offended him so deeply, claims Machiavelli, that he sought revenge on Florence by arguing that the *lingua patria* of Florence was not the basis of Italian. In doing so he failed in his highest duty as a citizen. For

> a man is under no greater obligation than to his fatherland; he owes his very being (*l'essere*), and all the benefits that nature and fortune offer him, to her. And the nobler one's fatherland, the greater one's obligation. In fact he who shows himself by thought and deed an enemy of his fatherland deserves the name of parricide, even if he has legitimate grievance. For if it is an evil deed to strike one's father and mother for any reason, it necessarily follows that it is still more criminal to savage one's fatherland. You owe her every advantage you have, and she can be guilty of no persecution that justifies your injuring her; indeed, if she disposes of some of her own citizens you should rather be thankful for those that remain than blame her for those she has banished.[20]

The portrait that Machiavelli draws of himself in the *Discourse* on language is that of a Florentine cultural imperialist. The fatherland is father and mother to you; she gives you your 'being'; she mediates all the good that you receive from 'nature and fortune'; she can commit no wrong; you can have no legitimate grievance whatsoever against her; she can banish you without being guilty of any fault; but you cannot revenge yourself against her without committing parricide; what is more, even when banished, you are bound by the obligations of piety and loyalty.

What are we to conclude from this brief consideration of the political and cultural tensions that exist between Machiavelli's Italian and Florentine patriotisms? All we can legitimately conclude is that the narrowly political and cultural aspects of Machiavelli's idea of fatherland do not give us its full meaning. To gain the full meaning we must realise that Machiavelli gives fatherland a theological and moral dimension. On the narrowly cultural, territorial and political basis there is always room for dispute and ambiguity. But there is no room for dispute or ambiguity when we look at Machiavelli's theological and moral meanings of fatherland. Whether one is speaking of Italy or Florence, it is not the territory or the language or the culture of these entities that make fatherland, fatherland in the full sense. What makes fatherland what it is, is the moral and theological ideas underlying it.

The Theological Meaning of Machiavelli's Fatherland

Machiavelli was well aware of the Christian notion of the fatherland. He was also aware that his notion conflicted with it. His celebrated attack on Christianity in the *Discourses* hinges on the question of the fatherland. As he saw it, Christianity opposed the paradise (*paradiso*) to the fatherland (*patria*). This, he asserted, was due to a false interpretation of Christianity's relationship to politics. According to such interpretation, Christianity taught men 'to esteem less the honour of the world', and to place man's *summum bonum* 'in humility, abnegation and contempt for human things'. The generality of men, 'in order to go to paradise' thought more about suffering injuries than avenging them, and turned the world over to wicked men. Machiavelli implies that the *patria* requires the principle of reciprocity of injuries, revenge and balance. But the idea of paradise, according to Machiavelli, interferes with these requirements of the fatherland. All this would have been quite unnecessary, he claims, had Christianity been interpreted according to *virtu*, instead of *ozio* (passivity). And had it been so interpreted, the Christians would have been permitted 'to exalt and defend their fatherland'.[21]

The 'exaltation' and the 'defence' of the fatherland — that was what Machiavelli wanted to accomplish, and Christianity was standing in his way. And the roots of the Christian obstacle went back to the New Testament. St Paul's statement to the Philippians was but one of many to be found in the New Testament: 'For us our homeland (*politheuma*) is in heaven.' The *Letter to the Hebrews* articulated the Christian position even better: the earth and the earthly fatherland could not be the true fatherland of the Christians: at best it could only be a place of pilgrimage, not the final resting place. Living by faith implied living like 'strangers and nomads' on earth. Abraham, Isaac and Jacob were to be the models of Christians: 'By faith they sojourned in the land of promise, as in a strange country . . . they were strangers and pilgrims on the earth.'[23] Man's ultimate concern on earth was the salvation of his soul, not the exaltation of the fatherland. 'What is a man profited, if he shall gain the whole world (*cosmos*) and lose his own soul? or what shall a man give in exchange of his soul?'[24] Or as St Thomas articulated the idea in theological language, 'Man is not ordained to the political community in his total self and in all that he has; and therefore it is not required that each of his acts should be well or ill deserving according as it is ordained to the political community . . . But all that a man is, all that he can do and all that he has is to be ordained toward God.'[25]

Machiavelli wrote in a Christian ambiance; he knew what he was up against. It was his mission to reverse the Christian order of importance of paradise and *patria*, the salvation of the soul and that of the fatherland. Love of the fatherland had to be absolute and unconditional — it meant a choice between the heavenly fatherland and the terrestrial fatherland.

We find several indications of where Machiavelli's priorities lay. He praised the Florentine patriots who fought against the papal states in the war of 1375-78, the so-called War of Eight Saints, who showed that 'they valued their fatherland more than their souls.'[26] He criticises Cosimo di Medici for loving himself more than his fatherland, and praises him for loving this world more than the other.[27] He notes that another well known Florentine, Rinaldo degli Albizzi, sought the 'celestial fatherland' only after he lost (by means of exile) his 'terrestrial one'.[28] Finally, he stated his own personal position in a letter to his friend Vettori, written shortly before his death: 'I love my fatherland more than my soul.'[29]

I want to underline the fact that Machiavelli's patriotism had a theological dimension: it sought, that is, to free patriotism from its Christian connection. Hannah Arendt does not seem to grasp this fully. In a noted commentary on this point she seems to think that Machiavelli did not deny the Christian position.[30] Arendt's mistake is based on the confusion of what Machiavelli means by 'love of self' and 'love of soul'. 'The question, as Machiavelli saw it,' Arendt writes, 'was not whether one loved God more than the world, but whether one was capable of loving the world more than one's own self. And this decision indeed has always been the crucial decision for all who devoted their lives to politics.'[31] As can be seen from the theological dimension of Machiavelli's thoughts on fatherland, he was contrasting not only *the love of the self* but also the *the love of soul* against *love of the fatherland*. Both self love and love of soul, according to Machiavelli, were inconsistent with love of the fatherland. And Machiavelli knew very well the difference between self-love (*amare se medessimo*), which he reproved in Cosimo, and love of the soul (*amore della anima*), which he dismissed as inferior to the love of the fatherland. Arendt's mistake was to equate 'love of oneself' with 'love of one's salvation'. For she writes: 'Most of Machiavelli's arguments against religion are directed against those who love themselves, namely their own salvation, more than the world; they are not directed against those who really love God more than they love either the world or themselves.'[32] It is not theologically valid to say that one can risk the loss of one's soul and at the same time claim to love God. Love of the salvation of the soul, in the theological sense, was founded upon and required by, the love of God. Arendt underestimated the implications of what Machiavelli called 'the love of this world' and 'the love of the fatherland'. For Machiavelli these meant and these required the rejection of the love of the soul, the salvation of the soul and the love of God. His patriotism, in other words, is completely atheistic. And Leo Strauss is correct when he states that Machiavelli is more concerned with the salvation of the fatherland than with the salvation of the soul, and his patriotism 'presupposes a comprehensive reflection regarding the status of the fatherland on the one hand and of the soul on the other.'[33] The Machiavellian man, in other words, must be prepared to risk the salvation of his soul for the love and service of the fatherland.

That Machiavelli's conception of the fatherland required the rejection of the heavenly fatherland was recognized by thinkers and commentators of the nineteenth century, when his patriotism became a rallying point for the national movements in Germany and Italy. 'Having entirely scrapped the superhuman and the supernatural', wrote De Sanctis, 'he [Machiavelli] sets up fatherland as the basis of life.'[34] 'God had come out of Heaven and descended to the earth, and had changed His name to Fatherland . . .'[35]

The Fatherland as the Basis of Machiavellian Political Ethics

The critique of the Christian view of the fatherland was a necessary precondition for the elevation of the fatherland as the absolute norm of politics. Machiavelli's immediate audience was Christian. The major challenge to his view would come from Christian quarters. He had, therefore, to show that the Christian notion of the greater importance of paradise was an obstacle to the problem of defending and exalting the fatherland. The defence and exaltation of the fatherland required aggression, imperialism, and revenge as a way of settling political injuries. He had to argue that the right of a fatherland to come into being and to maintain itself was an unconditional right, and the right to revenge was part of the right to exist. As De Sanctis writes, 'Just as the ascetics saw the individual absorbed into the Godhead, and just as the Inquisitors burned heretics in the name of God, so for one's country everything was lawful . . . This right of the country above every other right was commonly known as "reasons of state", or "public welfare" . . . country was supreme, its will and interests were *suprema lex* . . . '[36] Ranke also saw the connection between the idea of the fatherland and Machiavelli's moral theory: Machiavelli 'was capable of maintaining an attitude of indifference with respect to Good and Evil — that is to say, of being prepared, when his Fatherland was in a desperate condition, to be bold enough to prescribe poison for it.'[37] One of Machiavelli's major ethical achievements is the identification of the political good with the interests of the fatherland, and the justification of human actions in relation to the interests of the fatherland. His most sweeping statement on this point appears in the *Discourses:*

> One's fatherland is properly defended in whatever way she is defended, whether with disgrace or with glory . . . This idea deserves to be noted and acted upon by any citizen who has occasion to advise his fatherland, because when it is absolutely a question of the safety of one's fatherland, there must be no consideration of just or unjust, or merciful or cruel, or praiseworthy or disgraceful; instead, setting aside every scruple, one must follow to the utmost any plan that will save her life and keep her liberty.[38]

As far as the ethical doctrine of the fatherland is concerned, the differences in regimes make no difference to its ethical quality. Whether the regime in question is a republic or a monarchy or a tyranny, the patriotic obligation is the same. The form of government does not alter the ethical rule. Thus, the doctrine of *The Prince*, Chapter 18, is substantially the same as that cited above from the *Discourses*. What *The Prince* calls 'the maintenance of the state' is ethically the same as defending and exalting the fatherland. Thus, the statesman is free to break his promises and treaties when to keep them would work against him. And a shrewd statesman will never lack 'justifying reasons to make his promise-breaking appear honorable.'[39] Machiavelli wants to leave no doubt about the scope of this new ethical injunction. Promise-breaking applies not only to promises made under duress but also to those freely entered into: 'not only are forced promises not kept among princes when force is removed, but also other promises are not kept when their causes are removed. Whether this is praiseworthy or not, and if such methods should be used by a prince or not, we debate at length in our treatise on *The Prince* . . . '[40]

There is no parallel to this moral doctrine either in classical or in medieval political theory. In these political theories, *jus gentium* was the norm for the relations between states. However, the Machiavellian fatherland is not bound by *jus gentium*. For him revenge is a more reliable and safer guide to international security than the law of nations.[41] Similarly, the classical and medieval notion of just war, *bellum justum*, has no restraining power on Machiavelli's fatherland. According to the theory of *bellum justum*, war is an instrument or servant of justice and, therefore, ultimately to be governed by the dictates of justice. However, the justice of war, for Machiavelli, is not dictated by any justice that transcends the interests of the state, but is dictated by necessity as interpreted by the state: 'Let a prince therefore act to conquer and to maintain the state, his methods will always be judged honourable and will be praised by all . . . '[42]

The law of necessity replaces, according to Machiavelli, the rule of *jus gentium*: 'that war is just that is necessary, and those arms are holy (*pia*) when there is no hope apart from them'.[43] Machiavelli is quite flexible in his understanding of what constitutes necessity: it could include such a cause as the liberation of the fatherland from external aggressors, as was the case with Italy.[44] Or it may include conspiracies undertaken to liberate it from internal enemies such as those led by Rinaldo Albizzi.[45] Or it may include the use of any ruse which one thinks will be to the advantage of one's fatherland.[46] The matter of what constitutes necessity at any given time is to be determined by the statesman.

Machiavelli's rejection of the obligatory nature of *jus gentium* and his adherence to the rule of necessity preclude the possibility of a universal community of fatherlands. For Machiavelli the plurality of fatherlands is merely a question of fact. He sees nothing in nature that suggests the idea of a community of fatherlands. That being the case, world order is possible only on the imperial principle, as for example, that exercised by Rome. Only arms, wars, necessities can define the political relations between fatherlands. International society — if society it can be called — is a war society. 'Among private individuals, laws and writings and agreements make them keep their word; but among princes nothing but arms make them keep it.'[47]

Just as the notion of the fatherland gives us an idea of Machiavelli's conception of international community, so it also gives us an idea of the status of the individual in relation to the state. As we have already seen, the citizen owes his very 'being' to the fatherland; he has to be at its service 'in thought and deed'; he can have no 'legitimate grievance' against it; it can do no wrong toward him; it may disown him; but he cannot disown it without being guilty of parricide. The 'greatest good' that any man can do is that which he does for his fatherland.

The fatherland also enters into Machiavelli's definition of the good citizen. The distinction between the good man and the good citizen, fundamental to Aristotle, is dropped by Machiavelli: for him the good citizen is one who loves his fatherland; one whose patriotism is able to overcome his egoism. In the *Discourses*, where he devotes an entire chapter to this point, he exhorts 'everyone' to overcome even private injuries through the love of fatherland (*carita della patria*).[48]

What emerges from Machiavelli's moral theory is an organic conception of the relationship of the individual to the state. What binds the individual to the state ultimately, is not any utilitarian interest expressed by social contract; nor is it natural sociability. What binds the individual to the state is the fatherland. It is the fatherland, not fellow-citizens, that is the direct object of the Machiavellian citizen's love. The individual is as it were absorbed by the collectivity; he has no right that is underived from the fatherland. As De Sanctis points out, Machiavelli's conception of freedom does not include 'the rights of man'. Man for Machiavelli is not an autonomous being, an end in himself; he is an 'instrument' of the fatherland; and when he ceases to be that, the fatherland would simply smash him.[49]

Conclusion

Machiavelli's idea of fatherland has implications for both domestic and international politics.

With respect to domestic politics, it obviously provides the citizens with a basis for ethical behaviour. Through the fatherland the citizen can transcend his egoism and attach himself to a higher norm than mere self-interest. This ethic in its best form — in the form of civic humanism or classical republicanism — stipulates freedom and equality of citizens within the fatherland. But republican freedom and equality, as conceived by Machiavelli, are not the results of the *rights* of citizens. They are based on the pragmatic or utilitarian consideration that a fatherland of free and equal citizens — a republic — is stronger and happier than a fatherland governed by tyrants or oligarchs.

Machiavelli is very emphatic that the citizen has no rights against the fatherland. The citizen is related to it as the cell to the organism. The citizen, therefore, can and must be sacrificed for the salvation of the fatherland. The unity of the state is for the sake of the fatherland rather than for that of the citizens.

Turning to international politics, it is beyond dispute that Machiavelli's notion of the fatherland stands in the way of the emergence of a community of fatherlands. As his fatherland recognises no principles superior to its interests, any relationship that it establishes with other fatherlands must rest, ultimately, only on the principles of 'national interest' and power. And the world order that corresponds to such a view of the collectivity of fatherlands is either that of hegemony or that of balance of power. Machiavelli preferred the hegemonial system to the other, and Rome remained for him the supreme example of a successful hegemonial power.

In concluding this discussion the question may be raised as to why Machiavelli's notion of fatherland finds favour in modern history, as Meinecke has rightly claimed. A number of possible answers may be suggested. First, there is Machiavelli's emphasis. or overemphasis, on the phenomenon of insecurity. Fatherlands seek to remedy this primordial insecurity of human collectivities. Secondly, the insecurity in question may be derived from his faulty conception of human nature, namely that, ultimately, man is always led by his appetites, and that he desires to have and to acquire and to possess more than he needs, and that therefore, he is always subject to anxiety and insecurity. Thirdly, this view of human nature itself may be derived from his faulty conception of the world, i.e. from his cosmology. He rejects a teleological conception of the world, and subscribes to what must be called the astrological conception of the world, in which human affairs, or at least half of them, are subject to the rule of fortune. In the final analysis, the explanation of Machiavelli's hypostatisation of fatherland must be sought in his anthropology and his cosmology. And an adequate criticism of his notion of fatherland must begin with a critique of his anthropology and cosmology.

Notes

1. The notion of *patria* must be distinguished from that of *nazione* which he occasionally uses. For example, Venice and other Italian states are referred to as *nazione*. (Machiavelli, *Legazione e commissarie, Opere Complete*, IV, p. 654). Florence itself is referred to as a *nazione*, ibid., pp. 591, 593). The ambassadors at the court of Julius II are called "i *imbasciadori di tutte le nazioni*" (ibid., p. 661). In the *Discourses*, the French and Germans are referred to as nazione (III, 43, p. 497). In the *Discourse on the Language*, the foreign people composing the Roman legion are called 'the nations', *nazioni (Opere Complete*, VIII, p. 194). According to the same *Discourse*, a 'nation' is distinguished by its 'language' (ibid.). The fact that Machiavelli uses the term *nazione* does not mean that we can find in him the modern doctrine of nationalism. The Machiavellian fatherland is compatible with any regime, including the autocratic dynastic one, whereas the modern nation-state is compatible only with certain types of regime. Similarly, Machiavellian patriotism is not the same as modern nationalism: his patriotism is compatible with any type of government, whereas modern nationalism is not.

2. The *Discourses*, p. 124.All references to Machiavelli are to Sergio Bertelli and Franco Gaeta, (eds.), *Opere Complete*, 8 vols., (Milan, Feltrinelli, 1961-65).

3. Ibid., p. 415.

4. *The Prince*, p. 31.

5. Ibid., p. 42, 47.

6. The *Discourses*, p. 502.

7. It is interesting that in the *Art of War*, p. 519, Italy is referred to as a *provincia*.

8. *The Prince*, p. 105.

9. Ibid.

10. See, for example, *Discorso fatto al magistrato dei dieci sopra le cose di Pisa; Parole da dirle sopra le provisione del denaio, fatto un poco di proemio e die scusa; Del modo di trattare i popoli della Valdichiana ribellati; Provvisioni della republica di Firenze per instituice il magistrato de'nove ufficiali dell'Ordinanza e militia fiorentina.

11. *Discourse on Remodelling the Government of Florence, Opere Complete*, II, pp. 275-6.

12. See, for example, The *History of Florence*, pp. 65,69.

13. For an account of the debate on the origin of the Italian Language see Robert A. Hall, Jr., *The Italian Questione della Lingua*, in Studies in the Romance Languages and Literature, (University of North Carolina, 1952), no. 4, pp. 1-107.

14. Ibid., p. 16.

15. *Discourse or Dialogue on Our Language, Opere Complete*, VIII, p. 195. An English translation is found in J.R. Hale (ed. and trans.), *The Literary Works of Machiavelli* (London, Oxford University Press, 1964), pp. 173-91.

16. Ibid., p. 196.

17. Ibid., pp. 197-8.

18. See *The Prince*, p. 65.
19. *Discourse or Dialogue on Our Language*, p. 187.
20. Ibid., p. 183.
21. The *Discourses*, pp. 282-3.
22. St Paul to the Philippians, 3:20.
23. The Epistle to the Hebrews, 11:8-13.
24. Matthew, 16:26.
25. *Summa theologiae*, I–II, q. 21, art. 4, ad.3.
26. The *History of Florence*, p. 225.
27. Ibid., p. 462.
28. Ibid., p. 384.
29. Letter of 16 April 1527, *Opere Complete*, VI, p. 505.
30. See George Kateb, *Hannah Arendt: Politics, Conscience, Evil* (Totowa, N.J., Bowman and Allenheld, 1983), p. 13.
31. Hannah Arendt, *On Revolution* (New York, Viking Press, 1965), p. 290.
32. Ibid., p. 290.
33. Leo Strauss, *Thoughts on Machiavelli* (Seattle, University of Washington Press, 1969), p. 10.
34. Francesco De Sanctis, *History of Italian Literature* (Joan Redfern, trans; New York, Basic Books, 1959), 2 vols., vol. 2, p. 545.
35. Ibid., p. 547.
36. Ibid.
37. Friedrich Meinecke, *Machiavellism: The Doctrine of Raison d'Etat and Its Place in Modern History* (W. Stark, trans; New Haven, Yale University Press, 1957), p. 380. See also G.W.F. Hegel, *Hegel's Political Writings* (T.M. Knox trans., with an Introduction by Z.A. Pelczynski; Oxford, The Clarendon Press, 1964), pp. 219-23.
38. The *Discourses*, p. 495.
39. *The Price*, p. 73.
40. The *Discourses*, p. 496.
41. Ibid., pp. 363 and 380.
42. *The Prince*, p. 74.
43. *justum est bellum quibus necessarium, et pia arma quibus nisi in armis spes est*: this statement of a Samnite Captain, quoted in Livy, *History*, IV,1, finds great favour with Machiavelli. He repeats it thrice in three different works, thus indicating how consistent he was in his adherence to the principle of military necessity. See *The Prince*, ch. 26, The *Discourse*, Book III, ch. 12, and The *History of Florence*, Book V, ch. 8).
44. *The Prince*, p. 103.
45. The *History of Florence*, p. 338.
46. The *Discourses*, p. 427.
47. Machiavelli, *Opere Complete*, II, p. 60.
48. The *Discourses*, p. 502.
49. De Sanctis, *History of Italian Literature*, pp. 547-8.

4 ROUSSEAU: WILL AND POLITICS

J.M. Porter

One would be hard pressed to find another thinker who has presented his political philosophy in as dense and compact a fashion as Rousseau does with the *Social Contract*. This classic work, unlike any work of Plato or Mill or Marx, not only discusses the perennial questions and goals of man's political existence but presents the political system for their realisation, all in one short work. The very density of the manuscript contributes to the difficulty in comprehending and evaluating Rousseau.

There is an understandable tendency for students of Rousseau to view him through the eyes of those who were influenced by him, directly or indirectly, and, in this manner, to provide a coherent and intelligible explication of Rousseau's original and heady but rather mysteriously concocted political philosophy. This method of analysis could be called the successor hermeneutic: through the eyes of Kant, Hegel, or Marx one can see more clearly and thus unravel the essential themes compressed by Rousseau. Certainly, Kant and Hegel explicitly found in Rousseau themes which they used. Of especial importance to them, for example, was the idea of the rational development of the free will as the road to man's freedom and happiness.[1] With Marx the influence of Rousseau was not clearly acknowledged, but Marxian categories are used by commentators: 'What Rousseau is . . . describing in the *Social Contract* is the best possible polity that might be formed within the state of alienation characteristic of market society.'[2]

Another approach is to see how Rousseau uses the ancient societies of Sparta and Rome plus the teachings of Plato in order to criticise modern society and to construct a legitimate political system. This method of analysis could be called a predecessor hermeneutic. It seems obviously helpful in understanding Rousseau's social institutions, which have the strikingly non-modern but classical trait of combining the moral with the political. Rousseau's many laudatory references to Rome and Sparta are well known. There have been many interpreters, particularly of Rousseau's political system, who have also found it illuminating to read Rousseau in conversation with Plato.[3]

Nevertheless, particularly with a thinker as genuinely original as

Rousseau, one must be wary of assuming that his political philosophy is undistorted by a successor or predecessor hermeneutic. I propose to approach Rousseau through a study of his concept of the will. Indeed, if there was any one overwhelming factor which could cast doubt on the view that Rousseau is working fundamentally within the Greek or Roman philosophic and political traditions, it surely would be the clear primacy Rousseau places on the will over reason. Because the concept of will undergirds his model of a legitimate political system, this perspective should more clearly demonstrate the coherence and originality of Rousseau's thought and should make possible a more adequate assessment of the consequences of his political system. First, the coherence of Rousseau's political project will be shown through an explanation of the model political system outlined in the *Social Contract*.[4] Second, some key features of the will, as understood by Rousseau, will be delineated in order to indicate more fully Rousseau's intentions. Third, on the basis of the political model and the supporting concept of the will an assessment will be made of some of the consequences for man's political existence.

Rousseau's Model Political System

Men will be true citizens, Rousseau reasons, only when society is reconstructed to mirror the relationship of man and nature found in the original state of nature. The unintended transformation from the state in which man was born free to the political society in which man is in chains can in principle be corrected by a deliberate transformation of society. The original independence or liberty man had as a primitive non-rational brute in nature can be metamorphosed into moral liberty, which man can enjoy as a rational, virtuous being in society. This new mode of existence, promising moral liberty, depends upon individuals willing and acting in a manner purportedly consistent with and guided by distinct features of the state of nature; yet, these same willing and acting individuals are substantially transformed through the social contract into citizens. The promise of society depends upon the lessons of nature. Thus, it is necessary to examine, first, what Rousseau means by liberty or free agency as seen in both nature and society, and, second, to delineate those characteristics of the state of nature which are to be replicated by the social contract.

In the *Social Contract* (Book 1, ch. 8) Rousseau distinguishes between three kinds of liberty: natural, civil, and moral. Natural liberty is derived from an individual's physical power and is found in the state of nature: 'The right to anything that tempts him and that he can take.' Civil liberty is found in society and is derived from the laws of the state and, as Rousseau says, 'is limited by the general will'. Moral liberty is unique to a society based upon the social contract. Moral liberty 'makes man the master of himself; for to be governed by appetite alone is slavery, while obedience to a law one prescribes to oneself is freedom'. Moral liberty provides one with a sense of self-sufficiency ('master of himself') through combining will ('prescribe to oneself') with law.[5]

These three kinds of liberty can be distinguished by the place or context in which each can be found: state of nature, civil society and society formed by the social contract. In other words, each occurs within certain boundaries: natural liberty within the boundaries of the power of the individual; civil liberty within the boundaries of the general will; and moral liberty within the boundaries of the laws one prescribes for oneself. The last is of the greatest significance since its realisation constitutes the transformation from individual to citizen.

Moral liberty, or autonomy, requires the conjoining of will and law. Rousseau's use of law is unremarkable, but his use of will is strikingly original. There are three discernible meanings to liberty of the will. One can be called procedural, that is, there is liberty of the will when one voluntarily prescribes. A person is dependent — lacks free will — when obeying even a 'good' law if he has not voluntarily prescribed it. A second meaning to liberty of the will is created when man enters society. The will, for Rousseau, has almost no content in the state of nature because it is under the influences of particulars and appetites. Its potentiality, however, can be seen. Within civil society one can escape the appetites and particulars, and will the general and universal. Man substitutes a 'rule of conduct in the place of instinct', 'duty takes the place of physical impulse', and man 'consults his reason rather than studies his inclinations' (Book 1, ch. 8). Here is a rational and formal element to the will in that reason is the source, not instincts or appetites, and the object is general and universal, not particular and contingent.

The final meaning is contained in the idea of self-mastery. Liberty of will in this experiential or substantive sense is found in the state of nature ('everyone is there his own master') as well as in the civil society formed by the contract where moral liberty makes 'man the master of himself'. This explains why Rousseau believes that he has provided a solution to his central problem: find a form of association in which 'each one, uniting with all, nevertheless obeys only himself and remains as free as before' (Book 1, ch. 6). We can be free as *before* only in the procedural and the substantial or experiential senses. We have also gained, through the rational and formal element, moral liberty, which we did not have as primitive men in the state of nature. The rational and formal element becomes the means for retaining in society the core experience of being a free actor: control and mastery.

In order to obtain moral liberty, law must be prescribed by the citizen, and true law must in form be both general and abstract: 'When I say that the province of the law is always general, I mean that the law considers all subjects collectively and all actions in the abstract; it does not consider any individual man or any specific action' (Book 2, ch. 6). In addition to formal attributes, true law must be derived from the general will, that is the will created in the formation of the civil society. The general will as the source of law contains the objective, general interest of the whole community. So, both the source and the form of law make it objective, rational and universal.

Law and will, so defined, coalesce. Within the social contract the will is guided by reason rather than appetite and is directed at the general rather than the particular; the law instantiates through its rational form and ontological source the objective and general interest.[6] This internal coherence among the structural features of law and will provides moral liberty with an analytical as well as experiential or psychological meaning.

Moral liberty, or autonomy, would remain hypothetical were Rousseau unable to show how the conditions of nature can be transferred into civil society through the contract and its articles of association. The state of nature imposes three major conditions on man: (1) There is an unconditional dependence on the impersonal, objective, general laws of nature. The authority and force of nature are indiscriminate and equally felt by all. (2) There is no personal subjection. Men are isolated and independent of each other. The laws of nature are general, not personal in their applicability. (3) There is, in sum, a fundamental equality in that the generality of conditions is the same for all: all have mastery over themselves by only willing what they have the power to obtain. The articles of association for the social contract repeat these conditions: (1) There is an unconditional dependence on the general will. (2) There is no personal subjection, 'since each man gives himself to all, he gives himself to no one'. (3) There is, in sum, a fundamental equality within the social compact because the conditions are the same for all. These conditions established by the articles of association are not merely a mirroring or reflection of nature. They can be duplicated and reenacted in society through the general will; a new mode of existence, objective and rational, can thus be created.

The general will that creates the new mode of existence is 'connected' with individual moral liberty or autonomy in two ways. First, Rousseau explains that the relationship is analytic. Because each person 'gives his entire self' without reservation (Book 1, ch. 6), the individual escapes dependence and inequality: by definition all rights and powers are given to the whole community, which is to no one. Rousseau describes this act as a tautology: 'a contract, as it were, with himself'. 'An obligation to oneself', he adds, is not like 'having an obligation to something of which one is a member' (Book 1, ch. 7). Analytically, individual autonomy is preserved. Second, the new mode of existence, provided by the community under the general will, preserves the crucial experiential or substantive sense of freedom: control and mastery. The total alienation 'by each associate of himself and all his rights to the whole community' keeps each person independent and a master of himself: by the alienation of his private interest each person conceives of himself in terms of the other, that is, in terms of the general or common interest, and this enables his private or individual will now to will the general or common good, which is to prescribe a law to himself. These are the ingredients for autonomy: a subjective sense of individual mastery and control is retained while willing the objective general interest.

The analytical and experiential ties between autonomy and the general will are, for Rousseau, only different sides of the same bond. It is because the act of alienation can be conceived in analytic terms that the individual experiences no loss of his sense of control and mastery. The rational character of the act of alienation, an imposing of one's will on reality and oneself, accentuates psychologically the sense of control and mastery: one is a slave to passion, but by binding oneself through reason (a law prescribed to oneself) one is free, that is, experiences a sense of control and mastery.

For the general will to be a solution there must be a rationally coherent object to be realised; also, the general will must have a source or foundation which can provide some objectivity. Nature, in short, must still undergird the articles of association. With respect to the object, it is certainly Rousseau's claim that there is a true, objective, realisable, general interest: 'it should spring from all and apply to all' (Book 2, ch. 4). The possibility of collating private interests so that a general interest can be given force is a major concern of modern social science and philosophy. That this is a logical possibility — assuming that the premises are carefully stipulated in order to avoid the voter's paradox — is clear, although one may question whether there are many issues in politics for which a general interest can be found. An objective, general interest on an issue is possible; it is another question to determine if there are many such issues or if one should try and mold political and social existence so that a general interest can be formed.[7]

I will explore the foundation or ontological source of the will in more detail later. It needs to be noted, though, that the general will is possible because it builds upon two particular components of man's nature: *amour de soi* and free agency or liberty of the will. Each becomes distorted in society and requires the social contract to be perfected. *Amour de soi* is distorted into *amour propre* through the development of society. *Amour de soi* is not destroyed, however, and can be recovered and completed with a social contract 'under the supreme direction of the general will'. Under the general conditions of the state of nature, the private will was sufficient for attaining natural liberty and a concomitant happiness fitting that primitive mode of existence.[8] But, with the evolution of man and society, the advent of private property, and the growth of *amour propre*, neither liberty nor happiness could be sustained. When the conditions found in nature — equality, a dependence on nature, a lack of personal subjection — are established by the articles of association, then the human essence can be perfected through a new mode of existence: *amour propre*, which is selfish and particular, becomes virtuous and general.

The second component of man's nature, free agency or liberty of the will, also changes in the move from nature to society and, finally, to the social contract. Liberty in both the procedural or voluntary sense and in the substantive or experiential sense of mastery is distorted as man leaves the state of nature. The *Second Discourse* tells the story of man's corruption. There is only the illusion of free agency, as temptation and excessive desires predominate, and men experience a loss of the sense of mastery. With the social contract, however, willing and acting are fortified and transformed through the articles of association and the act of incorporation. In particular, the rational and formal elements in 'true' law and in the general will enable man to again experience himself as a free actor with a sense of control and mastery but this time within a 'moral and communal existence'. Moral liberty, not found in nature, fulfills the potential in the liberty of the will. Thus, *amour de soi* and liberty are not merely restored but are completed and enriched. Through the artificiality of the articles of the articles of confederation — that is, through their rationality, abstractness and generality — the potentiality of man can be realised.

Rousseau's Concept of the Will

The *Social Contract* is designed to show how social institutions can be made legitimate through the 'true principles of political right' (Book 4, ch. 9). Legitimacy, in short, is achieved by 'taking men as they are' and by creating institutions which then form men within society so that both individual moral liberty and a communal identity are attained.[9] One of the essential questions that is often posed for examining Rousseau's project is 'Has Rousseau created a unitary or pluralistic system?'A traditional way of approaching this question has been to describe the powers, processes and institutions of Rousseau's political system and draw conclusions about the consequences for political life. The unending controversies that characterise this approach result in part from a lack of agreement about Rousseau's philosophic premises and about their influence on the development of democracy.[10] The fact that Rousseau's premises themselves are often viewed as in tension further compounds the difficulties in assessing his political system. For example, it is said that Rousseau attempted to combine the virtue of the ancient city with the lessons of nature.[11] Another formulation is that he tried to unite ancient cohesiveness with modern voluntarism.[12] One can plausibly stress one or the other of these paired premises. Inevitably, there are more conflicting interpretations. One can understand why some interpreters have concluded that Rousseau was never able to reconcile his own premises.

A more fruitful approach is to begin an analysis with Rousseau's central philosophic concept, the will. The will serves as a prism for revealing Rousseau's intentions in creating his political system.

While Rousseau's concept of the will differs in several respects from Augustine's, he is, nonetheless, closer to the Judeo-Christian theological tradition than he is to that of classical Greece.[13] With the latter there was no clear idea of will or free agency independent of the functioning of the mind. Albrecht Dihle draws the contrast:

Our term "will" denotes only the resulting intention, leaving out any special reference to thought, instinct, or emotion as possible sources of that intention. Greek, on the other hand, is able to express intention only together with one of its causes, but never in its own right.[14]

Thus, the intention behind a human action is always conflated with the originating reason or emotion.[15] The ideal of moral freedom, which is for Rousseau the mark of a full and uncorrupted self, is for the Greeks a consequence of intellectual activity: 'freedom is brought about when the human intellect has chosen the aim of action according to the true order of being, and has not been hindered in its efforts by error, emotion, or compulsion'.[16] The opposite also holds, that is, when man's intellectual activity is restricted and the 'rational order of being' has been inadequately perceived, then to that degree man's freedom of action has been diminished.[17]

Perhaps the key difference between the philosophical anthropology of the Judeo-Christian tradition and that of classical antiquity is that willing or free agency was conceived as independent of, although related to, man's intellectual activity. The concept of the will remains notoriously problematic, but with the Judeo-Christian formulation will has been clearly differentiated from the functioning of the mind.[18] In examining the will by itself, usually two dimensions are articulated. One is the epistemological dimension. Here attention is focused on free choosing or deciding. Willing, in this sense, is viewed as undetermined or uncaused. It is often argued that a condition for moral autonomy is just such a free or uncaused will. Patrick Riley captures this position:

> One must assume the possibility of a free action that is binding for the reason that morality depends in part on undetermined choice: not undetermined in the sense that there is no reason for such willing but in the sense that we are free to accept or reject the reason, thereby earning justifiable praise or blame, and that the will is not determined, in the strictly causal sense in which a stone is necessitated to fall, by anything whatsoever.[19]

This autonomous or voluntaristic feature of the will, of course, is evident in Rousseau and is particularly stressed in Kantian interpretations.[20]

A second dimension of the will is ontological or experiential. The will is described as an organ or faculty with experiential content and structure. It is common in the Judeo-Christian tradition, beginning with Augustine, for thinkers to discuss the constituting experiences of the will. It is this second dimension of the will that needs to be explored, for it is the ontological or experiential conceptualisation which provides the point of reference for defining the self. With this second dimension of the will one can see most clearly Rousseau's originality and understand the intentions behind his model of a legitimate political system.

John Charvet correctly points out that for Rousseau free-will is as redundant in the state of nature as is reason. Instincts are sufficient for natural man. But, as Charvet explains Rousseau, there is present throughout all stages of man's development self-consciousness: 'The consciousness of oneself as an individual set apart from the rest of the world, arising out of one's own consciousness merely as subject to, but at the same time capable of resisting, the impulses of nature.'[21] What constitutes this self for Rousseau? Free-will is a feature of man, certainly in the later stages of man's development. It is the experiential or ontological dimension of will, however, which is the key to his understanding of the self.

Materialism cannot explain the existence or the nature of this self. Rousseau asks: 'if it is true that all matter senses, where shall I conceive the sensitive unity or the individual *I* to be? Will it be in each molecule of matter or in the aggregate bodies?'[22] Neither can the self be reduced to instincts. In the famous quotation from the *Second Discourse*, Rousseau claims: 'Nature commands every animal, and the Beast obeys. Man meets with the same impetus, but he recognises himself to be free to acquiesce, or to resist, and it is above all in the consciousness of this freedom that the spirituality of his soul shows itself.'[23] The origin of this capacity of the will cannot be discovered, or so implies the Savoyard Vicar:

I know will only by the sentiment of my own will, and understanding is no better known to me. When I am asked what the cause is which determines my will, I ask in turn what the cause is which determines my judgement; for it is clear that these two causes are only one; and if one clearly understands that man is active in his judgements, and that his understanding is only the power of comparing and judging, one will see that his freedom is only a similar power or one derived from the former . . . What, then, is the cause which determines his will? It is his judgement. And what is the cause which determines his judgement: It is his intelligent faculty, it is his power of judging: the determining cause is in himself. Beyond this I understand nothing more.[24]

The will, then, cannot be understood by looking for some deeper level from which it can be derived. Rather, Rousseau provides a phenomenology of the will.[25] There are three essential attributes to his conception: it is grounded in nature and passion; it is self-sufficient; and it emanates a sense of mastery.[26]

Rousseau's genealogy of man's moral character begins with natural man and with the one original passion: 'The source of our passions, the origin and the principle of all the others, the only one born with man and which never leaves him so long as he lives is self-love – a primitive, innate passion, which is anterior to every other, and of which all others are in a sense only modifications.'[27] Further, this natural origin guarantees that man begins good and potentially perfectible.

> Let us set now as an incontestable maxim that the first movements of nature are always right. There is no original perversity in the human heart. There is not a single vice to be found in it of which it cannot be said how and whence it entered. The sole passion natural to man is *amour de soi* or *amour-propre* taken in an extended sense. This *amour-propre* in itself or relative to us is good and useful; and since it has no necessary relation to others, it is in this respect naturally neutral. It becomes good or bad only by the application made of it and the relations given to it.[28]

As Rousseau reconstructs the story of man's progress, the initial unity of the will becomes fragmented in society when man abandons his 'true needs' and when the insatiable *amour propre* expands through comparisons with others: 'What makes man essentially good is to have few needs and to compare himself little to others; what makes him essentially wicked is to have many needs and to depend very much on opinion.'[29]

The skeleton description of a unified and good self applies only to natural man. In society imagination increases man's needs and dependence on others, the will becomes corrupted and man becomes unhappy. It is essential to note that man's unhappiness cannot be explained by a division or flaw within the will, such as depicted by the doctrine of original sin. Also, man's unhappiness cannot be traced to a failure of reason or a lack of knowledge. In fact, it is more the opposite: 'Reason engenders *amour propre* and reflection fortifies it.'[30] In the first explanation of unhappiness, one would need God's help to unite the will and provide happiness, and in the other, better reasoning or information would be necessary. Since Rousseau does not accept either the Christian doctrine of original sin or the Greek view of the potential primacy of the rational faculty over passion, he finds the causes and solutions of man's unhappiness elsewhere.

In brief, 'alien causes' corrupt man's natural passions, including *amour propre*, and these occur with the very development of civilisation.[31] In place of a Christian catechism Emile is given a more appropriate one: 'Let him know that man is naturally good; let him feel it; let him judge his neighbour by himself. But let him see that society depraves and perverts men.'[32] Why does man's 'fatal progress' lead to suffering and evil?[33] The answer is found in the peculiar nature of the will. The will needs boundaries or an order, and in nature there are provided just such boundaries through non-personal necessity. No self in this state experiences a debilitating loss of power or worth. There is a natural order for the will. In society there is only conventional order, and the self is constantly experiencing unrealised desires and a debilitating loss of power and worth. Rousseau agrees: 'Dependence on things, since it has no morality, is in no way detrimental to freedom and engenders no vices. Dependence on man, since it is without order, engenders all the vices, and by it, master and slave are mutually corrupted . . .'[34] Without boundaries and order the will, initially united and good, succumbs to the temptations of society. Why does it succumb? Augustine in his own exploration of the will had noted that to will and to be able are not the same, and Rousseau comes to a similar conclusion:

> I always have the power to will, I do not always have the force to execute. When I abandon myself to temptations, I act according to the impulsion of external objects. When I reproach myself for this weakness, I listen only to my will. I am enslaved because of my vices and free because of my remorse. The sentiment of my freedom is effaced in me only when I become depraved and finally prevent the voice of the soul from being raised against the law of the body.[35]

If the cause of evil and suffering is not in man's will but in external causes, there also must lie the solution. The external order must be so constructed that a will (of this nature) can regain its strength (the force to execute), its unity, and its happiness:

> In what then, consists human wisdom or the road of true happiness? [It] is in diminishing the excess of the desires over the faculties and putting power and will in perfect equality. It is only then that, with all the powers in action, the soul will nevertheless remain peaceful and that man will be well ordered.[36]

With this statement one can recognise the intention which permeates
the *Social Contract*.

Implicit in the view that the will is grounded in nature and passion
is the second key attribute of Rousseau's phenomenology of the will:
self-sufficiency. It is a premise necessary for Rousseau's notions of
happiness, perfectibility, goodness, immortality and freedom. 'Whoever
does what he wants', says Rousseau, 'is happy if he is self-sufficient.'[39]
There are, in Rousseau's account, no structural flaws in nature or in
man's will, and, as a consequence, Rousseau provides a highly original
explanation of the existence of evil and corruption: the fall from self-
sufficiency with the dependence on others. Unhappiness results.
Personal wickedness is traced to weakness of the will relative to the
temptations of the imaginations engendered by society. The causes are
'alien' to the will. In principle, the will is self-sufficient. Man only needs
the proper context — the *Social Contract* or the educational programme
of Emile — in which to develop: 'his potential faculties were to develop
only with the opportunities to exercise them . . . '[38] Indeed, the
'faculty of self-perfection', which caused man's facade of progress but
real moral decline, logically requires a premise of self-sufficiency,
otherwise self-perfectability would be impossible.[39]

Self-sufficiency is also a necessary condition for his conception of
the good and of immortality. Rousseau constantly tells his readers that
the will's first natural impulse is sound, and this can be the case only if
the will is self-sufficient: it needs no other grounding or ethical injec-
tion from a transcendent source. The idea of goodness is a derivative
of a will so conceived, whether it is the will of man or of God: 'Now,
goodness is the essential effect of a power without limit and of the self-
love essential to every being aware of itself. The existence of Him who
is omnipotent is, so to speak, coextensive with the existence of the
beings.'[40] Since the will and goodness in man parallel the relationship
in God, it is not surprising that immortality is explained in terms of
attaining self-sufficiency of the will:

> I aspire to the moment when after being delivered from the shackles
> of the body, I shall be *me* without contradiction or division and shall
> need only myself in order to be happy. While waiting, I am already
> happy in this life because I take little account of all its ills, because
> I regard it as almost foreign to my being, and because all the true
> good that I can get out of it depends on me.[31]

Rousseau's uses of freedom in the sense of self-choosing and in the sense of right-choosing depend upon the attribute of self-sufficiency. 'Even in the state of nature', according to Rousseau, children 'enjoy only an imperfect freedom' precisely because their needs surpassed their strength, and this situation, he concludes, is 'similar to that enjoyed by men in the civil state'.[42] Rousseau clearly thinks that the greater the self-sufficiency, the greater the freedom. Thus, he constantly advises man to perfect the balance between desires and strength, needs and wants. When the balance is achieved, as it was in the state of nature, man is self-sufficient and free. When the balance is lost, the choosing self is propelled by 'alien causes' which destroy the capacity for free-choosing. Only the self-sufficient will can freely choose. Freedom in the sense of autonomous self-choosing presumes the self-sufficiency of the will. The notion of freedom as right-choosing also builds upon the critical attribute of self-sufficiency. With its grounding in nature, a free will would by its very nature only want the good. For Rousseau, undetermined self-choosing and substantive right-choosing are but two dimensions of the will: 'Doubtless, I am not free not to want my own good; I am not free to want what is bad for me. But it is in this precisely that my freedom consists — my being able to will only what is suitable to me, or what I deem to be such, without anything external to me determining me.'[43]

In addition to self-choosing and right-choosing, freedom has another dimension, and this comprises the third key attribute of Rousseau's phenomenology of the will: the experience of mastery. Without this experience no self can be complete, free and happy. In short, no other experience is as essential to being a full person. This, of course, is not mastery in some vulgar and possessive sense. Attempts to overreach oneself — to extend desires over needs — negate the development of the sense of mastery. Rousseau asks: 'Does it follow that I am not my own master, because I am not the master of being somebody else than me?[44] In actuality, the sense of mastery serves to restrain human desires and action: 'I have never believed that man's freedom consisted in doing what he wants, but rather in never doing what he does not want to do . . . '[45] This negative formulation accentuates purposeful mastery as creating the essential sentiment of freedom, in contrast to simply the absence of impediments. The ultimate goal of the educational regimen of Emile is to create this very sense of mastery. Only a will developed to attain this sentiment can be called truly free. Emile is repeatedly 'forced' by dramas and schemes engineered by the tutor to develop his various faculties, including the will. The culmination of his education occurs at the end of the novel when Emile is taught to control his desires for Sophie by obeying the tutor's command to not see Sophie for two years. The tutor tells Emile: 'Up to now you were only apparently free. You had only the precarious freedom of a slave to whom nothing had been commanded. Now be really free. Learn to become your own master.'[46] Emile is told to exert his will over man's most powerful drive: 'try your strength' and 'exercise for battle'. The tutor explains to Emile that it is not 'within our control to have or not to have passions. But it is within our control to reign over them'.[47] The experience of mastery is coeval with recognising and accrediting this exercise of the will. such an exercise, though, is not merely subjective. It must have an objective component. In man's primitive state man's boundaries or limits are objective, grounded in necessity and nature. In society, it is nearly impossible to find the equivalent boundaries. The institutions of the *Social Contract*, grounded in the general will, address this need for an objective component. In *Emile*, the tutor both shows Emile boundaries and is himself one of the boundaries.[48] Emile is told that true freedom comes through the mastery of his desire, and, further, that this final exercise is applicable to all of man's potentialities and faculties:

> All passions are good when one remains their master . . . What is forbidden to us by nature is to extend our attachments further than our strength; what is forbidden to us by reason is to want what we cannot obtain; what is forbidden to us by conscience is not temptations but rather letting ourselves be conquered by temptations.[49]

Rousseau's lesson, then, is that the minimally-conscious self found in nature – united, good, free and happy, and with a sense of mastery – can in principle still endure in society.

The Political Consequences of Rousseau's Ideas

Rousseau believes that the will properly understood and then properly educated produces virtues that lead from the family to the state. Plato, in abolishing the family, is criticised by Rousseau for not understanding this crucial point:

> . . . as though there were no need for a natural base on which to form conventional ties; as though the love of one's nearest were not the principle of the love one owes the state; as though it were not by

means of the small fatherland which is the family that the heart attaches itself to the large one; as though it were not the good son, the good husband, and the good father who make the good citizen![50]

What kind of human association or relationship is possible, assuming that man's will is formed and operates as Rousseau declares? The nature of the Rousseauian virtues helps provide an answer. There are virtues that primarily depict relationship *with* others and those that are responses *to* others. Pity and love, for example, are two modes of establishing bonds with others; repentance and gratitude are types of responses to others. Rousseau's analysis of these four virtues is derived from his phenomenology of the will, and they illuminate the kind of human relationships Rousseau wishes to nourish.

The most striking feature of these four virtues, as defined by Rousseau, is that they are peculiarly non-personal, that is, the practice of these virtues does not sensitise one to acknowledge a distinctive other person. The psychic operation of pity, as reported by Rousseau, will serve to illustrate. Pity is the emotion engendered through imaginatively comparing one's own superior position with one who suffers, and it is the reverse of envy:

> Pity is sweet because, in putting ourselves in the place of the one who suffers, we nevertheless feel the pleasure of not suffering as he does. Envy is bitter because the sight of a happy man, far from putting the envious man in his place, makes the envious man regret not being there.[51]

Emile quickly learns to get an 'inner enjoyment' though the practice of pity.[52] This sweet emotion is not about or for the person suffering, but it is a particular emotion derived from the relative state of the person who has it. The emotion makes one aware of oneself; it does not 'focus' on another person. Further, this natural emotion can be safely utilised only when it is 'generalised and extended to the whole of mankind'.[53] Thus, pity is non-personal in two ways. First, it is not a concern for the other person but is derived from not being the other person. Second, in order to keep this natural impulse from being destroyed through excessive selfishness, or, as Rousseau says, 'to prevent pity from degenerating into weakness', it is the species, not the neighbour, toward whom pity must be directed.[54] Again, the virtue is non-personal. The self-sufficient will has been maintained: the virtue of pity does not sensitise one to a person nor does one become obligated through pity to a person, which would create a sense of dependence and a potential loss of the sense of mastery. Yet, one still has the natural sweet emotion without threat to one's self while joined with mankind: independent but united.

Love is another virtue depicting bonds with others, and it is traditionally held to be the strongest and most personal bond among humans. Nevertheless, as Rousseau plots this most complex of natural impulses, one is again struck by how curiously non-personal it becomes. After Sophie and Emile have come to know each other well and they have fallen in love, the query is made: What has Emile gained by his love and how has he changed? The answer must rank as one of the oddest in the history of human love: 'He has new reasons to be himself. This is the single point where he differs from what he was.'[55] In accounts of love, romantic or religious, it is invariably described as a 'desire' directed at something other than oneself. The person who loves is said to be drawn out by the beloved and made more worthy. Thus Portia tells of the effect of her love for Bassanio: 'To wish myself much better, yet for you . . . I might in virtues, beauties, livings, friends, exceed account.'[56] Emile, in contrast, has a self-sufficient will. But, as with pity, a psychic operation is performed through extending a natural impulse (sexual desire) to the idealised love of Sophie. By such sublimation the self does not lose its control. Allan Bloom correctly avers of Emile:

> He has an overwhelming need for another, but that other must be the embodiment of the ideal of beauty, and his interest in her partakes of the disinterestedness of the love of the beautiful. Moreover it is not quite precise to say that he loves an "other," for he will not be making himself hostage to an alien will and thus engaging in a struggle for mastery. This woman will, to use Platonic language, participate in the *idea* he has of her. He will recognize in her his own highest aspirations. She will complete him without alienating him.[57]

Gratitude and repentance are virtues designed to bridge two properties of the human condition: man's sense of isolation and his need of others. The two virtues have a common feature respecting the self in that both depend upon an uncaused offering of one self to another. Gratitude occurs, for example, when a person recognises that he is not self-sufficient but limited and thus can receive from another. This customary understanding of gratitude, though, is not taught Emile;

rather, gratitude is redefined to be consistent with the Rousseauian will: 'If you grant him what he asks of you, he will not thank you, but he will feel that he has contracted a debt.'[58] When the idea of gratitude is transformed to the metaphor of a cash debt, the person becomes objectified. Then, the self is not in question for either party. Repentance, a harder virtue, is also clearly anathema to the Rousseauian will, since it requires the sacrifice, however momentary, of one's sense of self-sufficiency and mastery. Not surprisingly, Emile experiences only a 'sentiment of wrong'. The wrong comes from his adolescent 'ardor', but there is no sense of knowingly committing a wrong for which he is responsible.[59] Weakness is the source of any wrong-doing, not the will itself, as Rousseau constantly reiterates. His own *Confessions* are noteworthy for not providing one example of a real confession or of repentance. Each famous episode is excused by a concatenation of alien causes and temptations. In sum, the traditional view has been that by admitting self-deficiency, the practice of gratitude and repentance enabled men to establish a personal dependence and thus temper their sense of isolation and mutual injustice. Virtues so understood would be incompatible with Rousseau's phenomenology of the will.[60]

It is clear that the psychic operation of extension is crucial to Rousseau's project for taking a natural man and forming a free, moral and happy man. The extension enables a natural impulse, distorted by *amour propre* in society, to be general, rational, equitable and just:

> Let us extend *amour propre* to other beings. We shall transform it into a virtue, and there is no man's heart in which this virtue does not have its root. The less the object of our care is immediately involved with us, the less the illusion of particular interest is to be feared. The more one generalizes this interest, the more it becomes equitable . . . [61]

The individual psychic operation of moving from the person to the species in order to obtain virtue is structurally identical to the act of association where the individuals together move from the particular to the general and form the social contract. It would be tedious to cite all of the obvious parallels but two points should be mentioned: both individually and collectively, the particular and selfish will is transformed through attachment to a non-personal, abstract or general whole; the inducement for this critical act is the goal of freedom and a sense of mastery. That there could be an asymmetry between private and collective willing, responsibility and accountability does not appear to

trouble Rousseau. Nor does he hold that the type of association significantly changes the operation of the will. He literally holds, as he said
in his rebuke of Plato, that the good son, husband, father, make a good
citizen. The idea that different roles and human contexts require different faculties or that different types of human associations may have
different goals and be in tension, if not conflict, is not seriously entertained. Indeed, his conception of the will serves to undermine such
concerns. It is precisely because of the key attributes of the will that
amour propre can be extended into virtue, that Emile can safely love
Sophie, and that a social contract is possible.

Thus, to understand the kind of political association intended by
Rousseau requires constant reference to the will. Its nature and operation clarify Rousseau's intention in creating his model of a legitimate
political system. There are two features of the association which particularly become clear. First, the intention of the compact is to create a
true unity. Second, the association is designed to solve social tension.[62]

First, the political association attains legitimacy — the individuals
are free but united — when each individual is able to will without
respect to persons. To obtain virtue, our care is extended to the species;
to obtain a legitimate association, our interest is extended to the whole.
What is required in both cases is an identification with a non-personal
unity. The idea of identification is meant to be taken seriously by
Rousseau. Only by identification with mankind can a natural impulse
become a virtue: 'For the sake of reason, for the sake of love of ourselves, we must have pity for our species still more than for our neighbour . . . '[63] The weakness of the will is thereby strengthened. The same
steps are taken in creating a social compact. For example, the Legislator, emulating Emile's tutor, must transform each individual who is a
solitary whole 'into a part of a larger whole from which this individual receives, in a sense, his life and his being'. By 'altering man's constitution' one will have 'strengthened it' (Book 2, ch. 7). Legitimacy
could not be achieved without true identification and unity with the
whole.[64] Citizenship itself is contingent upon identification and unity.
By definition, breaking the unity or even hypocritically identifying
('lying before the laws') entails a loss of citizenship and even one's
standing as a moral person. One becomes 'but a man' (Book 2, ch. 6;
Book 4, ch. 8).

That the association is designed to solve social tension can be seen
through recalling again the operation of the will. In the *Confessions*
Rousseau asserts that he was taught one great moral maxim which he

incorporated into his writing: 'to avoid situations which place our duties in opposition to our interests, and show us where another man's loss spells profits to us'.[65] As we have seen, Rousseau was able to do precisely this for the individual will through the extension of *amour propre* to the species or to an ideal. Emile only attains true freedom when he can experience his love for Sophie through the idea of love. With the social contract, 'duties and interests equally obligate' (Book 1, ch. 8). The particular will is transformed through the act of association into the general will. This transformation requires law and reason in order to establish the formal and rational features of the general will, and the result, as with Emile, is freedom: 'obedience to the law one prescribes for oneself is freedom' (Book 1, ch. 8). In principle, at least, natural impulse and right, interest and duty, can be tied. It is not rhetorical excess when Rousseau claims that 'the most general will is also always the most just, and that the voice of the people is in fact the voice of God'.[66] Given the key attributes of the will, man's nature is not perceived as constituted by faculties and desires in inescapable tension, nor is society visualised as having perpetual tension among generations, classes, interests and purposes. A solution to man's wretchedness in society is thus possible, and freedom can be attained.

An association which provides a non-personal unity and a solution to the tensions in man's social existence transforms the meaning of the 'political'. First, this is an association in which it makes little sense to talk of a public space. When the voice of God inheres in the will of the people, there is no need for the give and take of public discourse. The rhetoric of persuasion inevitably turns into the litany of belief. A public space is required precisely because rightness is not attainable; in other words, something less than a solution must be sought. Secondly, the legitimacy of Rousseau's political system is dependent upon achieving a true unity, one not born from simple agreement but from an identification. Here collective action is not the result of joint endeavours but is more aptly characterised as a community of believers.

Notes

I am grateful to my colleague Steve Lewis for his comments.

1. An excellent assessment of the mass of literature which stresses the Kantian themes in Rousseau is provided by Stephen Ellenburg, 'Rousseau and Kant: Principles of Political Right,' in R.A. Leigh (ed.) *Rousseau After Two Hundred Years*, (Cambridge, Cambridge University Press, 1982), pp. 3-22.

2. Asher Horowitz, 'Will, Community and Alienation in Rousseau's *Social Contract,*' *Canadian Journal of Political and Social Theory* (forthcoming). Robert Wokler provides a careful analysis of the influence of Rousseau on Marx and of the secondary literature on this topic: 'Rousseau and Marx,' in David Miller and Larry Siedentop (eds.) *The Nature of Political Theory*, (Oxford, Clarendon Press, 1983), pp. 219-46.

3. Regrettably, no one has written an essay critically examining the claim of Plato's influence on Rousseau. M.J. Silverthorne cites the various interpreters since 1918 who do see significant Platonic influence on Rousseau's thought. Silverthorne himself documents Rousseau's use of the *Laws*. 'Rousseau's Plato,' *Studies on Voltaire and Eighteenth Century* 116 (1973): 235-49. In addition to these citations, one should add the recent works by Allan Bloom (ed. and trans.) *Emile* (New York, Basic Books, 1979), and Hilail Gilden, *Rousseau's Social Contract: The Design of the Argument* (Chicago; University of Chicago Press, 1983). Leo Strauss, mentor of Gildin and Bloom, had used the phrase, 'listening to the conversation between the great philosophers'. *Liberalism: Ancient and Modern* (New York, Basic Books, 1968), p. 7.

4. Even in his practical works on Corsica and Poland, the model remained the *Social Contract*: 'For the rest, I have discussed this matter in the Social Contract, and for anyone who wants to reckon well my sentiment on anything, this is where it is necessary to search.' This is a passage cut from the final version of the essay on Poland. Quoted in James Miller, *Dreamer of Democracy* (New Haven, Yale University Press, 1984), p. 129.

5. John Plamenatz warns: 'It is worth noticing that Rousseau, who was among the first to try to show in any detail how men develop the capacities peculiar to their species through activities which make social and moral beings of them, who recognized that society (at least in its earlier stages) must be the largely unforeseen and unintended product of forms of behaviour which may be voluntary and purposeful but are not consciously directed to social aims, and who urged men to control and transform society to achieve a kind of freedom which he called *moral* and defined as obedience to a law prescribed to oneself, never used such expressions as "self-realization", "self-fulfillment", and "self-improvement".' *Karl Marx's Philosophy of Man* (Oxford, 1975), p. 323. 'Self-sufficiency' or a derivative was perhaps his most common phrasing. See the thorough study by Ronald Grimsley, 'Rousseau and the Ideal of Self-Sufficiency,' *Studies in Romanticism* 10 (Autumn, 1971), pp. 283-99.

6. In the *Geneva Manuscript* Rousseau notes this connection between the form of law and will: 'when the entire people enacts something concerning the entire people, it considers only itself . . . without any division of the whole. Then the object of the enactment is general like the will that enacts, and it is this act that I call a law.' Roger D. Masters (ed.), *On the Social Contract with Geneva Manuscript and Political Economy* (New York, St. Martin's Press, 1978), p. 190.

7. W.G. Runciman and A.K. Sen have argued that the two-person, non-zero-sum, non-cooperative game known as the 'prisoner's dilemma' illustrates the logical structure of the general will and demonstrates its potential objectivity. 'Games, Justice and the General Will,' *Mind* 65 (1965), p. 554. Brian Barry, less successfully, examines theories of decision-making to illustrate an objective element in the general will. 'The Public Interest,' in Anthony Quinton (ed.), *Political Philosophy* (Oxford, 1967), pp. 119-25.

8. Stephen Salkever has argued that happiness, not freedom, is Rousseau's goal. Freedom, though, describes the 'mode of existence' and entails happiness. See, 'Freedom, Participation and Happiness,' *Political Theory* 5 (1977), pp. 391-413; 'Rousseau and the Concept of Happiness,' *Polity* 11 (1978), pp. 27-45.

9. One of these institutions – the Legislator – is not created but found. The idea that human nature must be changed to fit the legitimate government occurs also in Rousseau's practical works. In the *Constitutional Project for Corsica*, Rousseau advises 'form the nation to fit the government', and in *The Government of Poland*, Rousseau praises the great lawmakers – Moses, Lycurgus and Numa – for creating a people through rigorous institutions, 'peculiar rites and ceremonies'. F.M. Watkins (ed.), *Rousseau: Political Writings* (New York, Nelson, 1953), pp. 277, 165.

10. James Miller provides a useful synopsis of the arguments and literature, *Rousseau: Dreamer of Democracy*, 'Epilogue: Democracy After Rousseau.'

11. Leo Strauss, *Natural Right and History* (Chicago, University of Chicago Press, 1953).

12. Patrick Riley, *Will and Political Legitimacy* (Cambridge, Harvard University Press, 1982); Nannerl O. Keohane, *Philosophy and the State in France* (Princeton, Princeton University Press, 1980).

13. Karl Jaspers, *Plato and Augustine* (ed. Hannah Arendt) (New York, Harvest Book, 1962).

14. Albrecht Dihle, *The Theory of Will in Classical Antiquity* (Berkeley, University of California Press, 1982), pp. 25-6.

15. 'Intention itself, whether originating from reasoning or from emotion, can never be named, in the language of Homer, without reference to one or the other of these origins.' Dihle, p. 26.

16. Dihle, p. 71.

17. Dihle, p. 47.

18. Augustine is usually held to be the 'discoverer' of the will as a distinct concept. Dihle, pp. 123-44; Hannah Arendt, *The Life of the Mind*, vol. 3, *Willing* (New York, Harcourt, Brace, Jovanovich, 1978), pp. 84-110; Jaspers, pp. 88-99.

19. Riley, *Will and Political Legitimacy*, p. 12.

20. F.M. Barnard has probed the relationship in Rousseau between self-choosing, right acting, and political rationality. 'Will and Political Rationality in Rousseau,' *Political Studies* 32 (1984), pp. 369-84.

21. John Charvet, *The Social Problem in the Philosophy of Rousseau* (Cambridge, Cambridge University Press, 1974), p. 10.

22. *Emile*, p. 279. After his criticism of materialism the Vicar concludes that man is 'animated by an immaterial substance' (p. 281).

23. 'Discourse on the Origin and Foundation of Inequality,' in *The First and Second Discourse*, R.D. Masters and J.R. Masters (trans.) (New York, St. Martin's Press, 1964), p. 114.

24. *Emile*, p. 280.

25. The paternity of Rousseau's concept of the will is too complicated a task to pursue here. Patrick Riley argues that 'Rousseau is not conceivable without Augustine and various seventeenth-century transformations of Augustinianism.' *Will and Political Legitimacy* (N.J., Harvard University Press, 1982) p. 5. Also, Nannerl O. Keohane, pp. 420-49. Riley further shows how the 'general will' was a notion used by many of Rousseau's immediate predecessors and some of his contemporaries: Pascal, Montesquieu, Malebranche, Leibniz, and Diderot. 'The General Will Before Rousseau,' *Political Theory* (November 1978), pp. 485-516.

26. I am accepting Rousseau's oft repeated claim to being consistent in his writings. Although there is a discussion of the will in the *Second Discourse* and in the *Social Contract*, *Emile* is his masterpiece on the phenomenology of the will. It should be added that it would have made little sense for Rousseau to have provided his summary in *Emile* of the *Social Contract* if he did not view the latter as constructed for Emile. *Emile*, p. 462. For a discussion of Rousseau's consistency, see: John Charvet, 'Rousseau and the Ideal of Community,' and

Robert Wokler, 'A Reply to Charvet: Rousseau and the Perfectibility of Man,' *History of Political Thought* (Spring, 1980), pp. 69-90.

27. *Emile*, pp. 212.13.

28. *Emile*, p. 92. In the *Second Discourse* (p. 95), Rousseau posits two principles in human nature — self-love and pity — but in *Emile* self-love is the original natural passion and pity is derivative.

29. *Emile*, p. 214.

30. *Second Discourse*, p. 132.

31. *Emile*, pp. 212-13.

32. *Emile*, p. 237.

33. *Emile*, p. 237.

34. *Emile*, p. 85.

35. *Emile*, p. 280. With Augustine there is a counter will, as it were, but with Rousseau the will is simply weak relative to the temptation. See the analysis by Walter B. Mead, 'Will and Moral Faculty,' in Francis Canavan (ed.), *The Ethical Dimension of Political Life* (Durham, Duke University Press, 1983), pp. 61-77.

36. *Emile*, p. 80.

37. *Emile*, p. 85.

38. *Second Discourse*, p. 127.

39. *Second Discourse*, p. 118.

40. *Emile*, p. 282.

41. *Emile*, p. 293.

42. *Emile*, p. 85.

43. *Emile*, p. 280.

44. *Emile*, p. 280.

45. Jean-Jacques Rousseau, *The Reveries of the Solitary Walker*, Charles E. Butterworth (trans.), (New York, New York University Press, 1979), Sixth Walk, p. 83.

46. *Emile*, p. 445. Without belabouring the point, man in the state of nature is 'forced' by accidents and by nature to develop his will and other faculties. *Second Discourse*, pp. 114-15. The *Social Contract* creates the institutional structure for civil society, and again man can be 'forced to be free'. Although the comparison helps to illustrate the intention behind Rousseau's notorious phrase, it is not meant to justify or defend Rosseau's position.

47. *Emile*, p. 445.

48. Judith Shklar, 'Rousseau's Images of Authority,' *American Political Science Review* 58 (December, 1964), pp. 919-32.

49. *Emile*, p. 445.

50. *Emile*, p. 363. The same point is made in *Political Economy*, p. 223.

51. *Emile*, p. 221.

52. *Emile*, p. 253.

53. *Emile*, p. 253.

54. *Emile*, p. 253.

55. *Emile*, p. 433.

56. *Merchant of Venice*, III, ii. I am grateful to Susan M. Porter for this citation.

57. Allan Bloom, 'Introduction,' *Emile*, p. 22. See also, Joel Schwartz, *The Sexual Politics of Jean-Jacques Rousseau* (Chicago: University of Chicago Press, 1984), pp. 74-102.

58. *Emile*, p. 161.

59. *Emile*, pp. 220-1.

60. John Charvet argues that Rousseau cannot logically move from a self-consistent ego to altruism. If Rousseau were interested in altruism, then his position would be contradictory. But, the extension of the self-contained ego is

not to other persons. The 'identification' repeatedly mentioned by Rousseau (*Emile*, pp, 222-3) has no more to do with persons than does the identification found between immature identical twins: there is neither self nor an other. If this is altruism, it is not a moral virtue. John Charvet, "Rousseau and the Ideal of Community."

61. *Emile*, p. 252.

62. Rousseau is a pessimist about the chances of establishing and maintaining his legitimate state, but this does not change his claim that the just state is in principle realizable.

63. *Emile*, p. 253.

64. 'Good social institutions are those that best know how to denature man, to take his absolute existence from him in order to give him a relative one and transport the I into the community unity, with the result that each individual believes himself no longer one but a part of the unity and no longer feels except within the whole.' *Emile*, p. 40.

65. *The Confessions of Jean-Jacques Rousseau*, trans. J.M. Cohen (Harmondsworth: Penguin Books, 1965), pp. 61-2.

66. *Political Economy*, p. 213. Given Rousseau's conception of the Will, it is impossible to conclude that his intent with the general will was to 'merely designate that part of our experience as individuals which moves each of us, in certain contexts, to say 'We,' and to act in accordance with that identification.' James Miller, *Rousseau: Dreamer of Democracy*, p. 62. The conclusion of Arthur Melzer is equally difficult to accept: 'With its strict equality, the General Will or popularly enacted law must be sovereign, not because it is just or moral – it is not – but because it is a realistic, political means – and the only means – of preventing widespread oppression.' 'Rousseau's Moral Realism: Replacing Natural Law with the General Will,' *American Political Science Review* (September 1983): 650.

5 A PUBLIC GOODS APPROACH TO THE THEORY OF THE GENERAL WILL

David Braybrooke

The general will easily turns into a metaphysical mystery. Is it the will of society or the body politic, hypostatised as a Person superior to any of its members, none of whom might have a will coinciding with it? If this is not a mystery, it may be said that it is at least 'a fiction. What is the State? Always a set of people, maybe only one, who command; the many must obey willy-nilly. It is not possible for everybody to be at once the subject of his own law and the sole author. Rousseau's determination to moralize politics can only overload it with an excessive finality foreign to it, offering to regenerate humanity but never succeeding. The pursuit of Virtue or Fraternity ends in Terror.'[1]

Sabine, citing Rousseau's language in the Encyclopedia article on Political Economy, is justified in asserting that the idea of the general will presupposes 'the theory that a community has a corporate personality or *moi commun*, the organic analogy for a social group'.[2] Rousseau himself, in that article, maintains, 'The body politic . . . is . . . a moral being possessed of a will.'[3] Indeed, it 'can be considered as an organized body, living and like that of a man'. This language, with the organic analogy fully exploited, leads not only to mystery, but also, in the course of so doing, to rejection of the problem of social choice theory as formulated in our time by Arrow. Violation of the anti-imposition axiom easily follows, with violation of the anti-dictatorship axiom an additional possibility.

Rousseau's language in the final version of *The Social Contract*, however, is much more sober, and need not be taken to have sinister consequences. The general will there becomes the will of 'a being of Reason because it is not a man',[5] phrasing that already betokens a shift away from the organic analogy. More important, Rousseau explicitly characterises the general will as formed from the wills of individual citizens, when these aim at their own interests in a certain way. With this characterisation, the theory of the general will, or at any rate the ingredient of that theory most basic in the *Social Contract*, invites treatment as an intuitive exercise in what we know as the theory of public goods. It is not a mystery at all. It is intelligible and prescient.

Moreover, it establishes a perspective for understanding the rationale of voting that reduces the impact of Arrow's theorem, even if it does not escape the impact entirely. Arrow himself, in a sympathetic though inconclusive discussion already present in the first edition of *Social Choice and Individual Values* allows for such a use for Rousseau's theory. 'Voting, from this point of view, is not a device whereby each individual expresses his personal interests, but rather where each individual gives his opinion of the general will', and this is to be found in 'consensus' on a 'moral imperative'.

Rousseau's Distinction Between the General Will and the Will of All

The general will, Rousseau tells us, aims at what is in everyone's own interest.[7] Yet it is not, he insists, to be confused with the will of everyone, in which everyone may aim just at his own interest.[8] Is there anything that can figure as the object of the one without being the object of the other? We have to find something that is in everyone's own interest, yet susceptible of being disregarded when everyone's own interest is, nevertheless, being pursued. This may sound impossible. But there is such an object, and it vindicates Rousseau in giving us a trenchant distinction between the general will and the will of everyone.

What is in everyone's own interest, as the object of the general will, is to be found, according to Rousseau, by taking away from the particular wills directed at the private interests of individual citizens 'the pluses and the minuses that are mutually destructive to themselves'.[9] I take it that what he means are the interests that people may have in gains associated with losses of equal amounts reckoned in physical terms or money income, not utility, for other people. Such gains all involve limitative benefits, that is to say, benefits which some can enjoy only if others are forestalled from enjoying them. They fall into two categories: first, gains by expropriative transfer that imply other people must give up goods in their possession; second, what I shall call 'other limitative benefits', breaking these down into two subcategories: benefits from goods that would be present in any case though not yet firmly appropriated; benefits that would not be present, for example, because they would not have been produced, had there not been some prior agreement to respect allocating them to those who hold them.

I shall for the time being take the condition about pluses and minuses in a strong sense, embracing all these categories and subcategories. Hence, I shall be supposing that in aiming the general will at its proper objects, not only are transfers or possible transfers of goods by force, fraud, and the abuse of political power ruled out, but also all goods the benefits from which are limitative. Limitative benefits are characteristic of private goods, the consumption of which in any instance is to the benefit of one person and to the detriment of anyone else. What Eve ate of the apple, it was impossible for Adam to eat. By contrast, the benefits characteristic of public goods (like a lighthouse, a broadcast of classical music, monetary stability, a safe environment) are such that consumption by one person does not impair or limit consumption by others.[10]

Now we can say, the will of everyone may aim wholly at private goods. The general will, by contrast, aims at public goods. The latter are certainly in everyone's own interest, and may be willed accordingly, by persons who give them due attention. However, people may disregard them in favour of pursuing private goods, which also are in their own interest. They may be preoccupied with private goods because of a certain lack of vision. Or they may be, as Rousseau explicitly notes, tempted to get what they can of public goods as free riders.[11]

The general will must not only be distinguishable from the will of everyone. It must be coherent and immutable.[12] Will aiming at public goods guarantee these properties? It is true that one person may benefit more from consumption of a public good than another person. Indeed, for everyone who rejoices in hearing a Bach concerto over the air, there may be a dozen who obtain at most only a mild pleasure. But this is not in itself an obstacle to everyone's willing to have the public good, in his own interest. A more telling objection lies in the possibility that people vary in their preferences for mixes of public goods. Some, for example, may favour pure air and water more than a public radio broadcasting string quartets, while others want relatively more resources to go into broadcasting; and these in turn may differ as to what programmes they want.

This difficulty can be turned by granting Rousseau the assumption that the general will aims not at all public goods, but at a subset of public goods that everyone wants. To get full value from this assumption, we need to rule out variations between people respecting their preferences for public goods as against private ones. On Rousseau's conception of the problem, this is to be done by appealing to the full development, sooner or later, of a feeling for the common interest, a matter that I shall take up in a moment. For now, I shall just assume that once the subset has been identified, everyone (or at least a majority) will demand that each good in the subset be produced in some substantial quantity.

We need to rule out something else: conflicts of preferences among the public goods in the subset, compared with each other. We could do this by assuming that though the benefits received from any good in the subset vary from person to person, the order of benefits from the subset is the same for all, in their own eyes. Without denying that an intelligible conception of the general will could be worked out on this assumption, I shall work with the stronger and simpler assumption that the order of benefits from the subset is the same for all and that everyone (in a sense that I am about to specify) gets an equal benefit from each good.

There are public goods that arguably fit into the set so circumscribed. They include public goods that are of chief importance in the work of governments: having a legal system; having police and (in at least some aspects) fire departments; having means of national defence; having a safe environment in other respects; having monetary stability. Government, in a sufficiently simple society, might be entirely occupied in providing such goods. We need not invoke the concept of utility, with its difficulties, refined or unrefined, to explain how the benefits from these goods are equal. We need not, and the citizens engaged in aiming the general will at its proper objects need not, depend on any subjective estimates of benefits to oneself. They may consider, respecting the goods mentioned, that it is reasonable to ascribe to everyone an equal benefit. Everyone, they may hold, benefits equally in having his life and limbs protected. They may hold further that everyone benefits equally from having their property protected. If the property varies in amount, it may be considered that the loss of any item of property from larger possessions would do less to jeopardise life-plans than the loss of any item from smaller possessions. With this inverse variation in jeopardy, the benefit from having the property protected may be held, by a reasonably pragmatic stipulation, to remain always the same.

For the moment, I leave the general will at the point of having identified some of the goods in the subset of public goods that on the most narrow view form its proper objects. Noting only that the citizens may mistake the answer, I leave open the question whether other public goods should be recognised as belonging to the subset: for example, provisions for civic education. I postpone the question of what level of production of the goods shall be decided upon. Even on the most narrow view, the general will should resolve this question; but how it is to go about doing so is best discussed on a broader view, because there the thinking that goes into the decision is most convincing.

Public and Private Goods

Can more than the subset of public goods just mentioned be embraced among the objects of the general will? I think we can find more to be embraced, if we return to the condition about taking away the pluses and the minuses and if we are willing to brave certain complications that we need not face with a general will aimed solely at a restricted subset of public goods. It is unrealistic to leave private goods (and other public goods) entirely out of account among the concerns of politics. On the other hand, they can become objects of the general will only insofar as that will contemplates them within a framework of distributive justice and as matters of common interest. Complications arise in both of these connections; and the framework of distributive justice becomes determinate for the general will, if it does become determinate, only by grace of argumentation something less than apodictic.[13]

We made some sense of the condition about pluses and minuses by taking the condition in a strong sense of setting aside both gains by transfer and other limitative benefits. We can make further sense of the condition by taking it more weakly, as setting aside expropriative transfers only. That is to say, we may take it as setting aside just those objects of one's own interest in which one aggrandises one's own benefits by taking private goods away from other people. The general will certainly could not aim at these benefits. Could it aim at any limitative benefits?

With public goods, by contrast with goods obtainable only by expropriative transfers, one could not deny anyone else the goods and still consume them oneself. The second subcategory of other limitative benefits, which are present only as a result of an agreement to respect the allocation of private goods from which they arise, meets something like the same condition. For to deny these goods to anyone by refusing to agree to an allocation and thus forestalling their presence implies denying the goods to oneself; indeed, it implies denying any goods to oneself that one might gain depending on an agreement about allocation. Everyone would have an interest in any scheme for producing private goods under which everyone substantially shared in the output.

Any such scheme would have a dual aspect: it would be a scheme for producing and distributing private goods some or all of them answering to self-interest of the narrowest sort; but having a scheme of some sort, in which everyone had a substantial share of private goods, would be a matter of common interest. Would having a scheme be a public good? The shares that people have are shares that they could be denied; and one person's consumption of his share stands in the way of another person's consuming it. On the other hand, the benefit of having some share or other does not impair anyone else's having the benefit of having some share or other. Everyone can enjoy the scheme in that respect simultaneously, and like everyone else, benefit from it fully. Nor could anyone be excluded from having a share unless the scheme were transformed into another scheme that did not fit the definition of giving everyone a substantial share. Either having a scheme is a public good, of a somewhat attentuated sort; or having one is an analogue of a public good.

Unfortunately, it is not, if it is a public good, necessarily one that belongs to the restricted subset considered earlier. It is not necessarily a public good from which it could be held that everyone got equal benefits in every respect that it was reasonable to take into account. The general will would be intelligible, free of mystery, if it stopped with the conclusion that it was in the common interest to have some such scheme, and did not try to choose which one. Yet to stop there would be a disappointment. The general will would not be doing all the work that Rousseau or we might ask of it; and it would leave no ready alternative way of making a justifiable choice. Can we get it to make a choice among schemes? I shall go about answering this question indirectly, by way of a closer analysis of the common interest and a discussion of the role that a cognitive standard for the common interest designates to voting.

The Common Interest

Nannerl Keohane, in an interesting discussion of Rousseau's conception of the common interest, distinguishes three types: one embracing the parallel interests that are served by a common scheme of co-operation, as in the example of the deer hunt; a second embracing interests that people have in the shared pleasures of social intercourse; the third embracing the interests that citizens have in the general — 'abstract and lofty' — benefits of having a political community that upholds liberty, equality and the rule of law.[14] I shall elaborate on this scheme, consistently I think with its basic insights, and distinguish four types of common interest: parallel but solitary interests served by a common scheme of co-operation; interests in joint consumption, with pleasure taken in the presence and concurrent consumption of other people; interests in joint consumption,with pleasure taken not merely in having other people present, consuming too and contributing to the noise and jollification, but also, vicariously, in having the others enjoy themselves, too; finally, shared interests resting on loyalty to the other members of the community and the community itself.

In effect, what I have done is mainly to subdivide Keohane's second category. It may be thought that the division is artificial: how plausible is it that people could enjoy having other people present during joint consumption without sympathising with their enjoyments? But, in fact, people can use others as instruments of pleasure without caring whether the others are pleased; this is notoriously a possibility in sexual intercourse. So the division marks off real possibilities. However, I agree that people's feelings naturally move across the distinction. More often than not, they come to care for the enjoyments of their sexual partners. It is just my point in elaborating Keohane's distinctions to bring out the natural tendency, which she herself has in mind, for people to develop common interests of all four types. Were people to begin with parallel interests only, they would tend to develop the others in the order given. In reality, the priorities are no doubt not so simple. At the very least, one could not expect people to be fully cognisant of the earlier types until after they had begun to be attached to some of the later ones. Nevertheless, on the essential point reality will vindicate Rousseau: in what he would reasonably consider a healthy community, the common interest will be generally felt to comprise all four types; and everyone's own interest will be shaped accordingly.

Social intercourse, properly managed, will, according to views in which *The Social Contract* corroborates *Emile*, induce in any individual person a sympathetic concern with the happiness of others.[15] Even without the development of a sense of joint efforts, this concern for other people enlarges one's conception of one's own interest to coincide at least in part with other people's. Hence the interest that each has in having a scheme for producing private goods that answers to the general interest becomes an interest attached not just to parallel objects but to shared ones. But the same enlargement of concern may occur with the subset of public goods that were discussed earlier. There, too, the goods become objects of shared (overlapping) interests rather than of interests merely parallel.

The development of a sense of joint efforts goes hand in hand with this shift from parallel interests to shared ones. If, by living with other people, one acquires a sympathetic concern with their interests, one will be helping them out from time to time, and receiving help from them in turn. Thus starts up a foundation for regarding the association with other people as a community of mutual aid. On the other hand, when specific new projects for co-operation are broached, one of the attractions for any individual person of participating in them will be the opportunity that they offer of benefitting others.

Sooner rather than later, it will be recognised that foremost among such projects are the undertakings of government to supply the public goods mentioned earlier: a legal system; internal protective services; national defence; monetary stability. Like Keohane, we can conceive of recognising them as something that is superimposed upon the recognition of the shared interests in private goods just mentioned. Recognising them may be looked upon simultaneously as an outgrowth of the loyalty of each member of the community to the others with whom he shares the efforts of mutual aid as well as in joint consumption of the results of those efforts. Upon mutual loyalty is built loyalty to the community as a whole.

Thus a rich notion of the common interest, each element of which is a clear and simple idea, answers to the general will. Moreover, the common interest, as Rousseau conceived it, offers a foundation for choosing, among the schemes that give everyone a substantial share of private goods, a just scheme. 'Justice' (like kindness), Rousseau says, is 'a true affection of the soul enlightened by reason, and nothing but an orderly development of our primitive affections,'[16] which 'of all the virtues [is] the one that conduces most to the common good of men.'[17]

Contemplating schemes for producing and distributing private goods everyone might find an interest in a scheme of subsistence farming or of fending for oneself in the market, in either case with provisions for security brought in with a government. We have a more robust sense of a common interest, and hence of something answering closely to Rousseau's conception of the general will, however, with schemes that prescribe a just distribution of the proceeds of joint efforts. What joint efforts are in this connection is not, however, something entirely given by nature. What joint efforts are depends on what the participants are willing to recognise as joint efforts. Do they think of each other as contributing something to producing the private goods produced under the scheme, if the contribution is only to maintaining the scheme, and that perhaps only by refraining from sabotaging it? An economy of subsistence farming or a *laissez-faire* market economy might be looked upon in this way. No doubt, however, it is easier to cultivate a sense of joint effort in a society with substantial public undertakings that enlist widespread participation. There everyone might be satisfied that the scheme was in their own interest if it prescribed equal incomes, or Rawls's Difference Principle, or equality in meeting needs plus the Difference Principle to distribute a surplus answering to matters of preference only. In suitable circumstances, it seems to me, the general will would gravitate toward adopting some such scheme as its object. But that is to say, simultaneously, every person whose individual will is combined in the general will would find it to their own interest to have such a scheme. The citizens would thus tend to converge on a unanimous endorsement, founded on a cognitive standard, of the idea of having some such scheme or other. I shall consider in a moment how the endorsement can be narrowed to fix, among approximately just schemes, upon a single one of them.

Voting, and Choice of a Scheme

What role, however, is left for voting in the expression of the general will? To some — for example, Riker — the fact that the general will offers a cognitive standard implies that voting is superfluous.[18] Yet Rousseau insists upon it. Every citizen must vote; every vote must be counted;[19] no representatives must intervene between the voting and the choice of general social policy.[20] Rousseau might join Riker in finding some use for voting as a means of throwing representatives out of office, if there were representatives;[21] or of replacing magistrates in the executive that he does assume will administer the day-to-day business of government.[22] For Rousseau, though not for Riker, recourse to voting would be a means not just of unsettling things. It would be a means of making sure that the magistrates do not deviate too far from the cognitive standard of pursuing the objects aimed at by the general will.

However, this is not in Rousseau's eyes the primary task of voting. The primary task in his eyes is to establish what the proper objects aimed at by the general will are and to prescribe their production. This may not be a very hard problem, especially if we suppose the general will aims only at a restricted subset of public goods. It does require some calculation, that is to say, some consideration as to what must be set aside as matters of conflicting particular interests. Thus, in my account so far, limitative benefits must be set aside unless they figure in schemes of production that redound to the substantial interest of everyone; and set aside also must be interests in those public goods in respect to which people's preferences conflict. The goods that remain will be the objects aimed at by the general will, though it has not yet been settled whether the general will will choose any particular scheme for producing limitative benefits. But these goods may be wrongly or incompletely identified if the calculation of what is to be set aside goes astray. Rousseau's view is that the best chance of getting the calculation right lies in having everyone attempt the calculation and vote accordingly. Assembled to deliberate on the calculations. the citizens are to be asked, 'What is to the advantage of the State;'[23] I would rather ask, 'What is to the advantage of the political community?' One could also ask, 'What is in the common interest?' However expressed, it is not a question to which the voters, either by majority or in unanimity, can return an infallible answer.[24] It is a question requiring an analysis at least as complicated as the one that I have been giving; and on all the points coming up in the analysis, any citizen, or all of them together, may be mistaken.

Yet Rousseau was not being blindly enthusiastic in holding, empirically, that the closer the voting results approach unanimity the closer is the approach to expressing the general will. By ruling out private 'communication' among the assembled voters, he does something to rule out coalitions, and with them a good deal of the instability to which the results of voting are ordinarily subject.[25] Furthermore Condorcet's theorem about juries gives some formal support to the notion that on a cognitive issue a majority is more likely to be correct than a minority, and a larger majority than a smaller one.[26] The argument for the theorem assumes that each participant has a probability of being correct greater than one half. Can we count upon rank-and-file citizens to be experts to this modest degree on what issues properly come before the general will and how they are to be decided?

In respect to recognising conflicts of interests and preferences, I think they are experts enough. At least in a society simple enough to open up no opportunities for elaborate swindles, they can recognise, with tolerable accuracy each speaking for him or herself, when they are liable to be victimised by the aggrandisement of another. Each can recognise with tolerable accuracy when a scheme for producing private goods does not promise substantial benefits for himself. Each can recognise with tolerable accuracy when a conflict with others in preferences among public goods has cropped up. (One way of bringing such conflicts to light would be to have a straw or trial vote before proceeding to a would-be definitive expression of the general will.) On all these matters they may be mistaken, even when they are sincerely trying to make the proper calculations and vote accordingly. Yet by and large most of them may be expected to reach the right answers, setting aside the objects that the general will cannot properly aim at, identifying its proper objects as including at least the provision of a restricted subset of public goods and as well the conclusion that some scheme or other affording everyone substantial shares shall be adopted for producing private goods.

Moreover, most of them may be expected to reach the right answers on the other issues that I have tentatively allowed may call for an expression of the general will. There is a class of questions, generally lost sight of in epistemology, for which the fact that a majority votes for one answer rather than another forms part of the evidence that it is the correct one. 'Is our climate a comfortable one?' is one question in the class. It must be quite a heterogeneous class if it includes also the present questions. Yet arguably it does. I have already provided a model of how it does in the question about what respects it was reasonable for the citizens to take into account when they judged whether or not equal benefits from a public good were to be ascribed to everyone. The view of a majority, if a majority took this view, that everyone was to be ascribed equal benefits, because everyone had a life to protect and plans equally dependent on whatever amount of property they have, deserves some respect. For those are respectable reasons, which the majority may well regard as decisive.

If we draw upon Rousseau's conception of how people acquire, progressively, richer and richer notions of the common interest, we can see how the reasons to which the majority give decisive weight might expand to resolve further questions. Even in a healthy community, we may suppose that it will take time for people to acquire such notions. It might take time for a majority of people with such notions to develop even after people reached adulthood and began playing their full part as citizens. But suppose that a majority of the citizens are brought up well enough to have a substantial attachment to every level of the common interest. Then one might expect this majority to increase, though perhaps only gradually, as everyone became more used to the effects of correct decisions by the general will in fostering more intense attachments on everyone's part to the common interest in every aspect.

One of the remaining issues tentatively allowed for is the issue about what level of production shall be fixed upon for any of the restricted set of public goods in respect to which it is held that people benefit equally. A criterion that the majority might regard as reasonable for fixing the level, given the nature of these goods, would be that the level should suffice to make the citizens feel comfortably secure. Are the police and fire departments large enough to meet this criterion? Are there enough administrators and judges and courts to uphold an effective system of legal protection? Every citizen is in a position to answer these questions in his own case.Those with a fully developed sense of common interest will take into account the feelings of others. Some others he will judge overanxious; some, too sanguine. Every citizen, moreover, is in a position to consider whether the provisions are ample enough to keep on creating feelings of security in the long run. The issue, in so far as it regards provisions for national defence, has since Rousseau's time become enormously complicated by technology.[27] But at least in a simpler world, with information of ordinary kinds about external threats, the estimates of a majority of citizens as to the adequacy of their armed forces would deserve some respect. They would not, as reasonable people attached to their common interests at every level, feel secure with a corporal's guard of untrained soldiers, if neighbouring states bristled with arms. On the other hand, if they themselves have pacific intentions, they would justifiably not consider it necessary to have every able-bodied man continuously mobilised while the neighbouring states ran down their forces.

The other issue tentatively allowed for was the issue about which scheme to choose in the range of schemes for producing private goods all of which, besides offering substantial benefits to everyone, meet some standard or other of distributive justice. Here, in the absence of arguments convincing everyone, or everyone imbued with a lively sense of the common interest, that one such standard is uniquely justified, the general will may have to make an arbitrary choice within the range specified. Such a choice, however, even if arbitrary, resolves the difficulty that if a unique scheme is not fixed upon, no benefits from any scheme will be realised. Moreover, offsetting the arbitrary features of the choice will be the fact that arguments reasonable if not conclusive exist for being content with any scheme within the range. For example, a scheme calling for equality in meeting needs plus the Difference Principle for matters of preference only can be backed by such arguments from the writings of Rawls and others.[28] The general will, adhering to such arguments, would have an appropriate foundation.

The private goods at issue in such schemes are other limitative benefits of the second kind, benefits that arise from goods that would not be present without agreement on some such scheme. But other limitative benefits of the first kind, where the goods are present regardless of such agreement, can be brought within the compass of the general will on the same approach. A majority, seeking to have them distributed in the way that most fully accorded with the common interest, would distribute them under the same ultimate scheme, for example, making sure of equality in meeting needs first and then considering whether any incentive effects (in the production of other goods) called under the Difference Principle for an unequal distribution in dealing with matters of preference only.

Have I, in opening up some room for shifts of judgement respecting ultimate schemes of distributive justice, fallen into inconsistency with Rousseau's stipulation that the general will is 'immutable'? But we need not foist upon Rousseau the notion that the general will gives the same answers regardless of circumstances. It would be immutable enough — no more immutable than is reasonable — if it gave the same answers in the same circumstances. It would also be immutable enough to make sense of Rousseau's stipulation if it was immutable in the end, though reached by successive approximations.

Conflicts of Preference

The general will, on the foregoing account, has already been given room to speak on the objects that it can speak to intelligibly — perhaps, given the problematic features of some of the objects mentioned, more room than it can properly use. The space accorded it embraces most perhaps of the issues that come up in politics. Yet there is something left over: issues about public goods about which people's preferences conflict, because they prefer different mixes of the goods. What shall be done about these issues? There are several possibilities. They could be ignored; or, what comes to much the same thing except for constitutional protection, assigned to private spheres set aside from social choice. People could form 'clubs' to produce them. Another possibility, realised under most governments nowadays, is to make use of the taxing, subsidising and organising powers of the state to produce a variety of public goods answering to the demands of different groups. Is there any way of rationalising such a practice as falling among the objects properly aimed at by the general will?

I think there is, though to avoid complications that would jeopardise the rationale one may have to assume that this extension is limited to a small set of issues, with simple alternatives. For example, public subsidies to making music, including broadcasting music, might be allocated among a number of kinds of music, categorised according to some simple scheme, relative to the proportions of the population most attached to each category. The scheme might lump together aficionados of baroque trio sonatas with those who delight most in Rachmaninoff and leave it to one broadcasting service for classical music to range over this variety. According to a prior scheme of allocation, the subsidies going to all categories of music might be related to those going to sports according to the relative proportions of music lovers and sports fans.

Leaving the various goods in question to be supplied to individual consumers in the market or as club goods may leave everyone with less of the goods that they most relish than would action through the state. If this is so (on the evidence), then the general will, calling upon the state to produce them according to some fair scheme of allocation like the one just described, advances everyone's interest in a non-limitative way. Very likely one could invent other allocations that would attract some people more and lead to cyclical voting; but the very prospect of confusing issues in this way stands against introducing other proposals for allocations unless they are in the circumstances cycle-proof improvements.

On the other hand, without flying in the face of this caution, it may be possible to form a firm majority for an allocation that skews the proportions in favour of goods of higher cultural aspiration. A majority might concur in doing this in order to discourage its professional elite from emigrating to other countries. Moreover, regardless of emigration, a majority, most of whom have other tastes, may be persuaded that the vitality of their society in the long run depends on having more robust provisions for high art and the higher learning than an allocation according to present tastes would warrant. The consideration is one, I fear, that is often abused by arguments that are specious even if successful. In principle, however, is not the long-run interest of the community one with which everyone, at least at the end of full moral development, can join his own? The joining is certainly something to be expected from the full development of the loyalties extolled by Rousseau. As such the long-run interest is a proper object of the general will. If, for the time being, only a majority of the people are ready to endorse it, that may be because they have a fuller view of the common interest. Their endorsement in this connection will be all the more impressive if it runs for most of them against their personal present tastes.

Conclusion

Whatever sense I have made of the general will has been made without trying to show just how it is to operate in a complex modern society or even, in a simpler society, in conjunction with specific forms of government as Rousseau conceived of them.[29] Moreover, if I have succeeded in showing that the general will need not be taken to be 'an ideal entity as indeterminate as it is absolute',[30] and, so taken, to license the sinister consequences that in some quarters it has been charged with, I by no means have offered to justify all the inferences to which Rousseau's doctrine has given some colour.

Most sinister of these have been the ventures of self-appointed prophets and tyrants to speak for the general will before even a majority have come to agree on the policies at issue. There is too much of an opening for repression and terror in the idea of forcing people to be free. But even a benign, spontaneous development of consensus about the common interest, of the kind that I have sketched, might lead to heavy pressures upon dissenters in opinions and ways of life. Rousseau stands for *Gemeinschaft*, not for the cosmopolitan liberties of *Gesellschaft*. A healthy democracy must have some combination of the two.[31]

Notes

1. Jean Roy, 'Burn with a Hard Gem-Like Flame!', *Bulletin de la société d'études rousseauistes* (September 1980), pp. 3-6.
2. George H. Sabine, *A History of Political Theory*, 3rd ed. (New York, Holt, Rinehart & Winston, 1961), p. 585.
3. Cited by Sabine, *Political Theory*; Jean-Jacques Rousseau, 'Political Economy' (1755), in Michel Launay (ed.), *Oeuvres Complètes*, vol. 2 (Paris, Senil, 1971), p. 278.
4. Rousseau, *Political Economy*, p. 278.
5. Jean-Jacques Rousseau, *Du Contrat social* (1762), in Launay (ed.), *Oeuvres Complètes*, vol. 2, p. 523.
6. Kenneth J. Arrow, *Social Choice and Individual Values* (New York, Wiley, 1951), p. 85.
7. Rousseau, *Du Contrat social*, p. 527.
8. Ibid. 'May' because though the will of everyone is 'often (*sic*) very different from the General Will' (ibid.), in happy circumstances the two may coincide

(ibid., p. 564). The coincidence, as my account of these matters will bring out; comes about through full enlargement of one's own interest to include all aspects of the common interest.

9. Ibid., p. 527.

10. John G. Head, *Public Goods and Public Welfare* (Durham, North Carolina, Duke University Press, 1974).

11. Rousseau, *Du Contrat social*, pp. 523 and 564.

12. Ibid., pp. 526 and 564.

13. We must also brave Plamenatz's contention that taken literally the condition about pluses and minuses is 'sheer nonsense'. Taking it literally, for Plamenatz, meant giving it a certain algebraic interpretation:

> Let John's will be $x + a$, Richard's $x + b$, and Thomas's $x + c$; x being what is common to them all, and a, b, and c, what is peculiar to each. If the general will is what remains after the "pluses" and "minuses" have cancelled each other out, it is x; but if it is the sum of the differences it is $a + b + c$. Whichever it is, it cannot be both; and the second alternative is too absurd to be considered.

This interpretation led Plamenatz to admonish, 'Beware of political philosophers who use mathematics, no matter how simple, to illustrate their meaning! God will forgive them, for they know [not?] what they do, but we shall not understand them' (Plamenatz, *Man and Society*, vol. I [London, Longmans, 1963], p. 393). It did not occur to Plamenatz that it might have been his algebraic interpretation rather than Rousseau's original statement that calls for the warning. Plamenatz defines a, b, and c without mentioning mutual destruction; and Plamenatz supplies no motivation for taking their sum as an alternative answering to the general will. Plamenatz goes on to recognise that x might answer without absurdity — thus making his consideration of $a + b + c$, or of this sum plus x as well, a wild aberrancy. However, he rules x out as unrealistic and as inconsistent with the possibility that people's opinions of what x consists of might change with the deliberation that Rousseau expects to precede the deliverances of the general will. Plamenatz would have done better to consider what x might consist of were the deliberation to run its course.

14. Nannerl O. Keohane, *Philosophy and the State in France* (Princeton, Princeton University Press, 1980), pp. 439-42.

15. Rousseau, *Du Contrat social*, 327.

16. Ibid., p. 305.

17. Ibid., p. 329. I owe this quotation, in the first instance, to Joshua Cohen.

18. William H. Riker, *Liberalism Against Populism* (San Francisco, Freeman, 1982), p. 526.

19. Rousseau, *Du Contrat social*, p. 526.

20. Ibid., p. 525-6; *cf*, the discussion in Andrew Levine, *The Politics of Autonomy* (Amherst, University of Massachussetts Press, 1976).

21. Riker, *Liberalism Against Populism*, pp. 241-6.

22. Rousseau, *Du Contrat social*, p. 539.

23. Ibid., p. 564.

24. Andrew Levine, in a discussion of the general will that is otherwise one of the most penetrating in the literature, holds that in Rousseau's view, 'The majority is *certainly* right, if only it is properly interrogated.' (Levine, *Autonomy*, p. 68). Neither the text of Rousseau nor Levine's own preceding discussion bears him out, unless we assume that 'properly interrogated' means the majority is to understand the question so well as to give the right answer. Rousseau himself gives some colour to this tautological interpretation by saying, 'If, when the people, suffi-

ciently informed, deliberate, the Citizens have no private discussions among themselves, from the great number of little differences the general will always results and the deliberation will always be good', (Rousseau, *Du Contrat social*, p. 527). But Rousseau also holds that the approach to being right varies with the size of the majority (ibid., p. 564). At the beginning of Book II, ch. III, of the *Social Contract*, he says, 'The General Will is always right and tends always towards public utility: but it does not follow that the deliberations of the people always have the same degree of correctness. One always wants one's good, but one does not always see what it is. The people are never corrupted, though they are often misled'. (ibid., p. 527).

25. A point stressed by Christopher Morris and John Ferejohn in various sessions of the summer institute on public choice theory held at Dalhousie University, August 1984. *Cf.* Rousseau, *Du Contrat social*, p. 527.

26. Levine follows Brian Barry in *Political Argument* (London, Routledge and Kegan Paul, 1965) in citing the theorem. Barry in turn cites Duncan Black, *The Theory of Committees and Elections* (Cambridge, Cambridge University Press, 1958). I rely on Black's account for the point that a larger majority is more likely to be right than a smaller one. Barry understands, as I do, Rousseau's reliance on majority voting as voting on an empirical hypothesis about its performance.

27. In most other connections, too, whether these have to do with public goods or with schemes for producing and distributing private goods, citizens must now deal with questions on which they might reasonably regard expert advice as decisive – if they could identify the right experts. I would not deny that in consequence the application of the theory of the general will is much less easy to carry through than Rousseau, with much simpler societies in mind, treats it as being. Before we consider how far the theory is relevant to our times, however, we need to see how far it is intelligible on the assumptions that Rousseau was working with.

28. In John Rawls *A Theory of Justice* (Cambridge, Massachussetts, Harvard University Press, 1971), consider not only the original position argument, but also the argument invoking fraternity and other considerations (pp. 103-6) and appealing to reasons why both those better off and those worse off under a current scheme of such a kind might be content to accept it. I rely in part on such arguments in David Braybrooke, 'Making Justice Practical' in Michael Bradie and David Braybrooke (eds.), *Social Justice* (Bowling Green, Ohio, The Applied Philosophy Program, Bowling Green University, 1982) and David Braybrooke , 'Justice and Injustice in Business' in Tom Regan (ed.), *Just Business* (New York, Random House, 1984).

29. Thus, as my colleague Robert Eden, in a stimulating comment, has pointed out to me, my analysis rests rather on Books I and II of *Du Contrat social* than on Book III.

30. Roy, 'Burn with a Hard Gem-Like Flame!'

31. I have benefited from comments of Joshua Cohen, Jules Coleman and Kurt Baier at the session of the summer institute on public choice theory at which this paper was read, as well as from the comments of Robert Eden afterward. Earlier, Russell Hardin and Jane Mansbridge helped the project forward with general encouragement. It was Jane Mansbridge who insisted that I take into account *Emile*. Most lately, I have had useful comments from audiences at the meeting of the Atlantic Provinces Philosophical Association at Acadia University, late in October 1984, and at the University of Western Ontario, where I read the paper early in the month succeeding. At Acadia, Serge Morin presented a long, acute and learned comment, which put my argument into an historical

perspective which I do not command, founded on the literature in French. It seemed to me that his comments were generally consistent with my argument. Finally, I have had some comments from Frederick Barnard, as well as the advantage of reading his recent article on Rousseau in *Political Studies* (1984), and taken some reassurance therefrom.

6 THE RISE AND FALL OF MARXIST IDEOLOGY IN COMMUNIST COUNTRIES*

Eugene Kamenka

Introduction

Karl Marx was the greatest thinker in the history of socialism. He gave socialism its intellectual respectability and its theoretical self-confidence. From divers sources and materials, from phrases in radical pamphlets and slogans at socialist meetings, from German philosophy, French politics and English economics, he created a socialist system of thought, a total socialist critique of modern society. He refined and systematised the language of socialism; he explained and expounded the place of socialism in history; he reconciled, or seemed to reconcile, its conflicting hopes and theoretical contradictions. His work — itself a process of self-clarification — set the seal upon the transition from the romantic revolutionism of the 1840s to the working-class movement that spanned the 1860s to 1880s. It fused into a single body of connected doctrine moral criticism and economic analysis, revolutionary activism and social science, the longing for community and the acceptance of economic rationality and industrial progress. It clothed the interests and demands of a still largely nascent and despised working class in the dignity of a categorical imperative pronounced by history itself. It laid the foundations for a critical account of the birth and development of modern society. For Marx correctly recognised the world-historical importance of the French Revolution and the Industrial Revolution. He saw that, in Europe at least, they were part and parcel of one development. He realised that they had inaugurated a new era in history, an era in which civil society — the world of industry and trade — had moved to the centre of the stage and was being driven by violent internal compulsions to ever more rapid change and expansion. Marx recognised more clearly than others the birth of modern society and the tensions and conflicts involved in its internal dynamic. Since the Napoleonic wars set the seal of destruction upon the old order and the old regime in Europe, we have been living through a continuing crisis which has spread outward from Europe until it engulfs the world. Marx was the first and in many respects greatest student of that crisis.

93

His predictions have proved at least partly false; his presentation of the issues may now seem far too simple; but he saw where the issues lay, not only of his time but of ours. The study of modern society still cannot bypass the work of Karl Marx.[1]

Marxism as social theory is one thing and Marxism as ideology another, though the two are related in a variety of interesting ways. The great success of Marxism, it has often been claimed, came when armed workers burst into the streets of Petrograd in October-November 1917 and established the first Marxist government in the world. That government has since grown from strength to strength; communist states now govern half the population of the world. Yet only some — and markedly a minority of — socialists in advanced industrial societies have seen this as a realisation of Marx's predictions and a vindication of his hopes. The communist revolutions took place at first sight in defiance of Marx's theory of history and not in accordance with it. The practical actions and theoretical proclamations of the governments that were brought into being have seemed to many a far cry indeed from Marx's vision of a free co-operative and ultimately stateless workers' community, in which class division, alienation and all forms of coercion would be totally overcome. Neither do those governments confront us as genuine 'workers' governments putting the interests of the proletariat first, cherishing proletarian organisation and proletarian freedom — confident and independent trade unions, for instance.

Karl Marx had, for much of his life, little time for the Russians. The Tsarist autocracy was, for him, the cornerstone of European reaction; in 1848 he called for war against it. Later he was to see in the British Foreign Secretary, Lord Palmerstone, a Russian spy. Russia's government and people he saw as products and carriers of Asiatic barbarism, shaped by the 250 years of Tartar overlordship but also, according to Marx in the 1850s, by the 'Mongolising and Tartarising nature of the terrain'. Russians were a spiritless, servile people, accustomed to the knout.

Paradoxically, it was in Russia that Marx gained the most attention and respect among serious intellectuals in his own lifetime. They welcomed his call for revolution, but they welcomed even more his implicit assurance that the capitalist, individualistic, competitive West was not the ultimate model for mankind, but would itself be replaced by a higher and communitarian society. By the 1870s, Marx was learning Russian and taking an intense interest in Russia as the country in which his doctrines 'have great currency'. In 1879, the English Liberal M.P., Sir Mountstuart Elphinstone Grant-Duff, reported to the Empress

Frederick of Prussia (eldest daughter of Queen Victoria) on a visit he had paid to Marx at his home. Marx spoke of her and of the Crown Prince with 'due respect and propriety' and his opinions, if slightly cynical, were largely correct when concerned with the past and the present. On the future Marx was vague and unsatisfactory. 'He looks, not unreasonably, for a great and not distant crash in Russia, thinks it will begin by reforms from above which the old bad edifice will not be able to bear and which will lead to its tumbling down altogether. As to what would take its place he had evidently no clear idea, except that for a long time Russia would be unable to exercise any influence in Europe.'[2]

As usual, Marx was partly right and partly wrong. Less than 70 years after the collapse of Tsarism, the Soviet Union remains the world's largest empire, the world's most secure and pervasive one-party dictatorship and one of the world's two great and terrifying super-powers, whose finger can be felt in every crumbling pie.

Marx died too soon to consider where his theories had led or what was new and what was old in the politics, system of government and national lifestyle of the Soviet citizen. There has been a flood of liter-ature since. There have been some splendid and eminently readable books that place today's Soviet reality in the context of Russian history: Tibor Szamuely's *The Russian Tradition* at the popular level and Richard Pipes' *Russia under the Old Regime* at the serious are among the best. Marx would have found them much more interesting, exciting and congenial than such typical centenary celebration talks on 'Marxism and the multi-nationals', 'Marxism and Feminism', 'Marxism and Gay Liberation', 'Marxism and the Counter-culture' as now engage the attention of many radicals. He would want to know about Russia rather than ignore it as an embarrassment for 'Marxism'. For history, Marx knew and said, was not made by 'the people' but by great 'historic' nations and by great socio-economic classes that were carriers, organisers and overlords of new productive forces and modes of production. Such classes were made and shaped by their role in history, i.e. by their role in production. That very general view of Marx's — that power (and not just ideas or ideals) shapes the course of history, and that revolutions have a logic independent of the will of those who make them — is not palatable to many people today, but it is thoroughly borne out by the history of communist states that his writing helped to create. The details of his theory of the coming socialist revolution, and of revolution generally, on the other hand, are not.

The rise and spread of communism, of communist revolutions and communist take-overs in the twentieth century bear out, without question, Marx's insistence that bourgeois society of industrial capitalism had an internal expansionary dynamic that would undermine and unsettle traditional, non-industrial nations throughout the world, that would drag all nations into the history of Europe. In spite of its subsequent concern with, and manipulative use of, the theme of national liberation, communism can be seen as a principal agent, in underdeveloped countries, of the practice and ideology of modernisation, industrialisation and the development of State economic and political power. Its most effective cutting edge, like that of Marxism, was directed not against capitalism, but against pre-capitalist modes and formations. Marx, however, saw the socialist revolution as far more than that. It would be a great historic advance upon capitalism and industrialisation and not simply an alternative route to the latter. It would occur in or depend upon support in the most advanced industrial societies. It would be the work of the proletariat, the most advanced, industrialised and consciously rational and collectivised part of the population. It would result in the abolition of private property and the disappearance of classes and, consequently, in the withering away of state and law. It would see, that is, the inauguration of a new unalienated co-operative society of human self-determination and freedom. The proletariat would bring this about because it was the truly universal class which had no particular standpoint or interest but represented the whole of humanity. The proletariat, indeed, as Shlomo Avineri has reminded us in a splendid presentation to the World Congress of Philosophy in Montreal in August 1983, became for Marx the philosopher-king, combining rational knowledge and rational action, knowing and doing in one. In Hegel, the great actors in history — Alexander, Napoleon, etc. — had served the cunning of reason, not themselves appreciating the significance and inevitable results of their action. The philosopher on the other hand, who understood the significance, was, like the owl of Minerva, wise only after the event. The proletariat would know and do rationally at the same time, and with increasing self-consciousness, as the revolution took shape.[3]

Both the rise and the development of communist states point, in the end, to the untenability of Marx's stage and essentialist theory of history and of his picture of the working class and the coming socialist revolution. The working class, in the one hundred years since Marx's death, and before that, have shown no signs of fitness for the role of philosopher-kings. They have shared in all the prejudices and confusions of their age and added many of their own. They have not been the bearers of rationality in industry but, on the contrary, frequent enemies of industrial progress and rationalisation. They have supported their countries in war and as industrial civilisation progressed they turned more and more to what Lenin called 'economism' – the pursuit of sectional material interests and of short-term goals. They neither made this century's communist revolutions nor did they come to control them. Affluence under capitalism, not deprivation, has widened their vision in recent years. The communist revolutions that can genuinely be called revolutions and not military take-overs – those in Russia, Yugoslavia and China, and more recently, the prospect of revolutions in South America – have not been the result of uprising by a conscious and disciplined proletariat, but the result of a collapse of the old regime, in war or financial incompetence, of the sufferings of the peasantry and the landless, and of the alienation of growing numbers of a special, non-Marxist class, the intelligentsia. They have been rebellions or revolutions against the old order, against pre-capitalist attitudes, traditions and ways of governing. They have been most strikingly successful not in societies where industrialisation is very advanced and the proletariat is a significant section of the population, but in peasant societies that can also plausibly be called authoritarian or even, in Marx's sense, asiatic despotisms – societies in which the state has long been stronger than the rest of society and the controller and initiator of all social and economic progress. The basis of communism is not Marx's vision of a spontaneous uprising by the working class that would represent the majority of the nation. It is Lenin's tactically brilliant elaboration of techniques for capturing state power through a disciplined and conspiratorial party that represents 'consciousness' instead of spontaneity; it is his blueprint for a system of one-party rule that would subordinate all significant social activity to the control of a one-party state. That is not what Marx intended; it is what many aspects of his theory and especially his conception of the proletariat's 'historical role' made possible.[4]

The outstanding thing about organised Marxists, as distinct from other socialists, has been their keen appreciation of the importance of power. The doctrine of the inevitability of revolution, the doctrine that state and law represented the will of the ruling class, the doctrine that the bourgeoisie would fight bitterly and relentlessly to retain its privileges and the doctrine that the economic arrangements of society were the key to everything else implied precisely what Lenin believed – that social progress was a matter of war, that the so-called dictator-

ship of the proletariat must be relentless and pervasive and that a disciplined conscious party that understood and used power could change
the character of society and control the destiny of mankind, provided
it understood the direction of economic organisation and development and the role that the state could play in this.

Marx's Implicit Totalitarianism

Soviet culture, both on the communist and the western view, is a
totalitarian culture. The communists, admittedly, object to the word
'totalitarian' in so far as it is used to imply that there is a specific
societal type transcending the orthodox Marxist classification or in so
far as it is used to suggest important parallels between communist
government on the one hand and fascist or nazi government of the other.
But they, too, will concede that Marxism-Leninism as the 'guiding ideology' of Soviet people and the Communist Party as the supreme expression of historical destiny and the true social interest do and they claim
should permeate and control all aspects of life in the Soviet socialist
society. The distinction between 'private' and 'public', the emphasis
on individual values abstracted from social life and the alleged autonomy of separate social or cultural spheres, they will argue, are categories based on the vicious separation of man from man that are characteristic of bourgeois production and bourgeois life.

The two fundamental features of Marxism that made it an effective
ideological weapon in the struggle against autocracies — its monism and
its progressivism — also combined to make it a suitable ideological
basis for totalitarian control. Marx's insistence on the absence of social
discontinuities, his emphasis on the social character of man and of all
human activities struck squarely and not ineffectively at the nineteenth
century liberal's elevation of the 'private' conscience and the 'private'
sphere of life. The Marxist classification of societies in terms of 'essential' characteristics and the Marxist view that historical developments
flowed in a single stream implied the view that any given society was a
finite whole, 'ruled' by pervasive principles, subject to domination
by a single class. That is why, in the face of all the evidence of complexity, Marxists — even in Australia — persist in talking about the
ruling class. Much as the Marxist doctrine of the class struggle may have
done to inspire and strengthen the development of truly pluralistic
views of society, this development took place entirely outside the
Marxist fold. For the Marxist, the doctrine of the class struggle carried

an essentially anti-pluralistic message — like Hegel's dialectic, class conflict was but a phase in the development on the One. The final goal of history lay in the coming to power of a single class that was no longer a class, but the whole of Man, in the creation of a society that was free, but no longer rent by competing interests and 'plurality of thinking'. Even before the achievement of this goal, the doctrine of a pervasive class struggle denied the autonomy or independence of any political field or demand, just as the — admittedly complex — strain of economic reductionism in Marxism denied the autonomy or independence of any social or cultural field. Nothing could claim the right to be considered apart from the 'social base' that gave it birth and the social interest it served.

'The member of the Russian intelligentsia,' M.O. Gershensohn wrote in the collection *Vekhi* after the abortive rebellion of 1905, 'in the literal meaning of the word lives outside himself, recognising as the only object worthy of his interest and concern something that lies beyond his own personality: the people, society, government.' The philosopher N. Berdyaev, in the same volume, complained that the attitude of the Russian intelligentsia might be summarised as — may truth vanish without a trace, if its abolition or suppression will remove one jot from the sufferings of the Russian people. Was not this the spirit in which the great critic Belinsky had written to (the admittedly senile) Gogol: 'The Russian people is right. It sees in the writers of Russia its leaders, defenders, and saviours from Russian autocracy, Orthodoxy and nationality. It can forgive a bad book, but not a harmful one'? Was it not the spirit in which, in 1913, Maxim Gorky assailed the Moscow Art Theatre for staging Dostoevsky's *Brothers Karamazov* and *The Possessed:* 'Dostoevsky . . . the evil genius of Russia . . . is great and Tolstoy is a genius, and all of you, gentlemen, are gifted and clever; but Russia and her people are more important than Tolstoy, Dostoevsky, and even Pushkin, to say nothing of ourselves'?[5]

Faced by autocracy and involved in revolutionary struggle, human beings tend to follow those who can point to a single, concrete and yet seemingly all-embracing aim. Because Marxist theory had been elaborated in the context of the advancing industrial economies of the west, and because Marx was more than a mere ideologue of revolution, it was not at all clear by Marxian standards that Russia had reached, in 1881, in 1905, or in 1917, the stage that made it ripe for a proletarian revolution. In fact, it was clear it had not and the decision to go ahead amounted to a radical *rejection* of Marxist 'materialism', of the Marxist belief that history could not be made by will and that the state only served and reflected economic realities independent of it. But once such doubts were suppressed or swept aside by the Bolshevik victory and Lenin's elaboration of the claims of 'consciousness' as opposed to those of 'spontaneity', Marxist essentialism − as expressed in the Marxian theory of revolutions and the doctrine of the dictatorship of the proletariat − was able to provide such an aim. From the transfer of power *everything* would follow: the dictatorship of the proletariat was the necessary and the sufficient ground for socialism, for communism, for the complete liberation of man. Combined with Marxist teleology, with the belief in history's progress toward an ultimate end, Marxist monism was also able to 'reduce' what others had thought of as the realm of values. The Revolution, and then the coming of communism, became the ultimate moral end in terms of which all was to be judged. Nor were such judgements mere individual judgements, they were the judgements of History itself. No wonder that the revolutionary Angelica Balabanoff could write, after reading Plekhanov's *The Development of the Monistic View of History* (the primer of a whole generation of Russian Marxists): 'I found it exactly what I needed at the time, a philosophy of method that gave continuity and logic to the processes of history and endowed my own ethical aspirations, as well as the revolutionary movement itself, with the force and dignity of an historical imperative.'[6] To rule in the name of history is to rule completely. To the imperatives of history there can be no opposition. The continuing importance and appeal of Arthur Koestler's *Darkness at Noon* lies in its appreciation of the role of this belief in the shaping of the Marxist mentality. But we know now, from the *Confessions of an Old Bolshevik* and other revelations about Bukharin's motives for 'confessing', that Koestler overrated, even then, the extent to which Old Bolsheviks still believed.

The logical structure and ambitions of Marxian theory made it easily convertible into the ideological foundation of totalitarian rule. But the empirical content on which it based much of its appeal was a content tied to specific social circumstances and events. Marxism was an ideology and a critique of the period of transition *into* fully-fledged industrial society − in the *Communist Manifesto*, one might almost say, Marx and Engels mistook the birth-pangs of a new social order for its death-pangs. Its claim to be a universal science reflects a period of cultural and technological development in which 'science' was beginning to replace religion and morality as the guide and hope of mankind, but in which the division of labour and the accumulation of knowledge had not yet reached the point where the conception of a 'universal science' absorbing and explaining all specialisms would become wildly implausible. Its emphasis on economic organisation and economic interests as the foundation and content of power was born of a period of almost violent economic and social change, in which tradition, custom and habits of ruling and of obedience seemed to have been swept away in a flood of economic innovation and re-organisation.

Karl Marx, as Dr. Alfred G. Meyer has argued,[7] for instance, wove three fundamental strands into a single, majestic system — a radical critique of bourgeois industrial civilisation as dehumanising man, an optimistic theory of progress pointing to the ultimate overcoming of all such dehumanisation and alienation, and a sober and respectably scientific investigation of society. The unity of this system, the suppression of contradiction between the three strands, depended upon Marx's conception of the historical role of the proletariat as the bearer of further progress, as the class that was yet more than a class (that could become humanity as a whole), as the group that would unite theory and practice to overcome the exploitation and dehumanisation of man. When events in the advanced industrial societies began to show that Marx's conception of the proletariat and its 'inevitable' destiny was false — as events indeed began to show from 1848 onward — the disintegration of 'classical' Marxism began.

The point may be approached in yet another way, as it has been approached by Professor Adam B. Ulam.[8] The birth and rapid development of industrial society in an initially agrarian social setting imposes enormous strain and social dislocation upon those who are torn out of their agrarian environment and the placid idiocy of rural life to become the new urban, industrial proletariat. The peasant's reaction to the new social role forced upon him, Professor Ulam suggests, is at first fundamentally anarchist in content: he combines strong hostility to the machine and industrial society with a longing for an idealised version of the village commune. But this only creates an unbearable tension in his daily life — slowly he must learn to stop dreaming that someone will smash the machines and accept the new industrialisation on which his whole power of earning has come to depend. It is at this stage that Marxism evolves as the ideology for the new working class. On the one hand, it promises the worker the same as the anarchists promise: a true community of mankind, in which the *Gemeinschaft* of agrarian life will be re-established in freer and more splendid form. On the other hand, it teaches the worker to accept industrialisation as the very means by which this truly human freedom will be brought about. It sings paeans to the role of the bourgeoisie in extending man's productive capacities. It deflects the worker's hostility away from the machine toward the owner of the machine and the government that protects the owner: it shows the worker the power he can have *within* the industrial system itself. Marxism, thus, 'receives its historical significance from its ability to combine anarchism — the most violent protest against industrialism — with an intense cult of technology and a conviction of the historical necessary and blessings of industrialism'[9]; it becomes (as it became in Germany) the inspirer and educator of the worker in his transition to a fully industrial life. But when the industrial society and the industrial ethos have become firmly established (as they did in Germany around 1900, and in England earlier), Marxism loses its relevance. The workers turn to labourism and the demand for better housing and higher wages; the middle classes look for status and security. The disintegration of Marxism referred to by Dr. Meyer sets in apace precisely because the proletariat ceases to perform the function vital for Marxist hopes. Thus, in Germany, from 1900 or so onward, the 'Marxism' of the German Social-Democratic Party served only to frighten the middle classes: it had less significant effect on social policies or even on the practical demands of the working-class and of the SPD itself. In Russia toward the end of the nineteenth century, on the other hand, Marxism was relevant as it is relevant in agrarian societies turning toward industrial-isation to-day. Russia was being rapidly precipitated into the industrial age, while its society was of the type to maximise anarchist reactions. It was on a wave of anarchist reaction that the Bolsheviks came to power in 1917, when Lenin deliberately deepened the anarchist content of Marxism to make a direct appeal to the peasant with his slogan of 'Land, Peace and Bread'; once in power, he used Marxism to intensify the cult of technology, to make socialism depend upon electrification. Just as Marxism could make bearable for the worker the smoke and misery of the growing industrial settlements of the west, so it could palliate for the Russian the 'crash programmes' of the Stalinist dictator-ship, just as it palliated the crash programmes of the Chinese dictator-ship in the period now called 'the rule of the Gang of Four'. (The revival of Marxism in western European societies in recent years is not based on the industrial worker, but on a new crisis of industrial society and of the cult of technology in general; it is based on the Marxism of 1844-48 rather than the Marxism of the 1870s.)

It is a matter of dispute, and it will no doubt remain a matter of dis-pute, to what extent the Bolshevik and Communist Chinese rise to secure power can be ascribed to the appeal and legitimating function

of their ideology and to what extent it was a result of cynical oppor-
tunism and single-minded use of terror even in those few communist
societies where communism was not imposed by the force of foreign
arms. There is no dispute among serious students of communist
societies that Marxism as a legitimating ideology disintegrates as those
societies pass beyond the mobilisational stages of rapid revolutionary
change and forced industrialisation into a modern industrial and post-
industrial ethos. Complexity, the need for state and legal organisation,
the emergence of classes, strata and interest groups become all too
evident. Marxism begins to be judged by its present achievements and
not its future claims and is found wanting − implicitly by the leader-
ship, explicitly by the population.

In the remainder of this paper I should like to look at the disintegration of Marxism in communist societies by looking at the course,
not of dissent or popular opposition, which is even more revealing, but
at the course of official ideology in the areas of Marxist philosophy
and the general theory of Marxism, in ethics and culture, in the theory
of the state and law.

The Ideological Breakdown

Prerevolutionary Russian philosophy (except, perhaps, for the philosophy of law, where Petrazicky's psychological theory of law and legal
norms had deserved, if brief, international standing) attracted no attention and acquired no standing above the remote provincial; Bolshevik
philosophy in the period 1919 to 1956 earned nothing but contempt
from serious philosophers of all nationalities. Bolshevik theory and
Bolshevik practice openly proclaimed goals that amounted to the complete politicisation, dogmatisation and vulgarisation of philosophy.
Dialectical materialism became the official philosophy of the Communist Party and the Bolshevik state, consistently invoked as the ultimate ideological foundation of all communist political activity and as
the only correct foundation for all science, whether social or natural.
The repression of non-Marxist philosophy became a necessary consequence of the dictatorship of the proletariat; Lenin's principle of
partiinost (party-mindedness) was taken to require of the philosopher
complete identification with both the general theoretical and specific
practical aims of the Communist Party. This view of philosophy as total
(though allegedly scientific) ideological *Weltanschauung* quickly led to
the blurring of all serious distinctions between the philosophical, the

ideological and the political. Bolshevism, insisting on the unity of theory and practice, made all the problems that arose in the building up of a communist society philosophical questions, whether they concerned military strategy, the nature of a 'Marxist' biology, or the raising of agricultural production. 'Philosophical' questions were discussed at meetings of factory workers and in popular publications; not only philosophers, but leading party administrators, not only philosophical publications, but the party press and the newspaper of the Red Navy played decisive roles at certain stages of 'philosophic' discussion.

The attempt to make philosophy a mass ideology — Soviet primers of dialectical materialism were published in editions of 250,000 or 500,000 copies and yet quoted as serious contributions to a difficult and technical subject — led (not unnaturally in these conditions) to a philosophical dogmatism organised along religious lines. Philosophy was seen as having its sacred texts (Marx and Engels, and then Lenin and Stalin), its unchallengeable ecclesiastical authority (the Communist Party), its officially recognised teachers (the approved party ideologists, strictly censored and promptly removed for deviation or independence), and its innumerable heresies suppressed and persecuted as such. (This trend paralleled the bureaucratisation of the party, and, like that bureaucratisation, had its roots in Leninism, but flourished most obviously from the Tenth Congress onward. The details of the process of dogmatisation have been insufficiently studied.) Consummated under Stalin, this dogmatic organisation of philosophy as a state ideology resulted in thinking which, as N.A. Berdyaev once put it, 'is purely anonymous'. Communist philosophers showered with praise any platitude or absurdity coming from their leaders; they attacked the disgraced or the unpopular in utterly unprincipled fashion; they confessed and recanted and attacked views they had themselves held a little earlier in the style made familiar by the Inquisition and heresy hunts. (Today, this is no longer the style of Soviet intellectuals or tertiary institutions when on their best behaviour; it is the style of secondary school instruction and of all Soviet chiefs when faced with opposition.)

The adoption of Lenin's political style into philosophy — by persons of infinitely less ability than Lenin — led to a *reductio ad absurdum* of all his worst intellectual traits. His abusive style, his impatience with complexity, his readiness to ascribe unworthy political motives to any opponent, his insistence on bringing everything down to a single issue, and his unprincipled readiness to distort the positions he was criticising, all became pervasive features of Soviet philosophy, features that these philosophers defended in the most philistine way. Amid this dogmatism and cynicism, it was constantly proclaimed that dialectical materialism was the only scientific world view. The suppression of all other philosophies and the failure to teach seriously even the history of philosophy were defended as being analogous to the suppression of medical quacks and the failure to teach the phlogiston theory to modern classes in chemistry. Yet to non-Marxist philosophers of the most divergent views, the scientific and intellectual content of dialectical materialism as a philosophy seemed remarkably slight and its basic propositions uninteresting in the light of contemporary philosophical developments. Substituting abuse for argument, constantly writing for a low-level audience, not subjected to intellectual criticism that counted in their eyes, Soviet philosophers seemed to their western counterparts to have regressed far behind the standards of criticism and analysis achieved by professional philosophers in Russia before the revolution, let alone by contemporary western philosophers. The attempt to reduce all philosophical conflicts to the conflict between idealism and materialism obscured more than it illuminated philosophical problems; difficulties both in the Soviet conception of materialism and in their exposition and criticism of other philosophers were constantly ignored, often by downright falsification of opponents who caused or brought out these difficulties. The concept of contradiction, so fundamental to Soviet philosophy, was never carefully examined, and technical criticism of Hegel's logic was never taken into account. The Leninist theory of 'reflection' – accompanied by an inability to grasp the force of Berkeley's criticisms – made Soviet epistemology remarkably naive. For all the bombast and self-congratulation with which Soviet ideologists accompanied their work, the 'philosophy' of dialectical materialism in their hands became a system of platitudes, half-truths and lies designed by unprincipled bureaucrats for semi-educated peasants.

We should also not forget that the October Revolution, unlike the February Revolution, did not represent the consummation of the revolutionary strivings and traditions of the Russian intelligentsia, even in its most radical form. The emigration from Russia in the years of the civil war included not only merchants and aristocrats, unpolitical poets and the liberal (Kadet) intellectuals, but much of the Menshevik and Social Revolutionary intelligentsia as well. To the majority of Marxist intellectuals it seemed clear from July 1917 onward (as it had been clear to Martov since 1903) that Lenin was appealing to the anti-intellectual forces in Russian life and that his victory would mean an age of barbarism. (Non-Russian Marxists, Kautsky, Luxemburg and the later Otto Bauer, held much the same view.) The Menshevik internationalist N.N. Sukhanov, one of the few revolutionary intellectuals present in St. Petersburg from the first days of the February to the last days of the October Revolution, brought this out graphically by contrasting the crudity of the people present at the Second Congress of Soviets summoned by the Bolsheviks on October 25 1917, with the membership of the First Congress, which had met a few months earlier.

The tone of Soviet philosophy between 1921 and 1953 was pervasive; so were its dogmatism and its pretensions to providing the 'key' to all problems. But the years between 1921 and 1930 did see a significant struggle between 'mechanists', who saw Marxist philosophy as a form of empirical science, and dialectical materialists, led by A.M. Deborin, who emphasised the Hegelian side of the dialectic and 'leaps' and 'transformations', as quantitative change produced qualitative breaks. Stalin, however, dealt with philosophy as he dealt with other Bolshevik leaders and rival programmes. The mechanists were condemned in 1930; Deborin was condemned in 1931 and forced to recant. The new line 'on the philosophical front' became entirely subservient to the day-to-day requirements of party policies and changed drastically as they changed. A crude economic reductionist version of Marxism and a simple stage theory of history were used to justify the historic role of the Communist Party, the dictatorship of the proletariat and relentless rejection of everything outside the communist fold, while the 'mystery' of the dialectic was constantly invoked to explain why dictatorship was really democracy, why the state had to become stronger before it withered away, why the enemies on the left were 'really' 'objectively' the enemies on the right.

In 1921, Lenin had called an end to the utopian anarchy of the period of War Communism and inaugurated a limited period of licensed capitalism under strict government control, the period of the New Economic Policy. It was called to an abrupt halt at the end of 1928 and a brutal forced collectivisation of the Soviet peasantry ushered in the period of the building of socialism and of Stalin's Five Year Plans. Then in 1936, Stalin abruptly proclaimed that the socialist stage had been reached and there was once more a revolution in the theory and philosophy of Marxism.

It showed the combined effect of Stalin's growing concern with ideology as a means of stabilisation and of the growth in technical and general education leading to increased specialisation and more postgraduate studies. The ideology of 'the one thing needful', so prominent in the period of revolutionary struggle and of the five-year plans, had been officially abandoned in 1936, but the purges and the war naturally enough gave it a great residual strength. The 1920s and even the early 1930s had been periods to stress the dependence of everything on economic change and economic progress. From 1936 onward, however, Stalin had turned toward converting the dialectic into the basis for a stable ideology of Soviet rule. Its task now was not to sharpen class struggle, but to help create consensus. The economic reductionism implicit in the materialist interpretation of history was, therefore, further modified. In 1938, in his *On Dialectical and Historical Materialism*, Stalin had stressed the capacity of the ideological superstructure for reacting back on the base; in 1950, in his *Marxism and Questions of Linguistics*, he went further and stressed the comparative independence of the ideological superstructure, its creative role in 'aiding the base', and insisted that some cultural phenomena, such as language, transcended class divisions and were, therefore, ideologically neutral. The pamphlet not only opened up the way for a study of formal logic as the ideologically neutral — though abstract and static — laws of thought, but symbolised generally the new stress on ideology.

The stress on ideology was accompanied by, and also reflected, a general growth in education and specialisation. The 1920s had been a period of educational 'crash programmes', designed to maximise literacy and basic skills. By the late 1930s, a more stable educational system producing more seriously trained people had emerged, but its impact on Soviet society was interrupted by purges and total and destructive war. The early postwar period had to undertake once again an enormous expansion of education, but this time at a (comparatively) much higher level. The demand now was not for literacy, but for more jurists, more teachers, more scientists, more administrators. The sophistication of Soviet society had enormously increased; so had the absolute numbers of people capable of reading serious work. In 1916 there were some 90 institutions of higher learning in all Russia; by 1959 there were 770, including 40 universities. By the 1960s there were well over 2,000,000 full-time or correspondence students of tertiary institutions, compared with some 200,000 in any year of the 1920s.

During the final years of Stalin's rule, when a build-up of philosophical teaching, discussion and publication began, the party was nevertheless extremely anxious to keep philosophers to a strictly partisan line, with the party as active arbiter on most philosophical and scientific questions. There was a campaign against 'objectivism'. The criticism of contemporary 'bourgeois' philosophy was encouraged, but carried on in the crudest and most vindictive terms; prerevolutionary materialist philosophy in the territories making up the Soviet Union was grossly overvalued. In 1948 the Central Committee of the Communist Party organised a conference for the purpose of condemning orthodox genetics and announcing that the Michurin-Lysenko school of biology, with its rejection of genes and its belief in the heritability of acquired characteristics, was the correct Marxist-Leninist view of biology. The Central Administration of the Statistical Institute had to recant the heresy that statistics was based on the mathematical relationships of large numbers and to concede that statistical relations had meaning only in the context of Marxist-Leninist social science. A.A. Maksimov and a group of philosophers of science attacked the physicists for using and defending the subjective-idealist theory of relativity, but were in this case successfully repelled. Then in 1950 came Stalin's shattering blow to Marxist linguistics, in which the theories of N. Ia. Marr (1864-1934) and his Marxist disciples − that languages unfolded by qualitative leaps − were proclaimed as nonsense, and his followers were accused of stifling Soviet linguistics. This pamphlet led to two years of hasty philosophical activities in which everything was brought into line with Stalin's new pronouncements on the relation between base and superstructure and the character of language and formal logic.

The year 1948, like the year 1931, did not produce any major revolution in the Soviet philosophical line; the dominant (Deborinist) trend in Soviet philosophy has never been repudiated wholesale in the way in which the Stuchka-Pashukanis-Reisner position on law was repudiated in 1936. There were differences in emphasis, a growing national chauvinism, increasing cold-war bitterness in writing on contemporary bourgeois philosophy, less tendency toward economic reductionism, and increasing stress on ethics and moral education and on the administrator's delusion that policies can remake society.

Only the death of Stalin saw the beginnings of a really new tone in Soviet philosophy, presaging the qualitative leap that became possible after 1955-56. Within a year laudatory references to Stalin as a great philosophical genius had disappeared from the journals and demands for a certain respect for professional competence and integrity began to be heard. While lawyers were publicly much more forthright than philosophers in demanding a certain professional standing and respect for their professional integrity, a certain section of leading philosophers − apparently with full party approval − began calling for more objective and creative philosophical work. In 1955, the journal *Kommunist* complained that of the 1,000 or more graduate philosophers then supposedly active in the Soviet Union, only about 100 published with any degree of regularity; the remaining 900 preferred to rest on their laurels. 'Their philosophical swords are covered with rust . . . bleak "quotology" has become their stock in trade . . . They are capable of making a deal with their conscience, they praise a book to the skies today and readily tear it to pieces tomorrow . . . We must put an end to such depravity.' In 1956, at the Twentieth Congress of the CPSU, N.S. Krushchev in his secret speech inaugurated the campaign for liquidating the cult of personality in Soviet cultural life. In 1961, at the Twenty-Second Congress, Stalin's murderous depravities and intellectual errors, including the error of dogmatically laying down positions in fields in which he was not competent, were exposed to the world. In general terms, this was an extremely important trend — of course, within the limits of ultimate party control — toward declassifying the specific details of professional disciplines and permitting professional discussion without the threat of political punishment for taking the wrong side. By 1958, the leading Soviet philosopher P.N. Fedoseev was emphasising the importance of concrete analysis in philosophy and the impropriety of importing methods appropriate to the struggle against hostile ideology into scientific discussions. But de-Stalinisation was at no stage permitted to become a critique of the effects of censorship, repression and one-party rule as such — and is not permitted to do so today, even in Poland, let alone the USSR.

The trend toward professionalisation and professional integrity becoming more evident in Soviet philosophical discussion after 1953 was accompanied by some important surrenders by dogma coming in contact with life. In 1955 discussions on the philosophy of science led to the acceptance of the theory of relativity (both the general and the special) as fully compatible, in its physical formulations, with the doctrines of dialectical materialism; it was taken to confirm the *diamat* view that geometry is a branch of physics, that space and time cannot be abstracted from matter, and that matter is not inert material but can also be energy. In these discussions the leading Soviet philosophers identified with the attack on relativity, A.A. Maksimov and R. Ia. Steinman, together with the anti-relativity physicist I.V. Kuznetsov, were branded as reactionary. The following year, cybernetics, previously condemned as a bourgeois pseudo-science, was fully accepted as the science of computers, bringing out certain important analogies with human thinking. In connection with this the development of mathematical logic and the truth-table technique were accepted by an increasing number of Soviet philosophers as an important expansion of formal logic — a development culminating in the decision by the Moscow University Philosophy Faculty in 1966 to accept Professor I.S. Narsky's recommendation that the Department of Logic in the Faculty confine itself to teaching formal and mathematical (symbolic) logic and that the teaching of dialectical logic be split off from it. At the same time, the regime of Lysenko in biology was overthrown in favour of orthodox genetics.

All these developments produced very significant signs of a new atmosphere in considerable areas of Soviet philosophy. Since, there has been emphasis on problems within dialectical materialism — the relation of formal and dialectical logic, the philosophy of physics, the relationship and co-ordination of the categories of dialectical materialism, and so on. An increasing amount of publication on these questions has been done by university presses and marketed in small editions of seven to ten thousand copies, thus enabling would-be authors to address a more technical audience. The standard argument in such works is mostly still by way of deduction from unquestioned fundamental principles of dialectical materialism, or from Lenin, whose philosophical writings have taken on a specially canonical character since the rejection of Stalin and the alleged return to Leninist norms. There is now a great deal of new nonsense in low-level Soviet philosophical teaching about the 'Leninist stage' in the history of philosophy, the philosophical critique of religion, epistemology, etc., but even the use of doctrinal authorities is now comparatively intelligent and increasingly looks to the context and spirit in which the cited pronouncements were made. But there is, in a host of fields, open recognition that Marxism is irrelevant. Extremely important in this connection have been the growth of contacts with the west through scholarly exchanges, somewhat less restricted travel opportunities for Russians, and a general rise in the sophistication of criticism that now demands some genuine acquaintance with the object of that criticism. Access to non-Marxist sources has been made much easier for senior students and post-graduate students, and there seems to be consistent pressure from members of the Institute of Philosophy and of the Philosophy Faculty at Moscow State University for the publication, in Russian, of non-materialist philosophers, of Marxist revisionist work, and of contemporary western philosophical work. Students are increasingly referred to original sources in non-Marxist philosophy; Plato, Hume and Kant have been published in Russian (Hume for the first time since the revolution); western texts in mathematical logic have been translated; as early as 1966 there was even a Russian translation, (available only on restricted order) of the American compilation *Sociology Today*, edited by Robert K. Merton,

Together with increasing professionalisation and partial de-ideologisation and significantly liberalised contact with the west has come an increasing stress on having dogma take more genuine account of most recent scientific and social developments. Rather important in this connection has been the ever-increasing stress placed by the party on the role of law and ideology as an educator for the conditions of the new life. Since 1951 there has been a growing concern with the problems of Marxist-Leninist ethics. The tendency here has been to soft-pedal or reject altogether the end-directedness of Marxist (especially Lenin's) ethics (good is what helps the revolution and the coming of communism) and to emphasise the specific categories of ethical living as expressions of the commonly accepted rules of social life, and more recently, of humanitarian ideals. The reaction against Stalinism among Soviet intellectuals produced, for a period, a climate in which the integrity of aesthetic and ethical qualities was stressed. This was reflected in the 1960 work by the Leningrad professor V.P. Tugarinov *On the Values of Life and Culture*. He argued there that in aesthetics, and to a lesser extent in ethics, there are categories of beauty and the good, logically independent of the categories of historical materialism, though they interact with the categories of historical materialism. Then, the Department of Ethics at Moscow began to turn its attention to axiology and to the *criteria* of progress. While Soviet theorists must still completely reject 'revisionism', and include in this any Marxist humanism that emphasises alienation as a fundamental category going deeper than mere economic exploitation, recent Soviet writing has put more emphasis on the early works of Marx and has attempted to take over, within the officially approved dogma, some of the humanist points. Such problems as industrial organisation, environmental pollution, drunkenness, etc., are treated as standing outside Marxism.

In law, where there was a trend toward treating more seriously (though only at the theoretical level) the rights of the accused, there have been studies on truth and the judicial process, and attempts to ask as a theoretical question how truth is best established. The growth of dissidence for a time made these questions more urgent, but also more muted as a result of renewed censorship. Further, sociology, previously rejected as a bourgeois substitute for Marxism, has now been accepted as a genuine science in the Soviet Union, and research into absenteeism, adaptation of workers from rural districts, and so on, is being undertaken in Soviet universities and reported in philosophical journals.

There is, indeed, considerable enthusiasm among undergraduate and post-graduate students about sociology, both as a radical critique of the shortcomings of Soviet society and as a means of providing some sort of empirical control over dialectical materialism, as a way of bridging the shocking gap that used to exist between the fantasy world of Soviet philosophy and the realities of Soviet life. This gap, it should be said, is being significantly narrowed. At conferences discussing sociology, even at those already held in Minsk and Leningrad in 1966, a group of younger people made determined attempts to suggest that sociology and sociological inquiry made necessary a reconsideration of the applicability of the traditional Marxist-Leninist definition of such concepts as 'class' to Soviet society. In private, I have found younger men very ready to argue that US stratification theory is a better tool for the sociological study of Soviet society than the traditional concept of classes.

The general position reached in the Soviet Union, then, is this: since 1953, and especially since 1956, there has been an enormous improvement in the quantity, style and professional competence of philosophical writing on technical philosophical questions and on the history of philosophy. In public, the fundamental principles of dialectical materialism are still treated as given and attested assumptions that cannot be challenged, but they are being interpreted and reinterpreted with specific problems in mind and all serious and creative development has consisted of the attempt to integrate non-Marxist treatments of this problems. In ontology and logic there is a serious awareness of problems; there is a steady and not unintelligent concern with the philosophy of physics. In all these fields, however, problems can still be dealt with only in the framework of a dialectical materialist view, which often involves the shirking or glossing over of problems. Soviet philosophers have not developed the precision of language, the scepticism about large-scale metaphysical answers, and the habit of examining limited problems, utterances and concepts in depth. In the fields that come closer to social questions – in ethics, aesthetics and the historical aspects of the history of philosophy – work is still rather poor and uncritical, vacillating between conventionalism and crude ideologising. Those who are allowed to write have learned not always to write what they think; and those who write what they think are not allowed to write. If they persist, they will be deprived, successively, of their jobs, their freedom, their health and threatened in their sanity by 'psychiatric treatment', or – if they are very well known internationally, expelled. Their crime, however, is the political crime of resisting authority. It is not the intellectual heresy of questioning an ideology which no one, in power or out, any longer seriously believes as an intellectual system.

The growing, decidedly non-Marxist, emphasis in Marxist-socialist societies on the importance and complexity of state organisation and law as a means of 'steering society' is well known. It has involved the rejection of the earlier view that state and law are by their essence coercive organs of class rule which lose their *raison d'être* once the division of society into antagonistic classes has been overcome. It has led, irresistibly, to the recognition that neither state nor law has a single unitary essence, or serves just one function. It has also led to ever-increasing emphasis on the necessary technicality of law and administration, on the importance of knowledge and training, the impossibility of totally overcoming the division of labour and on the specialisation of functions in this field. There is now clear, if guarded, recognition of the existence of concepts, techniques and principles, and of objective problems, that must form part of any serious concern with law and administration in modern societies, whether those of socialism or those of the 'bourgeois' and developing world. There is also increasing concern, as Professor F.-C. Schroeder has recently reminded us,[10] with the mechanism of legal regulation, with the legal and extra-legal dimensions of the translation of legal rules into social realities. Soviet bloc writers, especially in Poland, have turned to the sociology of law in a non-classical-Marxist sense. (They are also tending, as Schroeder suggests, in their enthusiasm for 'steering society' to exaggerate the social power of legal regulation and to identify law with management, with administration by the state.) Others, however, are concerned with the specifically legal — not just with norms, but with legal concepts and relationships, even if their concern is expressed in decidedly cautious and muted terms.

Of course, there are still countervailing trends in contemporary Marxist-Leninist theory: the continued insistence on the class interest of the bourgeoisie as ruling and shaping western societies and seeking, through imperialism and neo-colonialism, to dominate the world; the attack on the abstract and formal character of 'bourgeois' law as concealing and facilitating economic subjugation and inequality; the rejection of 'idealist' and 'natural law' elevation of justice as an abstract, formal, or moral concept true for all time; the refusal, in the Soviet Union especially, to see or respect law and legal theory as an independent, critical social tradition, with an in-built bias toward freedom, equality and the clear determination of rights. Nevertheless, Soviet and

East European theoreticians of state and law are now anxious to appear at world congresses and do appear there as professional colleagues of western lawyers, rejecting the 'juristic nihilism' which they treat as a slanderous distortion of Marxism. Nor, as we all know, do they all any longer put forward the same views — there are differences of substance, as well as of emphasis, on such questions as the extent and importance of non-class-based elements in the ethics and legal systems of class societies; the relation between form and content in law, and the character and status of the formal; the correct interpretation, in the light of modern developments, of the classical doctrine of the withering away of state and law as society moves from socialism to the final stages of communism. Thus, the Czech legal philosopher, Vladimir Kubes, agrees with the West German liberal social theorist and former Minister of the Interior, Professor Werner Maihofer, in emphasising that the younger Marx does not speak of the withering away of state and law at all. Kubes insists that replacing the government of men by the administration of things does not mean that one can do without a system of norms for regulating the system of production. Law and the state, he argues, are separate; the state may wither away, the law cannot do so as long as human society endures.[11] The Hungarian legal philosopher, Csaba Varga, argues similarly that the ideal of simple, rational laws immediately accessible to the population at large, the ideal of the laicising of law, is a utopian illusion that characterises the early stages of a revolution and does not survive subsequent development under a revolutionary regime.[12]

Behind all this, despite the vacillation and ambiguity, and the differences between individual Marxist-Leninist thinkers in the Soviet and east European fold, lies a recognition of administrative imperatives, of general social problems and needs, that cannot be reduced to the classical Marxist analysis of society in terms of class conflict, class morality and class interests. It is a recognition forced upon revolutionaries who can no longer live off focusing attention on the evils of the past or urging great leaps forward into an uncharted future, but who must pay real and serious attention to the needs of the present as a significant, complex and continuing social reality.

Western students of contemporary China, most of whom have put an enormous emotional investment into mastering a difficult language and a rich and complex intellectual tradition, have always been too ready to see developments in the People's Republic of China as intensely local or national, as *sui generis*. They have underrated the extent to which Maoist ideology has drawn on Soviet ideology of a different period, and the extent to which the logic of Marxism and the logic of revolutions, with their internal tensions and contradictions, operate in China as they did and do in the Soviet Union. Those who argued some years ago, as Professor A.E.-S Tay and I did,[13] that the mix and tensions of what, following Tönnies and drawing on Max Weber, we call *Gemeinschaft, Gesellschaft* and bureaucratic-administrative conceptions of law were to be found in China as in the Soviet Union, and that the greater Chinese elevation of *Gemeinschaft* procedures, though traditionally based, was inherently unstable and likely to give way to increasingly bureaucratic-administrative arrangements, have been proved right. The position, of course, is still not stable; the tensions have not been resolved. The geopolitical hostility between China and the USSR grows ever sharper, but the retreat from the mass line since the overthrow of the Gang of Four and the renewed emphasis on competent, complex and regularised administration is leading to a certain convergence of Soviet and Chinese perceptions of the role of state and law under socialism. There is perhaps no better index of serious progress in Marxist-Leninist philosophy of law, and of the increasing recognition of the complexity and (limited) integrity of law, than the willingness of theoreticians in communist countries to discuss as a theoretical problem the heritability of law.

In its early stages, or in mobilisation revivals, revolutionary ideology tends to emphasise the negation of law, and thus social and legal discontinuity between different social formations, and especially between 'pre-socialist' and 'socialist' stages. It sees the revolution, or each revolution, as a new beginning, a total overthrow, a purging of the old world. But this mood lasts only during the period of revolutionary enthusiasm, while the revolution is still fundamentally preoccupied with distinguishing itself from the past. Already in the 1920s, one of the early communist chairmen of the Soviet Supreme Court, P.I. Stuchka, noted, very perceptively, that every revolutionary government begins by enacting laws that are retroactive for all time — but when it has become stable, when it has come to be concerned with the future development of the post-revolutionary society, with stability and orderliness, it accepts the practice that laws should come into operation from a specific period. The increasingly critical attitude to the rule of law taken by a western university intelligentsia deprived of responsibility or social power, and taking public affluence and technological competence for granted, though perhaps sparked off by the Great Proletarian Cultural Revolution as well as by Vietnam, is now proceeding in inverse proportion to the stabilisation, to the growing acceptance of the importance of state and law, in communist countries. There, those classical Marxist doctrines that amount to 'juristic nihilism' (as communist theoreticians now call it) are being more and more flatly rejected as vulgar pseudo-Marxism, infantile left-wing communism, anarchistic Maoism (in China, corrupt Gang-of-Fourism) or as bourgeois misrepresentations of Marxist doctrine, invented for the purpose of discrediting it. The importance of law, let alone of the state, as a social category, as a means of regularising social life, steering society, safeguarding production and development, and protecting the individual is now proclaimed — at least in theory — in every communist capital from Berlin through Moscow to Peking. Law may have been, according to Marxists indeed it was, an instrument of class domination in past and present societies of class conflict, inluding early Soviet society. But it is now seen as having been even then not only or entirely that. In developed Marxist-Leninist societies in the stage of socialism, however, where class conflict has been overcome and the state is allegedly the State of All the People, law is now presented as an administrative imperative. It safeguards and secures the socialist system, and the life and values of citizens; it requires technical knowledge and scientific study — i.e. specialisation and expertise — as well as devotion to the practice of socialist legality and to the task of the creative development of socialist law. In China, it is now also seen as an integral part of the four modernisations.

In the USSR, many of the most liberal trends of the Khrushchev era — the elevation of general 'human' values, such as kindness, against Stalinist ruthlessness in a cause, the elevation of law as protecting the individual against the state — did not survive into the renewed bureaucratisation and growing repression of the Brezhnev period. (In China, they are currently prominent in officially-sanctioned literature showing the evils of the Gang of Four, but signs of renewed attacks on Marxist humanism are already appearing, quite apart from the persisting repression of genuine dissidents.) In the USSR, the view that state and law can express certain general social interests and general requirements has, however, been steadily strengthened, and it is now being strengthened in China. So has the professionalisation of Soviet and Chinese Marxist philosophy, and political and legal theory. The emphasis now is on complexity, on recognising continuity as well as discontinuity in historical stages and between socialist and non-socialist forms of society, and the relative independence and integrity of legal institutions, concepts and problems. Precisely because these are comparatively new waters for the Marxist theoretician of law not charted by the classics, there is considerable disagreement and discussion among communist legal philosophers on the precise implications of this — the extent to which pre-socialist and socialist law display continuity, heritability, or common problems; whether the state and law will wither away in a very distant future or, in any real sense, not at all; whether the future of law is to some extent a separate question from the future of the state.

The most interesting discussion of the problem of heritability or continuity in law — a basic but unadmitted problem for the old Marxism and an interesting one for the new — comes, surprisingly, out of Romania, Bulgaria and China, countries whose intellectual contributions to Marxist theory have not in the past been of great importance. The most substantial work is that of the Bulgarian scholar, Neno Nenovski, *Heritability in Law*.[14] It appeared in Bulgaria in 1973 and has commendably been translated into Russian, with a brief, partly critical and patently cautious introduction by the Soviet scholar, Iu. Zav'yalov. Nenovski himself grasps the bull firmly by the horns, taking his departure from an interesting and important series of articles by the Romanian legal theorist, the late Anita M. Naschitz, in the Romanian academic journal of law and legal theory in 1966. Law, Nenovski insists, does not have a single essence but a complex one, which displays internal contradictions or tensions. It cannot be reduced to class-rule — at best it can be reduced to two elements: a common social element and a class element, each standing in complex relation with the other. The class essence of law is a separate thing from the essence of law. The common social element in law explains why the transition from one social form to another is not accompanied, in law, by radical discontinuity, by a total rejection of earlier legal institutions, concepts and techniques. There is both continuity and discontinuity in the passage from one social formation to another. This is true not only in law, but in social life generally, even in those relations of production that law reflects. There are legal institutions and legal values which, within definite limits, have general significance, which are directly related to the general conditions of the existence of human society, and which, therefore, penetrate into both socialist and non-socialist law, creating the possibility of heritability between the two systems, just as they create the possibility of heritability between any two systems. The Chinese, who discussed these issues in the 1957 Hundred Flowers period and again after 1976, have come closest to officially endorsing, with qualifications, Nenovski's view.

With that, the disintegration of Marxism as universal social science and as practical legitimating ideology for the governance of Marxist-socialist societies is complete. The fact that Marxist hopes and analyses bear little relation to the reality of those societies may be morally to their credit. But it has shown that Marxism is far more effective as a battle-cry than as a general theory of society' or as a guide to the building of socialism.

Notes

*Fred Barnard, with whom I was privileged to spend some time as a visitor in the University of Western Ontario, is a historian of ideas in the grand tradition. He deals with great works and important ideas, recognising the extent to which they have shaped the world we live in without failing to understand that they are themselves shaped by circumstance and social setting, and not only other ideas. Such ideas can, as ideologies, be both overpowering and dangerous, leaving no room for honest men and women to breathe or think in. By coming to Canada, and in counterposing ideals of humanism and justice to both Marxism and Fascism, Fred has been able to breathe *and* think, knowing that much of the world is not so fortunate. This slight and rather general essay in the history of ideas is dedicated to him.

1. I have drawn here on my Introduction in Eugene Kamenka (ed.), *The Portable Karl Marx* (New York and Harmondsworth, 1983).

2. *The Portable Karl Marx*, p. 67.

3. Mr. David Lovell, who has successfully completed his Ph.D. thesis in the History of Ideas Unit at the ANU, has studied 'The Concept of the Proletariat in the Thought of Karl Marx' in detail. It is a subject surprisingly, or perhaps not surprisingly, neglected by Marxists. Lovell's work shows quite clearly how Marx sees the proletariat conceptually, reconciling the contradiction between socialism as the movement of the working class and socialism as the proclamation of the general social interest by making itself a 'universal' class. Philosophically, at first, and then politically and economically, 'the proletariat' is a vital component in Marx's system, its nature determined by the logical requirements of the system and not by the empirical development of the working class as an existing social group.

4. A recent addition to the multitudinous literature on this point is David Lovell, *From Marx to Lenin: Marx's Responsibility for Soviet Authoritarianism* (Cambridge University Press, 1984).

5. As cited by Helen Muchnic, *From Gorky to Pasternak* (London, Methuen, 1963), p. 15.

6. Angelica Balabanoff, *My Life as a Rebel* (London and New York, Hamilton, 1938), p. 13.

7. In his *Marxism: The Unity of Theory and Practice* (First published 1934; Michigan, Ann Arbor, 1963), *passim*.

8. In his *The Unfinished Revolution* (New York, Longman/Westfield, 1960), *passim*.

9. Ulam, *The New Face of Soviet Totalitarianism* (Russian Research Studies Centre, Harvard University Press, 1963), p. 21.

10. Friedrich-Christian Schroeder, 'Der "Mechanismus der rechtlichen, Regulierung" als Kategorie der sowjetischen Rechtstheorie', 10 *Rechtstheorie*, 1979,

No. 2, pp. 187-98.

11. V. Kubeš, 'Das Recht und die Zukunft der Gesellschaft', in F.C. Hutley, Eugene Kamenka and A.E.-S. Tay (eds.), *Law and the Future of Society*, Beiheft No. 11, *Archiv für Rechts- und Sozalphilosophie* (Wiesbaden, 1979), pp. 1-25.

12. C. Varga, 'Utopias of Rationality in the Development of the Idea of Codification', *ibid*., pp. 27–41.

13. See especially, Eugene Kamenka and A.E.-S. Tay, 'Beyond the French Revolution: Communist Socialism and the Concept of Law', 21 *University of Toronto Law Journal* 1971 pp, 109-40; A.E.S. Tay, 'Law in Communist China', Parts I and II, 6 *Sydney Law Review* 1969, pp. 153-72, and 1971, pp. 335-70; A.E..-S. Tay, 'Gemeinschaft, Gesellschaft, Mobilisation and Administration: The Future of Law in Communist China', *Asia Quarterly* 1971 No. 3, pp. 257-303; and A.E.-S. Tay, 'Smash Permanent Rules: China as a Model for the Future', 7 *Sydney Law Review* 1976, pp. 400-23. 'The development (in China) has its own distinctive history; but the tensions and theoretical problems are the same: China, as we can now see clearly, does not represent a *new* way', we wrote at the end of 1976 in Eugene Kamenka, R. Brown, A.E.-S. Tay (eds.), 'Socialism, Anarchism and Law', in *Law and Society: The Crisis in Legal Ideals* (London, Edward Arnold, 1978), pp. 48-80, at p. 77n. For the most recent and in some ways fullest statement of our typology, see Eugene Kamenka and A.E.-S. Tay, (eds.), *Law and Social Control* (London, St Martin's Press, 1980), pp. 3-26 and 105-16.

14. Neno Nenovski, *Preemstvennost v prave* (trans. from the Bulgarian by V.M. Safronov, with an introduction by Iu. S. Zavsyalov); (Moscow, 1977).

7 THE DECLINE OF UTOPIAN IDEAS IN THE WEST

Isaiah Berlin

My topic is utopianism. The idea of a perfect society is a very old dream, whether because of the ills of the present, which make men conceive of what their world would be like without them — to imagine some ideal state in which there was no misery and no greed, no danger or poverty or fear of brutalising labour or insecurity — or because these utopias are fictions deliberately constructed as satires, intended to criticise the actual world and to shame those who control existing regimes, or those who suffer them too tamely; or perhaps they are social fantasies — simple exercises of the poetical imagination.

Broadly speaking, western utopias tend to contain the same elements, where a society lives in a state of pure harmony, in which all its members live in peace, love one another, are free from physical danger, from want of any kind, from insecurity, from degrading work, from envy, from frustration, experience no injustice or violence of any kind, live in perpetual, even light, in a temperate climate, in the midst of infinitely fruitful, generous nature. The main characteristic of most, perhaps all, utopias is the fact that they are static. Nothing in them alters, for they have reached perfection: there is no need for novelty or change; no one can wish to alter a condition in which all natural human wishes are fulfilled.

The assumption on which this is based is that men have a certain fixed, unaltering nature, certain universal, common, immutable goals. Once these goals are realised, human nature is wholly fulfilled. The very idea of universal fulfilment presupposes that human beings as such seek the same essential goals, identical for all, at all times, everywhere. For unless this is so, utopia cannot be utopia, for then the perfect society will not perfectly satisfy everyone.

Most utopias are cast back into a remote past: once upon a time there was a Golden Age. So Homer talks about the happy Phaeacians, or about the blameless Ethiopians among whom Zeus loves to dwell, or sings of the Isles of the Blest. Hesiod talks about the Golden Age, succeeded by progressively worse ages, descending to the terrible times in which he lived himself. Plato speaks, in the *Symposium*, of the fact that men were once – in a remote and happy past – spherical in shape, and then broke in half, and ever since each hemisphere is trying to find its appropriate mate for the purpose of once again becoming rounded and perfect. And he speaks also of the happy life in Atlantis, gone, gone forever as a result of some natural disaster. Virgil speaks about *Saturnia regna*, the Kingdom of Saturn, in which all things were good. The Hebrew Bible speaks of an earthly paradise, in which Adam and Eve were created by God and led blameless, happy, serene lives, a situation which might have gone on forever, but was brought to a wretched end by man's disobedience to his Maker. When, in the last century, the poet Alfred Tennyson spoke of a kingdom where there is 'no hail nor rain nor any snow, nor ever wind blows loudly' – this reflects a long, unbroken tradition, and looks back to the Homeric dream of eternal light shining upon a windless world. These are poets who believed that the Golden Age is in a past which can never return. Then there are the thinkers who think that the Golden Age is still to come. The Hebrew prophet Isaiah tells us that 'In the last days, men shall beat their swords into ploughshares, and their spears into pruning hooks: nations shall not lift up sword against nation, neither shall they learn war any more. The wolf also shall dwell with the lamb and the leopard shall lie down with the kid. The desert shall bloom like a rose, sorrow and sighing shall flee away.' Similarly, St Paul speaks of a world in which there will be neither Jew nor Greek, neither male nor female, neither bond nor free. All men shall be equal, and perfect in the sight of God.

What is common to all these worlds, whether they are conceived of as an earthly paradise or something beyond the grave, is that they display a static perfection in which human nature is finally fully realised, and all is still and immutable and eternal.

This ideal can take social and political forms, both hierarchical and democratic. In Plato's Republic there is a rigid, unified hierarchy of three classes, based on the proposition that there are three types of human nature, each of which can be fully realised and which together form an interlocking, harmonious whole. Zeno the Stoic conceives an anarchist society in which all rational beings live in perfect peace, equality and happiness without the benefit of instituitons. If men are rational, they do not need control; rational beings have no need of the state, nor of money, nor of law courts, nor of any organised, institutional life. In the perfect society men and women shall wear identical clothes and 'feed in a common pasture'. Provided that they are rational, all their wishes will necessarily be rational, too, and so capable of total harmonious realisation. Zeno was the first utopian anarchist, the founder of a long tradition which has had a sudden, at times violent, flowering in our own time.

The Greek world generated a good many utopias after the city state showed the first signs of decline. Side by side with the satirical utopias of Aristophanes there is the plan for a perfect state of Theopompus. There is the utopia of Euhemerus, in which happy men live on islands in the Arabian Sea, where there are no wild animals, no winter, no spring, but an eternal, gentle, warm summer, where fruits fall into men's mouths from the trees, and there is no need for labour. These men live in a state of unceasing bliss on islands divided by the sea from the wicked, chaotic mainland in which men are foolish, unjust and miserable.

There may have been attempts to put this into practice. Zeno's disciple Blossius of Cumae, a Roman Stoic, probably preached a social egalitarianism which may have been derived from the earlier communist Iambulus. He was accused of inspiring anti-Roman revolts of a communist type, and was duly investigated, indeed, 'grilled', by a senatorial committee which accused him of spreading subversive ideas – not unlike the MacCarthy investigations in the United States. Blossius, Aristonicus, Gaius Gracchus were accused – the story ends with the execution of the Gracchi. However, these political consequences are merely incidental to my topic. During the Middle Ages, there is a distinct decline in utopias, perhaps because according to Christian faith man cannot achieve perfection by his own unaided efforts; divine grace alone can save him – and salvation cannot come to him while he is on this earth, a creature born in sin. No man can build a lasting habitation in this vale of tears: for we are all but pilgrims here below, seeking to enter a kingdom not of this earth.

The constant theme which runs through all utopian thought, Christian and pagan alike, is that once upon a time there was a perfect state, then some enormous disaster took place: in the Bible, it is the sin of disobedience – the fatal eating of the forbidden fruit; or else it is the Flood; or wicked giants came and disturbed the world, or men in their arrogance built the Tower of Babel and were punished. So, too, in Greek mythology, the perfect state was broken by some disaster, as in the story of Prometheus, or of Deucalion and Pyrrha, or of Pandora's Box – the pristine unity is shivered, and the rest of human history is a continuous attempt to piece together the fragments in order to restore serenity, so that the perfect state may be realised once again. Human stupidity or wickedness or weakness may prevent this consummation; or the gods may not permit it; but our lives are conceived, particularly in the thought of Gnostics and in the visions of the mystics, as an agonised effort to piece together the broken fragments of the perfect whole with which the universe began, and to which it may yet return. This is a persistent idea which goes through European thought from its earliest beginnings; it underlies all the old utopias and has deeply influenced western metaphysical, moral and political ideas. In this sense, utopianism — the notion of the broken unity and its restoration — is a central strand in the whole of western thought. For this reason it might be not unprofitable to try to reveal some of the main assumptions which appear to underlie it.

Let me put them in the form of three propositions, a kind of three-legged stool on which the central tradition of western political thought seems to me to rest. Again, I shall, I fear, simplify these matters too much, but a mere sketch is not a book, and oversimplification is — I can only hope — not always falsification; and often serves to crystallise the issues. The first proposition is this: to all genuine questions there can only be one correct answer, all the other answers being incorrect. If there is no correct answer to it, then the question cannot be a genuine one. Any genuine question must, at least in principle, be answerable, and if this is so, only one answer can be correct. No one question, provided it is clearly stated, can have two answers which are different and yet both correct. The grounds of the correct answers must be true; all other possible answers must embody, or rest on, falsehood, which has many faces. That is the first cardinal assumption.

The second assumption is that a method exists for the discovery of these correct answers. Whether any man knows or can, in fact, know it, is another question; but it must, at least in principle, be knowable, provided that the right procedure for establishing it is used.

The third assumption, and perhaps the most important in the context of this essay, is that all the correct answers must, at the very least, be compatible with one another. That follows from a simple, logical truth: that one truth cannot be incompatible with another truth; all correct answers embody or rest on truths; therefore, all the correct answers, whether they are answers to questions about what there is in the world, or of what men should do, or what men should be — in other words, whether they answer questions concerned with facts or with values (and for thinkers who believe this third proposition, questions of value are in some sense questions of fact) — can never be in conflict with one another. At best, these truths will logically entail one another in a single, systematic, interconnected whole; at the very least, they will be consistent with one another: that is, they will form a harmonious whole, so that when you have discovered all the correct answers to all the central questions of human life and put them together, the result will form a kind of scheme of the sum of knowledge needed to lead a — or rather, the — perfect life. It may be that moral men cannot attain to such knowledge. There may be many reasons for this. Some Christian thinkers would maintain that original sin makes men incapable of such knowledge. Or perhaps we lived in the light of such truths once, in the Garden of Eden before the age of sin, and then this light failed us because we tasted of the fruit of the Tree of Knowledge, knowledge which, as our punishment, is bound to remain incomplete during life on earth. Or, perhaps, we shall know it all one day, whether before or after the death of the body. Or again, it may be that men shall never know it: their minds may be too weak, or the obstacles offered by intractable nature may be too great, to make such knowledge possible. Perhaps only the angels can know it, or perhaps only God knows it; or, if there is no God, then one must express this belief by saying that in principle such knowledge can be conceived, even if no one has ever achieved it or is ever likely to do so. For, in principle, the answer must be knowable; unless this is so, the questions would not be genuine; to say of a question that it is in principle unanswerable is not to understand what kind of question it is — for to understand the nature of a question is to know what kind of answer could be a correct answer to it, whether we know it to be correct or not; hence the range of possible answers to it must be conceivable; and one in this range must be the correct one. Otherwise, for rationalist thinkers of this type, rational thought would end in insoluble puzzles. If this is ruled out by the very nature of reason, it must follow that the pattern of the sum (perhaps of an infinity) of the correct solutions of all possible problems will constitute perfect knowledge.

Let me continue with this argument. It is asserted that unless we can conceive of something perfect, we cannot understand what is meant by imperfection. If, let us say, we complain about our condition here, on earth, by pointing to conflict, misery, cruelty, vice — 'the misfortunes, follies, crimes of mankind' — if, in short, we declare our state to be short of perfect, this is intelligible, only by comparison with a more perfect world; it is by measuring the gap between the two that we can measure the extent by which our world falls short. Short of what? The idea of what of which it falls short is the idea of a perfect state. This, I think, is what underlies utopian thought, and indeed, a great deal of western thought in general; in fact, it seems central to it, from Pythagoras and Plato onward.

At this point, it may be asked where, if all this is the case, the solutions are to be sought — who are the authorities — who can show the rest of us the right path for theory and practice? On this (as might have been expected), there has, in the west, been little agreement. Some have told us that the true answers are to be found in sacred texts, or given by inspired prophets, or by priests who are the authorised interpreters of these texts. Others deny the validity of revelation or prescription or tradition, and say that only accurate knowledge of nature yields the true answers —to be obtained by controlled observation, experiment, the application of logical and mathematical techniques — nature is not a temple, but a laboratory, and hypotheses must be testable by methods which any rational being can learn and apply and communicate and check; science, they declare, may not answer all the questions we wish to put, but what it cannot answer no other method will supply: it is the only reliable instrument we have or will ever have. Again, some tell us that only the experts know: men gifted with mystical vision, or metaphysical insight and speculative power; or scientific skills; or men endowed with natural wisdom — sages, men of lofty intellect. But others deny this and declare that the most important truths are accessible to all men: every man who looks within his own heart, his own soul, will understand himself and the nature which surrounds him, will know how to live and what to do, provided he has not been blinded by the baleful influence of others — men whose natures have been perverted by bad institutions. That is what Rousseau would have said: truth is to be sought not in the ideas or behaviour of corrupt dwellers in sophisticated cities, but is more likely to be found in the pure heart of a simple peasant, or of an innocent child — and Tolstoy in effect echoed this; and this view has adherents today despite the work of Freud and his disciples.

There is almost no view about the sources of true knowledge that has not been passionately held and dogmatically asserted in the course of conscious meditation about this problem in the Hellenic and Judeo-Christian tradition. About these differences, great conflicts have broken out and bloody wars were fought, and no wonder, since human salvation was held to depend upon the right solution to these questions — the most agonising and crucial issues in human life. The point I wish to make is that all sides assumed that these questions could be answered. The all but universal belief which this amounts to is that these answers are, as it were, so much hidden treasure; the problem is to find the path to it. Or, to use another metaphor, mankind has been presented with the scattered parts of a jigsaw puzzle: if you can put the pieces together, it will form a perfect whole which constitutes the goal of the quest of truth, virtue, happiness. That, I think, is one of the common assumptions of a great deal of western thought.

This conviction certainly underlay the utopias which proliferated so richly during the European Renaissance, when in the fifteenth century there was a great rediscovery of the Greek and Latin classics which were thought to embody truths forgotten during the long night of the Middle Ages or suppressed or distorted by the monkish superstitions of the Christian ages of faith. The New Learning was based on the belief that knowledge and only knowledge — the liberated human mind — could save us. This, in its turn, rested on the most fundamental of all rationalist propositions — that virtue was knowledge — uttered by Socrates, developed by Plato and his greatest disciple Aristotle, and the principal Socratic Schools of ancient Greece. For Plato, the paradigm of knowledge was geometrical in character, for Aristotle biological, for various thinkers during the Renaissance it may have been neo-Platonic and mystical, or intuitive or mathematical, or organic or mechanical, but none doubted that knowledge alone offered spiritual and moral and political salvation. It was, I think, assumed that if men have a common nature, this nature must have a purpose. Man's nature could be fully realised if only he knew what he truly wanted. If a man can discover what there is in the world, and what his relationship is to it, and what he is himself, however he has discovered it, by whichever method, by whichever recommended or traditional path to knowledge — he will know what will fulfil him, what, in other words, will make him happy, just, virtuous, wise. To know what will liberate one from error and illusion, and truly understand all that as a spiritual and physical being one knows oneself to seek after, and yet, despite this, to refrain from acting accordingly, is not to be in one's right mind — to be irrational and perhaps not altogether sane. To know how to compass your ends and then not to try to do so is, in the end, not truly to understand your ends. To understand is to act: there is a certain sense in which these earlier thinkers anticipated Karl Marx in their belief in the unity of theory and practice.

Knowledge, for the central tradition of western thought, means not just descriptive knowledge of what there is in the universe, but as part and parcel of it, not distinct from it, knowledge of values, or how to live, what to do, which forms of life are the best and worthiest, and why. According to this doctrine — that virtue is knowledge — when men commit crimes, they do so because they are in error: they have mistaken what will, in fact, profit them. If they truly knew what would profit them, they would not do these destructive things — acts which must end by destroying the actor by frustrating his true ends as a human being, by blocking the proper development of his faculties and powers. Crime, vice, imperfection, misery, all arise from ignorance and mental indolence or muddle. This ignorance may be fomented by wicked people who wish to throw dust in the eyes of others in order to dominate them, and who may, in the end, as often as not, be taken in by their own propaganda.

'Virtue is knowledge' means that if you know the good for man, you cannot, if you are a rational being, live in any way other than that whereby fulfilment is that toward which all desires, hopes, prayers, aspirations are directed: that is what is meant by calling them hopes. To distinguish reality from appearance, to distinguish that which will truly fulfil a man from that which merely appears to promise to do so, that is knowledge, and that alone will save him. It is this vast Platonic assumption, sometimes in its baptised, Christian form, that animates the great utopias of the Renaissance, More's wonderful fantasy, Bacon's New Atlantis, Campanella's City of the Sun, and the dozen or so of the Christian utopias of the seventeenth century — of which Fenelon's is only the best known. Absolute faith in rational solutions and the proliferation of utopian writing are both aspects of similar stages of cultural development, in classical Athens and the Italian Renaissance and the French eighteenth century and in the two hundred years that followed, no less so in the present than in the recent or distant past. Even the early travellers' tales, which are held to have helped to open men's eyes to the variety of human nature and, therefore, to discredit the belief in the uniformity of human needs and consequently in the single, final remedy to all their ills, often seem to have had the opposite effect. The discovery, or example, of men in a savage state in the forests of America was used as evidence of a basic human nature, of the so-called natural man, with natural needs as they would have existed everywhere if men had not been corrupted by civilisation, by artificial man-made institutions, due to error or to wickedness on the part of priests and kings and other power seekers, who practised monstrous deceptions on the gullible masses, the better to dominate them and exploit their labour. The concept of the noble savage was part of the myth of the unsullied purity of human nature, innocent, at peace with its surroundings and itself, ruined only by contact with the vices of the corrupt culture of western cities. The notion that somewhere, whether in a real or imagined society, man dwells in his natural state to which all men should return, is at the heart of primitivist theories, and is found in various guises in every anarchist and populist programme of the last hundred years, and has deeply affected Marxism and the vast variety of youth movements with radical or revolutionary goals.

I must repeat that the doctrine common to all these views and movements is the notion that there exist universal truths, true for all men, everywhere, at all times, and that these truths are expressed in universal rules, the Natural Law of the Stoics and the Mediaeval Church and the jurists of the Renaissance, defiance of which alone leads to vice, misery and chaos. It is true that doubts were thrown on the idea by, for example, certain Sophists and Sceptics in ancient Greece, as well as by Protagoras, and Hippias, and Carneades and Pyrrho and Sextus Empiricus, and in a later day by Montaigne and the Pyrrhonists of the seventeenth century, and above all by Montesquieu, who thought that different ways of life suited men in different environments and climates, with different traditions and customs. But this needs qualification. It is true that a Sophist quoted by Aristotle thought that 'fire burns both here and in Persia, while customs change under our very eyes'; and that Montesquieu thinks that one should wear warm clothes in cold climates and thin garments in hot ones, and that Persian customs would not suit the inhabitants of Paris. But what this kind of plea for variety comes to is that different means are most effective in different circumstances toward the realisation of similar ends. This is true even of the notorious sceptic David Hume. None of these doubters wish to deny that the central human goals are universal and uniform, even though they may not be necessarily established *a priori*; all men seek food and drink, shelter and security; all men want to procreate; all men seek social intercourse, justice, a degree of liberty, means of self-expression, and the like. The means toward these ends may differ from country to country, and age to age, but the ends, whether alterable in principle or not, remain unaltered; this is clearly brought out by a high degree of family resemblance in the social utopias of both ancient and modern times.

It is true that a rather graver blow against these assumptions was directed by Machiavelli, who suggested doubts about whether it was possible, even in principle, to combine a Christian view of life involving self-sacrifice and humility, with the possibility of building and maintaining a powerful and glorious republic, which required not humility or self-sacrifice on the part of its rulers and citizens, but the pagan virtues of courage, vitality, self-assertion and, in the case of rulers, a capacity for ruthless, unscrupulous and cruel action where this was called for by the needs of the state. Machiavelli did not develop the full implications of this conflict of ideals — he was not a professional philosopher — but what he said caused great uneasiness in some of his readers for four and a half centuries. Nevertheless, broadly speaking, the issue he raised tended to be largely ignored. His works were pronounced immoral and condemned by the Church, and not taken altogether seriously by the moralists and political thinkers who represent the central current of western thought in these fields.

To some degree, I think, Machiavelli did have some influence: on Hobbes, on Rousseau, on Fichte and Hegel, certainly on Frederick the Great of Prussia who took the trouble of publishing a formal refutation of his views; most clearly of all on Nietzsche and those influenced by him. But, by and large, the most uncomfortable assumption in Machiavelli, namely, that certain virtues, and even more, certain ideals, may not be compatible — a notion which offends against the proposition that I have emphasised, that all true answers to serious questions must be compatible — that assumption was for the most part quietly ignored. No one seemed anxious to grapple with the possibility that the Christian and the pagan answers to moral or political questions might both be correct given the premises from which they start: that these premises were not demonstrably false, only incompatible: and that no single over-arching standard or criterion was available to decide between, or reconcile, these wholly opposed moralities. This was found somewhat troubling by those who believed themselves to be Christians but wished to give unto Caesar what was Caesar's. A sharp division between public and private life, or politics and morality, never works well. Too many territories have been claimed by both. This has been and can be an agonising problem, and, as often happened in such cases, men were none too anxious to face it.

There was also another angle from which these assumptions were questioned. The assumptions, I must repeat at the cost of boring you, are those of Natural Law: that human nature is a static, unaltering essence, that its ends are eternal, unaltering and universal for all men, everywhere, at all times, and can be known, and perhaps fulfilled, by those who possess the appropriate kind of knowledge.

When the new nation states arose in the course, and partly as a result, of the Reformation in the sixteenth century in the west and north of Europe, some among the lawyers engaged in formulating and defending the claims and laws of these kingdoms, for the most part reformers, whether out of opposition to the authority of the Church of Rome (or, in some cases, to the centralising policies of the King of

France) began to argue that Roman law, with its claim to universal authority, was nothing to them; they were not Romans; they were Franks, Celts, Norsemen; they had their own Frankish, Batavian, Scandinavian traditions; they lived in Languedoc: they had their Languedoc customs from time immemorial; what was Rome to them? In France they were descendants of Frankish conquerors, their ancestors had subdued the Gallo-Romans, they had inherited, they wished to recognise only their own Frankish or Burgundian or Helvetic laws; what Roman law had to say was neither here or there; it did not apply to them. Let the Italians obey Rome. Why should Franks, Teutons, descendants of Viking pirates, accept the dominion of a single, universal, foreign legal code? Different nations, different roots, different laws, different peoples, different communities, different ideals. Each had its own way of living — what right had one to dictate to the others? Least of all the Pope, whose claims to spiritual authority the reformers denied. This broke the spell of one world, one universal law, and consequently one universal goal of all men, everywhere, at all times. The perfect society which Frankish warriors, or even their descendants, conceived as their ideal might be very different from the utopian vision of an Italian, ancient or modern, and wholly unlike that of an Indian or a Swede or a Turk. Henceforth, the spectre of relativism makes its dreaded appearance, and with it, the beginning of the dissolution of faith in the very concept of universally valid goals, at least in the social and political sphere. This was accompanied, in due course, by a sense that there might be not only a historical or political but some logical flaw in the very idea of a universe equally acceptable to communities of different origin, with different traditions, character, outlook, concepts, categories, views of life.

But again, the implications of this were not fully spelled out, largely, perhaps, because of the enormous triumph at this very time of the natural sciences. As a result of the revolutionary discoveries of Galileo and Newton and the work of other mathematicians and physicists and biologists of genius, the external world was seen as a single cosmos, such that, to take the best known example, by the application of relatively few laws, the movement and position of every particle of matter could be precisely determined. For the first time it became possible to organise a chaotic mass of observational data into a single, coherent, perfectly orderly system. Why should not the same methods be used to apply to human matters, to morals, to politics, to the organisation of society, with equal success? Why should it be assumed that men belong to some order outside the system of nature? What holds good for material objects, for animals and plants and minerals, in zoology, botany, chemistry, physics, astronomy – all these new sciences well on the way of being unified, which proceed from hypotheses about observed facts and events to testable scientific conclusions, and together form a coherent and scientific system – why should not this also apply to human problems? Why cannot one create a science or sciences of man and here also provide solutions as clear and certain as those obtained in the sciences of the external world?

This was a novel, revolutionary and highly plausible proposal which the thinkers of the Enlightenment, particularly in France, accepted with natural enthusiasm. It was surely reasonable to suppose that man has an examinable nature, capable of being observed, analysed, tested like other organisms and forms of living matter. The programme seemed clear: one must scientifically find out what man consists of, and what he needs for his growth and for his satisfaction. When one has discovered what he is and what he requires, one will then ask where this last can be found; and then, by means of the appropriate inventions and discoveries, supply men's wants, and in this way achieve, if not total perfection, at any rate a far happier and more rational state of affairs than at present prevails. Why does it not exist? Because stupidity, prejudice, superstition, ignorance, the passions which darken reason, greed and fear and lust for domination and the barbarisms, cruelty, intolerance, fanaticism which go with them, have led to the deplorable condition in which men have been forced to live too long. Failure, unavoidable or deliberate, to observe what there is in the world, has robbed man of the knowledge needed to improve his life. Scientific knowledge alone can save us. This is the fundamental doctrine of the French Enlightenment, a great liberating movement which in its day eliminated a great deal of cruelty, superstition, injustice and obscurantism.

In due course this great wave of rationalism led to an inevitable reaction. It seems to me a historical fact that whenever rationalism goes far enough there often tends to occur some kind of emotional resistance, a 'backlash', if I may put it so, which springs from that which is irational in man.

This took place in Greece in the fourth and third centuries BC, when the great Socratic schools produced their magnificent rationalistic systems: seldom, we are told by historians of Greek cults, did mystery religions, occultism, irrationalism, mysticisms of all kinds flourish so richly. So, too, the powerful and rigid edifice of Roman law, one of the great achievements of human civilisation, side by side with the great legal-religious structure of ancient Judaism, were followed by a passionate, emotional resistance, culminating in the rise and triumph of Christianity. In the later Middle Ages there was, similarly, reaction to the great logical constructions of the Schoolmen. Something not dissimilar occurred during the Reformation; and, finally, following the triumphs of the scientific spirit in the west, a powerful countermovement some two centuries ago.

This reaction, which I should like to bring to your attention, came mainly from Germany. Something needs to be said about the social and spiritual situation in the Germany of that time. By the seventeenth century, even before the devastation of the Thirty Years War, German-speaking countries found themselves, for reasons which I have neither the time nor — a more compelling reason — the competence to discuss, culturally inferior to their neighbours across the Rhine. During the entire seventeenth century, the French seemed to be dominant in every sphere of life, both spiritual and material. Their military strength, their social and economic organisation, their thinkers, scientists and philosophers, painters and composers, their poets, dramatists, architects — their excellence in the general arts of life — these placed them at the head of all Europe. Well might they be excused if then and later they identified civilisation as such with their own culture.

If, during the seventeenth century, French influence reached an unexampled height, there was a notable flowering of culture in other western countries also: this is plainly true of England in the late Elizabethan and Stuart period; it coincided with the golden age of Spain, and the great artistic and scientific renaissance in the Low Countries. Italy, if not perhaps at the height which it reached in the Quattrocento, produced artists, and especially scientists of rare achievement. Even Sweden in the far north was beginning to stir.

The German-speaking peoples could not boast of anything similar; if you ask what were the most distinguished contributions made to European civilisation in the seventeenth century by the German-speaking lands, there is little enough to tell: apart from architecture and the isolated genius of Kepler, original talent seemed to flow only in theology; the poets, scholars, thinkers, seldom rose above mediocrity: Leibniz seems to have few native predecessors. This can, I believe, be explained, at least in part, by the economic decline and political divisions in Germany; but I am concerned only to stress the facts themselves. Even though the general level of German education remained quite high, life and art and thought remained profoundly provincial. The attitude to the German lands of the advanced nations of the west, particularly of the French, seemed to be a kind of patronising indifference. In due course the humiliated Germans began feebly to imitate their French models, and this, as often happens, was followed by a cultural reaction. The wounded national consciousness asserted itself, sometimes in a somewhat aggressive fashion.

This is a common enough response on the part of backward nations who are looked on with too much arrogant contempt, with too great an air of conscious superiority by the more advanced societies. By the beginning of the eighteenth century some among the spiritual leaders in the devout, inward-looking German principalities began to counter-attack. This took the form of pouring contempt on the worldly success of the French: these Frenchmen and their imitators elsewhere could boast of only so much empty show. The inner life, the life of the spirit, concerned with the relation of man to man, to himself, to God – that alone was of supreme importance; the empty, materialistic French wise-acres had no sense of true values: of what alone men lived by. Let them have their arts, their sciences, their *salons*, their wealth and their vaunted glory. All this was, in the end, dross – the perishable goods of the corruptible flesh. The *philosophes* were blind leaders of the blind, remote from all conception of what alone truly mattered, the dark, agonising, infinitely rewarding descent into the depths of man's own sinful but immortal soul, made in the semblance of divine nature itself. This was the realm of the devout, inward vision of the German soul.

Gradually this German self-image grew in intensity, fed by what might be called a kind of nationalist resentment. The philosopher, poet, critic, pastor Johann Gottfried Herder* was perhaps the first wholly articulate prophet of this attitude, and elevated this cultural self-consciousness into a general principle. Beginning as a literary historian and essayist, he maintained that values were not universal; every human society, every people, indeed, every age and civilisation, possesses its own unique ideal, standards, way of living and thought and action. There are no immutable, universal, eternal rules or criteria of judgement, in terms of which different cultures and nations can be graded on some single order of excellence, which would place the French – if Voltaire was right – at the top of the ladder of human achievement and the Germans far below them in the twilight regions of religious obscurantism and within the narrow limits of provincialism and dim-witted rural existence. Every society, every age, has its own

---

*For the interpretation of whose views Professor Barnard has done so much, and for which he deserves the gratitude of all English-speaking students, and of many others.

cultural horizons. Every nation has its own traditions, its own character, its own face. Every nation has its own centre of moral gravity, which differs from that of every other: there and only there, its happiness lies — in the development of its own national needs, its own unique character.

There is no compelling reason for seeking to imitate foreign models, or returning to some remote past. Every age, every society, differs in its goals and habits and values from every other. The conception of human history as a single universal process of struggle toward the light, the later stages and embodiments of which are necessarily superior to the earlier, where the primitive is necessarily inferior to the sophisticated, is an enormous fallacy. Homer is not a primitive Ariosto; Shakespeare is not a rudimentary Racine (these are not Herder's examples). To judge one culture by the standards of another argues a failure of imagination and understanding. Every culture has its own attributes, which must be grasped in and for themselves. In order to understand a culture, one must employ the same faculties of sympathetic insight with which we understand one another, without which there is neither love nor friendship, nor true human relationships. One man's attitude toward another is, or should be, based on perceiving what he is in himself, uniquely, not what he has in common with all other men; only the natural sciences abstract what is common, generalise: human relations are founded on recognition of individuality, which can, perhaps, never be exhaustively described, still less analysed; so it with understanding communities, cultures, epochs, and what they are and strive for and feel and suffer and create, how they express themselves and see themselves and think and act.

Men congregate in groups because they are conscious of what unites them — bonds of common descent, language, soil, collective experience; these bonds are unique, impalpable and ultimate. Cultural frontiers are natural to men, spring from the interplay of their inner essence and environment and historical experience. Greek culture is uniquely and inexhaustibly Greek; India, Persia, France, are what they are, not something else. Our culture is our own; cultures are incommensurable: each is as it is, each of infinite value, as souls are in the sight of God. To eliminate one in favour of another, to subjugate a society and destroy a civilisation, as the great conquerors have done, is a monstrous crime against the right to be oneself, to live in the light of one's own ideal values. If you exile a German and plant him in America, he will be unhappy; he will suffer because people can be happy, can function freely only among those who understand them. To be lonely is to be among men who do not know what you mean. Exile, solitude, is to find yourself among people whose words, gestures, hand-writing are alien to your own, whose behaviour, reactions, feelings, instinctive responses, and thoughts and pleasures and pains are too remote from yours, whose education and outlook, the tone and quality of whose lives and being, are not yours. There are many things which men do have in common, but that is not what matters most. What individualises them, makes them what they are, makes communica-tion possible, is what they do not have in common with all the others. Differences, peculiarities, nuances, individual character is all in all.

This is a novel doctrine. Herder identified cultural differences and cultural essence and the very idea of historical development, very differently from Voltaire. What, for him, makes Germans German is the fact that the way in which they eat or drink, dispense justice, write poetry, worship, dispose of property, get up and sit down, obtain their food, wear their clothes, sing, fight wars, order political life, all have a certain common character, a qualitative property, a pattern which is solely German, in which they differ from the corresponding activities of the Chinese or the Portuguese. No one of these peoples or cultures are, for Herder, superior to any of the others, they are merely different; since they are different, they seek different ends; therein is both their specific character and their value. Values, qualities of character, are not commensurable: an order of merit which presupposes a single measuring rod is, for Herder, evidence of blindness to what makes human beings human. A German cannot be made happy by efforts to turn him into a second-rate Frenchman. Icelanders will not be made happy by life in Denmark, or Europeans by emigrating to America. Men can develop their full powers only by continuing to live where they and their ancestors were born, to speak their language, live their lives within the framework of the customs of their society and culture. Men are not self-created: they are born into a stream of tradition, above all of language, which shapes their thoughts and feelings, which they cannot shed or change, which forms their inner life. The qualities which men have in common are not sufficient to ensure the fulfilment of a man's or a people's nature, which depends at least as much on the character-istics due to the place, the time and the culture to which men uniquely belong; to ignore or obliterate these characteristics is to destroy men's souls and bodies equally. 'I am not here to think. I am here to be, to live, to act.' For Herder, every action, every form of life, has a pattern which differs from that of every other. The natural unit for him is what he calls *das Volk*, the people, the chief constituents of which are soil and language, not race or colour or religion. That is Herder's life-long sermon — after all, he was a Protestant pastor — to the German-speaking peoples.

But if this is so, if the doctrine of the French Enlightenment — and indeed, the central western assumption, of which I have spoken, that all true values are immutable and timeless and universal — needs revising so drastically, then there is something radically wrong with the idea of a perfect society. The basic reason for this is not to be found among those which were usually advanced against utopian ideas — that such a society cannot be attained because men are not wise or skilful or virtuous enough, or cannot require the requisite degree of knowledge, or resolution, or, tainted as they are with original sin, cannot attain perfection in this life, but is altogether different. The idea of a single, perfect society of all mankind must be internally self-contradictory, because the Valhalla of the Germans is necessarily different from the ideal of future life of the French, because the paradise of the Moslems is is not that of Jews or Christians, because a society in which a French-man would attain to harmonious fulfilment is a society which to a German might prove suffocating. But if we are to have as many types of perfection as there are types of culture, each with its ideal constell-ation of virtues, then the very notion of the possibility of a single perfect society is logically incoherent. This, I think, is the beginning of the modern attack on the notion of utopia, utopia as such.

The Romantic movement in Germany, which owed a great deal to the influence of the philosopher Fichte, contributed its own powerful impetus to this new and genuinely revolutionary *Weltanschauung*. For the young Friedrich Schlegel, or Tieck, or Novalis, values, ethical, political, aesthetic, are not objectively given, not fixed stars in some Platonic firmament, eternal, immutable, which men can discover only by employing the proper method — metaphysical insight, scientific investigation, philosophical argument or divine revelation. Values are generated by the creative human self. Man is, above all, a creature endowed not only with reason but with will. Will is the creative function of man. The new model of man's nature is conceived by analogy with the new conception of artistic creation, no longer bound by the objective rules drawn from idealised universal nature (*la bella natura*) or by the eternal truths of classicism, or natural law, or a divine law-giver. If one compares classical doctrines — even those of such late neo-classical, somewhat Platonist, theorists as Joshua Reynolds or Jean Philippe Rameau — with those of their romantic opponents, this emerges clearly. Reynolds, in his famous lectures on the Great Style, said in effect that if you are painting a king, you must be guided by the conception of royalty. David, King of Israel, may in life have been of mean stature and had physical defects. But you may not so paint him, because he is a king. Therefore, you must paint him as a royal personage: and royalty is an eternal, immutable attribute, one and equally accessible to the vision of all men, at all times, everywhere; it does not alter with the passage of time or différence of outlook, somewhat like a platonic 'idea', beyond the reach of the empirical eye, and the business of the painter or sculptor is to penetrate the veil of appearance, to conceive of the essence of pure royalty, and convey it on canvas, or in marble or wood or whatever medium the artist chooses to use. Similarly, Rameau was convinced that the business of a composer was to evince in sound harmony — the eternal mathematical proportions — which are embodied in the nature of things, in the great cosmos, not given to the mortal ear, yet that which gives the pattern of musical sounds the order and beauty which the inspired artist creates — or rather, reproduces, 'imitates' — as best he can.

Not so those who are influenced by the new romantic doctrine. The painter creates; he does not copy. He does not imitate; he does not follow rules; he makes them. Values are not discovered, they are created; not found, but made by an act of imaginative, creative will, as works of art, as policies, plans, patterns of life are created. By whose imagination, whose will? Fichte speaks of the self, the ego; as a rule he identifies it with a transcendent, infinite, world spirit of which the human individual is a mere spatio-temporal, mortal expression, a finite centre which derives its reality from the spirit, to perfect union with which it seeks to attain. Others identified this self with some other superpersonal spirit or force — the nation — the true self in which the individual is only an element; or, again, the people (Rousseau comes near to doing this) or the state (as Hegel does), or it is identified with a culture, or the *Zeitgeist* (a conception greatly mocked by Goethe in his *Faust*) or a class which embodies the progressive march of history (as in Marx), or some other, equally impalpable movement or force or group. This somewhat mysterious source is held to generate and transform values which I am bound to follow because, to the degree to which I am, at my best or truest, an agent of God, or of history, or progress, or the nation, I recognise them as my own. This constitutes a sharp break with the whole of previous tradition, for which the true and the beautiful, the noble and the ignoble, the right and the wrong, duty, sin, ultimate good, were unalterable, ideal values and their opposites, created eternal and identical for all men: in the old formula, *quod semper, quod ubique, quod ob omnibus:* the only problem was how to know them and knowing, realise or avoid them, do good and eschew evil.

But if these values are not uncreated, but generated by my culture or by my nation or by my class, they will differ from the values generated by your culture, your nation, your class; they are not universal, and may clash. If the values generated by Germans are different from values generated by Portuguese, if the values generated by the ancient Greeks are different from those of modern Frenchmen, then a relativity deeper than any enunciated by the Sophists or Montesquieu or Hume will destroy the single moral and intellectual universe. Aristotle, Herder declared, is 'theirs' — Leibniz is 'ours'. Leibniz speaks to us Germans, not Socrates or Aristotle. Aristotle was a great thinker, but we cannot return to him: his world is not ours. So, three-quarters of a century later, it was laid down that if my true values are the expression of my class — the bourgeoisie — and not of their class — the proletariat — then the notion that all values, all true answers to questions, are compatible with each other, cannot be true, since my values will inevitably clash with yours, because the values of my class are not the values of yours. As the values of the ancient Romans are not those of modern Italians, so the moral world of medieval Christianity is not that of liberal democrats, and, above all, the world of the workers is not that of their employers. The concept of a common good, valid for all mankind, rests on a cardinal mistake.

The notion that there exists a celestial, crystalline sphere, unaffected by the world of change and appearance, in which mathematical truths and moral or aesthetic values form a perfect harmony, guaranteed by indestructible logical links, is now abandoned, or at best is ignored. That is at the heart of the Romantic movement, the extreme expression of which is the self-assertion of the individual creative personality as the maker of its own universe; we are in the world of rebels against convention, of the free artists, the Satanic outlaws, the Byronic outcasts, the 'pale and fevered generation' celebrated by German and French romantic writers of the early nineteenth century, the stormy Promethean heroes who reject the laws of their society, determined to achieve self-realisation and free self-expression against whatever odds.

This may have been an exaggerated, and at times hysterical, type of romantic self-preoccupation, but the essence of it, the roots from which it grew, did not vanish with the waning of the first wave of the

Romantic movement, and became the cause of permanent unease, indeed, anxiety, in the European consciousness, as it has remained to this day. It is clear that the notion of a harmonious solution of the problems of mankind, even in principle, and, therefore, of the very concept of utopia, is incompatible with the interpretation of the human world as a battle of perpetually new and ceaselessly conflicting wills, individual or collective. Attempts were made to stem this dangerous tide. Hegel, and after him Marx, sought to return to a rational historical scheme. For both there is a march of history – a single ascent of mankind from barbarism to rational organisation. They concede that history is the story of struggles and collisions, but these will ultimately be resolved. They are due to the particular dialectic of self-development of the World Spirit, or of technological progress which creates division of labour and class war; but these 'contradictions' are the factors which themselves are indispensable to the forward movement that will culminate in a harmonious whole, the ultimate difference in unity, whether conceived as an infinite progress toward a transcendent goal, as in Hegel, or an attainable rational society, as in Marx. For these thinkers history is a drama in which there are violent contenders. Terrible tribulations occur, collisions, battles, destruction, appalling suffering; but the story has, must have, a happy ending. For utopian thinkers in this tradition, the happy ending is a timeless serenity, the radiance of a static, conflict-free society after the state has withered away and all constituted authority has vanished – a peaceful anarchy in which men are rational, co-operative, virtuous, happy and free. This is an attempt to have the best of both worlds: to allow for inevitable conflict, but to believe that it is at once unavoidable and a temporary stage along the path to total self-fulfilment of mankind.

Nevertheless, doubts persist, and have done so since the challenge thrown out by the irrationalists. That is the disturbing heritage of the Romantic movement; it has entered the modern consciousness despite all efforts to eliminate or circumnavigate it, or explain it away as a mere symptom of the pessimism of the bourgeoisie made uneasy by consciousness of, but unable to face, its inescapably approaching doom.

Since then the 'perennial philosophy', with its unalterable objective truths founded on the perception of an eternal order behind the chaos of appearances, has been thrown on the defensive in the face of the attacks of relativists, pluralists, irrationalists, pragmatists, subjectivists, and certain types of empiricism; and with its decline, the conception of the perfect society, which derives from this great unitary vision, loses its persuasive power. From this time onward, believers in the possibility of social perfection tend to be accused by their opponents of trying to foist an artificial order on a reluctant humanity, of trying to fit human beings, like bricks, into a preconceived structure, force them into Procrustean beds, and vivisect living men in the pursuit of some fanatically held schema. Hence the protest — and anti-utopias of Aldous Huxley, or Orwell, or Zamyatin (in Russia in the early twenties), who paint a horrifying picture of a frictionless society in which differences between human beings are, so far as possible, eliminated, or at least reduced, and the multi-coloured pattern of the variety of human temperaments, inclinations, ideals — in short, the flow of life — is brutally reduced to uniformity, pressed into a social and political straitjacket, which hurts and maims and ends by crushing men in the name of a monistic theory, a dream of a perfect, static order. This is the heart of the protest against the uniformitarian despotism which Tocqueville and J.S. Mill felt to be advancing upon mankind.

Our times have seen the conflict of two irreconcilable views: one is the view of those who believe that there exist eternal values, binding on all men, and that the reason why men have not, as yet, all recognised or realised them, is a lack of capacity, moral, intellectual or material, needed to compass this end. It may be that this knowledge has been withheld from us by the laws of history itself: on one interpretation of these laws it is the class war that has so distorted our relations to each other as to blind men to the truth, and so prevented a rational organisation of human life. But enough progress has occurred to enable some persons to see the truth; in the fullness of time the universal solution will be clear to men at large: then pre-history will end and true human history will begin. Thus contend the Marxists, and perhaps other socialist and optimistic prophets. This is not accepted by those who declare that men's temperaments, gifts, outlooks, wishes permanently differ one from another, that uniformity kills; that men can live full lives only in societies with an open texture, in which variety is not merely tolerated but is approved and encouraged; that the richest development of human potentialities can occur only in societies in which there is a wide spectrum of opinions — the freedom for what J.S. Mill called 'experiments in living' — in which there is liberty of thought and of expression, views and opinions clash with each other, societies in which friction and even conflict is permitted, albeit with rules to control them and prevent destruction and violence; that subjection to a single ideology, no matter how reasonable and imaginative, robs men of freedom and vitality. It may be this that Goethe meant when, after reading Holbach's *Système de la Nature* (one of the most famous works of eighteenth-century French materialism, which looked to a kind of rationalist utopia), he declared that he could not understand how anyone could accept such a grey, corpse-like, Cimmerian affair, devoid of colour, life, art, humanity. For those who embrace this romantically tinged individualism, what matters is not the common base but the differences, not the one, but the many; for them the craving for unity — the regeneration of mankind by recovery of a lost innocence and harmony, the return from a fragmented existence to the all-embracing whole, is an infantile and dangerous delusion: to crush all diversity and even conflict in the interest of uniformity is, for them, to crush life itself.

These doctrines are not compatible with one another. They are ancient antagonists: in their modern guise, both dominate mankind today, and both are resisted: industrial organisation versus human rights, bureaucratic rules versus 'doing one's own thing'; good government versus self-government; security versus freedom. Sometimes a demand turns into its opposite: claims to participatory democracy turn into oppression of minorities, measures to establish social equality crush self-determination and stifle individual genius. Side by side with these collisions of values, there persists an age-old dream: there is, there must be — and it can be found — the final solution to all human ills; it can be achieved; by revolution or peaceful means it will surely come; and then all, or the vast majority, of men will be virtuous and happy, wise and good and free; if such a position can be attained, and once attained will last forever, what sane man could wish to return to the miseries of men's wanderings in the desert? If this is possible, then surely no price is too heavy to pay for it; no amount of oppression, cruelty, repression, coercion will be too high, if this, and this alone, is the price for ultimate salvation of all men? This conviction gives a wide licence to the infliction of suffering on other men, provided it is done for pure, distinterested motives. But if one believes this doctrine to be an illusion, if only because some ultimate values may be incompatible with one another, and the very notion of an ideal world in which they are reconciled to be a conceptual (and not merely practical) impossibility, then, perhaps, the best that one can do is to try to promote some kind of equilibrium, necessarily unstable, between the different aspirations of differing groups of human beings — at the very least to prevent them from attempting to exterminate each other, and, so far as possible, to prevent them for hurting each other, and to promote the maximum practicable degree of sympathy and understanding, never likely to be complete, between them. But this is not, *prima facie*, a wildly exciting programme: a liberal sermon which recommends machinery designed to prevent people from doing each other too much harm, giving each human group sufficient room to realise its own idiosyncratic, unique, particular ends without too much interference with the ends of others, is not a passionate battle cry to inspire men to sacrifice and martyrdom and heroic feats. Yet if it were adopted, it might yet prevent mutual destruction, and, in the end, preserve the world. Immanuel Kant, a man very remote from irrationalism, once observed that 'out of the crooked timber of humanity no straight thing was ever made'. And for that reason, no perfect solution is, not merely in practice, but in principle, possible in human affairs, and any determined attempt to produce it is likely to lead to suffering, disillusionment and failure.

8 MORAL PLURALISM AND THE LIBERAL MIND*

Richard Vernon

This paper hinges on a distinction between two principles, one political and the other moral. The political principle is that diversity in public opinion and private pursuits is acceptable, and that it is not the business of the state to impose uniformity. The moral principle is that diversity in moral judgement is inescapable, and that there are conflicts which moral philosophy cannot hope to remove. The question that I want to examine is this: to what extent, if at all, does the former principle depend upon the latter? Or, applying labels to the two principles which I hope are not misleading, to what extent, if at all, does liberalism depend upon moral pluralism? The answer that I shall argue for is that liberal political principles do not depend on pluralist moral principles at all, and that many recent interpretations of liberalism are wholly mistaken in the views which they advance regarding its moral foundations. This paper is, then, a critical one, but in the course of its argument some suggestions about what *could* supply liberalism with an appropriate foundation should emerge.

Moral Pluralism and Politics

It must be stressed at once that 'moral pluralism' as that term is used here is not a position but a category, of limited usefulness, into which a number of different and even exclusive positions may be placed. Let us simply survey some examples. According to Richard Wollheim, '[I]t has been characteristic of the civilised parts of Europe — their pride, some would say — to develop a theory of politics [which holds that] the identity, and continuity of a society resides not in the common possession of a single morality but in the mutual toleration of different moralities. This theory is called Liberalism.'[1] According to Basil Mitchell, liberalism (today at any rate) finds its 'basis' in 'the intrinsic value of ethical diversity,'[2] and he quotes P.F. Strawson in confirmation: 'What will be the attitude of one who experiences sympathy with a variety of conflicting ideals of life? It seems that he will be most at home in a liberal society, in a society in which there are variant moral environments, but

143

in which no ideal endeavours to engross and determine the character of the common morality.'[3] According to John N. Gray, who follows in part W.B. Gallie's well-known thesis of 'essential contestability', 'recognition of the chronic character of normative and epistemic dissensus . . . can provide the departure point for an endorsement of the basic values of a liberal civilization.'[4] According to Alasdair MacIntyre, moral dissensus is the root of 'the liberal attitude' that 'values are personal, values are private, values can be chosen', an attitude endemic in the morally and socially fragmented societies of today.[5] According to Joseph Raz, a coherent defence of liberalism and its central value rests upon a theory which is 'committed to moral pluralism, that is, to the view that there are many worthwhile and valuable relationships, commitments and plans of life which are mutually incompatible, so that autonomous people can and should choose between them.'[6] And according to Sir Isaiah Berlin, we can find no satisfactory ground for J.S. Mill's 'profession of faith', which is also 'the ultimate basis of liberalism', other than the belief, latent in Mill, 'that there are no final truths not corrigible by experience, at any rate in what is now called the ideological sphere — that of value judgements and of general outlook and attitude to life'.[7] For only belief in corrigibility, it would seem, can lead one to accept the rivalry of values. Here Ralf Dahrendorf, among many others, is in agreement: 'The individualism of the liberal has its meaning only in the context of the epistemological assumption that nobody knows all the answers, or rather, that there can be no certainty about the truth or falsehood of given answers.'[8]

The divergences among these views are of some interest. 'Toleration' is presumably a matter of thinking something to be bad while putting up with it for some overriding reason; but to believe in 'the intrinsic value of ethical diversity' is to set the question of tolerance aside, for what one values one can hardly be said to tolerate.[9] But if there is disagreement about the liberal's attitude to diversity there is also disagreement about the scope of diversity within a liberal society: Wollheim speaks of 'different moralities', while for Strawson there is a 'common morality' which exists alongside diverse and conflicting 'ethics' or 'ideals'. For some 'contestability' theorists — as for theorists of 'total ideology' or 'way of life' — normative and epistemic positions are conjoined and mutually reinforcing, so that there is no neutral epistemic ground on which normative disagreement can be resolved; a liberal society is one which experiences such radical conflict. For MacIntyre, on the contrary, the liberal experience is characterised by the logical heterogeneity of 'is' and 'ought', and by the conviction that epistemic agreement is available but does not translate into normative commitment. the liberal's view of values is an essentially subjectivist one.

That, however, is in turn strenuously denied by Raz, who makes the notion of autonomous choice central to liberal doctrine, and contends that the notion of choice is intelligible only in the context of positions which have value prior to our choosing, and whose rival claims we must weigh. Such a view may sometimes have been advanced by Berlin: it is to be distinguished, however, from the view attributed to Mill and liberalism in the passage quoted, and which Dahrendorf would apparently support. If corrigibility is inescapable in moral questions, presumably we should be open to correction even if there were moral consensus; the diversity of moral views would seem to be only a symptom of the impossibility of final proof, or else, perhaps, a reason for remembering that our moral beliefs are corrigible.

A rather disconcerting number of theses, then, are offered as necessary conditions for liberalism, and so varied are they that to consider them together may seem a hopeless task. But there is, as claimed above, a limited usefulness in doing so, in that despite significant differences they all display two features: first, they assume that political principles rest immediately on moral arguments, and reflect pre-existing moral commitments; second, they assume that the complement and source of politically legitimate diversity must be the undecidability of moral questions. If a political theory insists on the acceptance of differences that must be because moral philosophy — for one reason or another — finds diversity to be uneliminable. But such an approach, I believe, misrepresents the relationship between liberalism and diversity; it misrepresents the relationship between diversity and choice; and it misrepresents the relationship between political theory and moral philosophy. Those are the objections to be developed below.

The Limitations of Diversity

Liberals have objected to the enforced regimentation of life, and to the invasion of areas of private choice by public authority; they have objected, too, to the monopolisation of power as something which is peculiarly likely to lead to such invasions of rights. In several respects, then, we may identify liberalism as a critique of political monism: it does not suppose that all interests are somehow subsumed within a single unchallengeable common interest, and it seeks to expose power to the need to win consent. It recognises, then, the multiplicity of experiences, interests and wills in political society, and is in that (fairly minimal) sense a doctrine of plurality. But that, of course, does not permit any hasty (and surely mistaken) equation of the liberal and pluralist traditions;[10] nor does it tell us much about what kind of plurality is essential to the liberal conception of politics. For to stress plurality may be to say something about the properties (or attributes) of things, to say something about their relations; or to say something about their status.

To these modes or types of plurality different concepts attach. *Diversity* is a matter of the properties or attributes of things, and occurs when not everything that is attributed to one item can be attributed to each of the others. It is to do with the uneven distribution of features. *Separateness*, on the other hand, is a matter of the relations obtaining between things; things are separate to the extent that they exercise no significant or regular impact upon one another. Things can, of course, be separate whether they are diverse or similar; the extent to which things share attributes does not vary with the extent to which they exert causal influence on each other (unless, as is sometimes claimed, these vary inversely).[11] *Distinctness*, on the other hand, is a matter of the status of things as things (as opposed to parts or segments of a single thing). It is what Rawls, for example, has in mind in speaking of 'the plurality of persons'.[12] And it is clear that items can be distinct without being either separate or diverse. They can be distinct even though they exercise regular and significant mutual influence (and *must* be distinct if this influence is to be described as causal); they can be distinct without being diverse in their attributes or properties — people who resemble each other are no less distinct by virtue of their resemblance, and people who differ in their attributes are not in some odd way more distinct by virtue of their diversity.

All three modes of plurality may, of course, be detected in the classical writings of liberalism. That individuals are or tend to become distinct and separate without being diverse is one way of describing the central thesis of Tocqueville's *Democracy in America*. That they are distinct and should become diverse without becoming separate is, in effect, among Mill's contentions in *On Liberty*. But of the three modes, surely it is clear that separateness can be dispensed with, as a putative liberal value, whatever communitarian-minded critics may say or imply. There is no thesis of essential separation in Locke or Mill (let alone Green), but a thesis of interpersonal influence and mutual aid; that liberals do not think of community as having political expression does not mean that they see it as having no expression at all. In another trend of liberal thinking, from *Democracy in America* (or perhaps the *Persian*

Letters) to critiques of totalitarianism, the creation of communities is systematically valued as an obstacle to the engrossment of life by power; 'atomism' in the sense of separateness or dissociation is precisely what is *feared*, and what is meant by 'pluralism' in its *political* sense is at least as often intended as an alternative to fragmentation as to unity. To the extent that they have been pluralists, then, liberals have often conceived of groups not as dissociative but as associative media, and the object of fostering separateness has been distant indeed from their concerns.

Now it is sometimes proposed that distinctness, too, be eliminated as a candidate, a move that would certainly simplify the task of finding the root conception of plurality, only diversity thus remaining. But this would be mistaken. It is understandable, and perhaps even plausible, in the light of the excesses of theorists of 'methodological individualism', who certainly went too far in their effort to deduce crucial political alternatives from the recognition or non-recognition of individual identity. In reaction, it is claimed that nothing follows from this recognition at all: 'It is hard to conceive of a perspective from which the *fact* of individual identity could be denied.' And: 'liberal values . . . plainly require a less restricted account of what it is to be a human person.'[13] But while the second statement is true, in denying that the fact of distinctness can do all the work, the first errs in denying that it does any work at all. It is not too hard to conceive of perspectives in which significance is refused to distinct individual identity: note, to mention but two disparate examples, the patriarchalist view of women and children, and the Leninist doctrine of objective interest. These are political doctrines of subsumption, as they may be termed, in which some experiences or reasons have no weight because those who undergo or entertain them do not represent themselves, but are represented. Characteristically, liberals have viewed political society as a coming-together or (in Tocqueville's term) a *concours*[14] of agents whose experiences or interests or reasons are not subsumable under someone else's, but are their own. It is perhaps easy, but it is mistaken, to confuse this with an argument from diversity. In fact, that something is one's own does not in any way depend upon its being different. Your experience is *your* experience even if it is much the same as mine; my reasons are *my* reasons even if they are identical to yours, or even if I got them from you (and for certain special purposes have to recognise your copyright). To stress distinctness is simply to stress that political actors have their reasons, not someone else's, for acting, and that each self is a point from which the world is experienced.

The weight attaching to this is well brought out by Mill: 'If a person possesses any tolerable amount of common sense and experience, his own mode of laying out his existence is the best, not because it is the best in itself, but because it is his own mode.'[15] There is an important difference between valuing or respecting a mode of life or a belief because it is *someone's* and valuing it *because* it is different. Mill goes on at once to say that 'different persons . . . require different conditions', and that: 'Such are the differences among human beings in their sources of pleasure, their susceptibilities of pain, and the operation on them of different physical and moral agencies that, unless there is a corresponding diversity in their modes of life, they neither obtain their fair share of happiness, nor grow up to the mental, moral and aesthetic stature of which their nature is capable.' But he is not valuing diversity here; he is valuing individuality, and noting that diversity is a natural fact; uniformity is a sign that nature has been suppressed, and that what is one's own has been denied.

'Valuing diversity' is, anyway, a somewhat odd notion which – in the absence of qualification – has unacceptable implications. In a discussion we may or may not know, and it may or may not matter to us, that particular alternative views originated with particular people. Very approximately, perhaps, our concern with *who* said what varies inversely with the formality of the situation, the most rigorously formal kinds of discussion becoming 'subjectless'. But if we are concerned with who said what, that is because of some feature of theirs, not because of some feature of what they say; we think people deserve respect, we think they have a right to speak their minds, we do not want to offend, and so on. Alternatively, if our concern is strictly with the content of different communications, that is because we are interested in exhausting alternatives as thoroughly and efficiently as possible. So we may give weight to the speaker or to the message (or both), but in neither case does it make any apparent sense to speak of valuing diversity. We give certain kinds of respect to people for any of a number of possible reaons, but not because they are different; we do not respect only those who have something novel to say, and we do not find it regrettable if the same view is held by more than one person. Nor is it because they are different that we give weight to different views; we do so as long as there is some prospect that they are in part at least right, or at the very least are provocative, and the relevant 'value' is clearly that of truth. 'The intrinsic value of diversity' is best understood as a shorthand expression for something in which diversity is not itself a value but is in one way or another attendant upon a value.

Now there are, of course, portions of *On Liberty* which are strongly diversitarian in flavour at least, so much so that Mill has been credited (if that is the word) with a belief in 'the sanctity of idiosyncracy'.[16] There is, moreover, the whole utilitarian dimension of Mill's argument, which — successfully or otherwise — seeks to justify liberty by assessing the consequences of permitting or prohibiting diversity of opinion. This is not the place for an exploration either of Mill's rich concept of individuality or of his complex doctrine of utility: but two things have surely been established. First, Mill's concept of individuality is not reducible to a concept of idiosyncracy; and if it *were* a concept of idiosyncracy it would provide an extremely poor vehicle for the argument which he wishes to advance. As one commentator has said: 'In the absence of all pressure of coercion or undue influence, persons may and in fact often do choose to imitate others rather than to make themselves unique; this tendency to conformity could be countered by authoritative order requiring the cultivation of diversity.'[17] Second, the argument from the utility of diversity has a crippling defect to the extent that it renders freedom conditional, for when the conditions do not hold the argument does not support freedom; and the conditions, as even Mill believes, do not always hold.

The logic here was interestingly anticipated by Comte, who likewise — as Mill was well aware — had argued that diversity must be permitted in times of uncertainty. When we do not know, Comte argues, we must be free to think and speak without restriction, for we could sensibly impose restrictions only if we knew already what was worth thinking and saying, which *ex hypothesi* we do not.[18] When this consideration applies, he continues, the liberty of thought and speech must be absolute. But the illiberal corollary is drawn out by Comte in another and more famous passage: when the consideration does not apply — when in any sphere positive understanding is attained — then there is no case for liberty at all.[19] Such a (Comtean) condition of unqualified truth-attainment is envisaged, too, in *On Liberty*; but in speaking of it, Mill foresees a need for the artificial simulation of diversity, so that the grounds of true belief will continue to be understood.[20] This is again to give primacy to one's beliefs being 'one's own', not, obviously, in the sense that they are unique, but in the sense that one has explored them for oneself, that one experiences their truth, that one does not merely receive them but that one enters actively into their demonstration. Diversity of taste is simply a natural fact; diversity of belief, ultimately, is simply a means by which truth can be vivified; in neither case is diversity valued for itself.

It is intriguing to compare the Comtean argument with that of Tocqueville, Comte's contemporary, and also Mill's correspondent. For Comte, liberty is justified in a troubled or transitional age in which diverse views cannot be reconciled, and in which what is at issue between competing hypotheses cannot be resolved. For Tocqueville, precisely to the contrary, the idea of freedom needs to be advanced and protected in an age of consensus, such as had, in his view, already arrived. America, which is everyone's future, displays a condition of moral consensus and uniformity: 'in the moral world', he wrote, 'everything is classified, co-ordinated, foreseen, and decided in advance'. But he also found in America political conditions which were in no sense a simple extension of moral experience: 'In the political world, everything is in turmoil, contested, and uncertain. In the one case obedience is passive, though voluntary; in the other there is independence, contempt of experience, and jealousy of authority.'[21] Why, in the light of moral consensus, should political independence be important? What Tocqueville wants is not unrelated to what Mill calls individuality, if this carries the sense of being an agent rather than a patient, of using and developing one's powers rather than relying on others'. But it has nothing to do with individuality if this carries the sense of diversity, for diversity, according to Tocqueville, is just what we can no longer expect. In comparison with the old regime, society has become homogeneous, irrevocably; a homogeneous society offers only weak obstacles to the central engross-ment of power; but it is both vain and regressive to seek to restore diversity. What we can do, instead, is to try to create a sense of self-worth and personal efficacy, so that citizens will decline to become mere subjects.

To say this is to imply that more than social outcomes, in the aggre-gate, are important: that importance attaches to the relationships between individuals and their roles and beliefs, which should be actively and responsibly assumed. To say that is in turn to imply the importance of what Rawls calls the 'plurality of persons' or what above was called distinctness − it is to take seriously the fact that each member of a polity represents a distinct locus of experience. It does not at all imply that their experiences, or the conclusions which they draw from experi-ence, are diverse.

Choice and Diversity

To think of liberalism in the way that has just been suggested may well suggest that choice has a central place in liberal political theory, a view which is certainly plausible and has been proposed in, for example, the case of Mill himself: 'At the centre of Mill's thought and feeling lies . . . his passionate belief that men are made human by their capacity for choice.'[22] This, however, may appear to reintroduce diversity as a root principle in that in one way or another choice and a diversity of options are held to be inseparably linked. So, it would seem, if we deny that diversity is primary and offer personal distinctness as a necessary precondition, we may quickly be met with the objection that personal distinctness is of interest, and can figure in a normative argument, only to the extent that normative diversity is assumed; our valuing of choosing, and our belief that there are moral choices to be made, are interdependent. There are, however, at least two distinct ways of making such an argument.

In one version, it is the awareness of choice that generates respect for diversity. If we believed, in a Platonic manner, that while error is multiple, truth is one, we could see nothing good in diversity of opinion. Only if we grasp that there is a discretionary component in our understanding of things, that different choices can intelligibly be made, will we have reason to see in diversity something to be accepted or welcomed. In another version, the direction of argument is rather the reverse. Only if there is diversity, it is claimed, and only if we regard diversity not as a mere fact but as a legitimate and necessary feature of the world, can we speak meaningfully of choices being made. Let us examine examples of these arguments in turn.

The very idea of 'choosing values' may itself be problematic,[23] but certain versions of it seem problematic to an unacceptable degree. It is not clear that it is right to speak of 'choosing' when the alleged 'choices' are held to be made between attitudes of a subjective and wholly prescriptive kind: *or* between ways of life which are totally self-reinforcing and mutually insulated in both cognitive and normative terms − a version which appears different merely in substituting shared for solitary prescriptions. Perhaps there is an extended sense in which one could be said to 'choose' between such things; just as there is an extended sense in which someone induced to go through certain motions could be described as, say, 'voting', even if he did not have the remotest idea of the point of the procedure. But the core of the idea of choosing contains notions such as weighing, balancing, guessing, doubting, predicting, testing, hoping and so on, and could one do much or any of this if only prescriptions, and no descriptive elements, were involved? And even if one could, could a moral rationality attenuated to such a degree provide a foundation for the sort of political theses that are said to be built upon it? It seems incongruous to suppose that a position which insists so much on contingency of choice at the base should insist no less on ineluctable entailments in the superstructure.

To avoid these difficulties, let us consider an example which, to its credit, does insist that there are discursive elements in choosing: W.B. Gallie's influential account of 'Essentially Contested Concepts'.[24] This account stresses the discretionary element in the application of evaluative ('appraisive') concepts; an attractively pluralistic philosophy of history is put to use in support of a political therapy. The intention is, however, to show, in opposition to prescriptivist claims, that there are discursive elements, attempts to explain the world, in choice: rival proposals do not merely prescribe, they describe intelligibly; but they do not do so decisively. Different uses of evaluative concepts such as 'democracy' or 'justice' are intelligible in that each can be sustained by evidence when confronted by rival uses; but criteria of evidence are indecisive because these concepts are internally complex, and no ranking of their features in order of importance can be agreed upon. Thus, different features of the concepts can be 'aggressively' advanced as primary and their primacy 'defended' without demonstrable error. Because of this, in turn, each feature is vigorously elaborated and our understanding of it deepened. If so, there are grounds for valuing this process, and if its participants can be brought to understand this historical model, they will respect those with whom they disagree, will not regard them as 'perverse, bestial or lunatic', but will understand the indispensable value of their criticism.

Of the many things to be said about this very intriguing model, two are of special relevance here. First, in view of later attempts to present such 'essential contestability' as the philosophical foundation of liberalism,[25] it should be noted that it is not Gallie's claim that a philosophy of contestability *underlies* the process of contestation. While the participants may realise what kind of activity they are engaged in — as Gallie hopes they or some of them will — they need not; they may be unwitting tools of a cunning of reason. So there must be some principle of legitimacy *other* than essential contestability itself if the model is to work; they must have found some non-philosophically grounded way of rubbing along together; and desirable though it is that they should cease to regard one another as 'perverse, bestial or lunatic' they must also — before their moment of enlightenment — have evolved some way of restraining themselves in the face of opposition from people whom, apparently, they regarded as lunatics or beasts. There must, then, be political principles of legitimacy which are distinct from moral-philosophical (or epistemological) criteria of justification. Moral pluralism, therefore, cannot be a necessary condition for the acceptance of pluralism in its political sense.

Second, if and when the moment of enlightenment arrives, a problem will arrive with it. For contestation depends upon rival definitions of shared concepts: but enlightenment brings with it a perfectly adequate and incontestable account of concepts' meaning — that is, historical descriptions. When one knows that 'democracy' is an internally complex concept, that such things as representation, participation and equality figure in it in varying proportions at various times, what else — apart from more detail — needs to be supplied in answer to the question, 'What is "democracy"?' How could anyone know this, and persist in saying 'Democracy really means maximum participation'? Are we in an essentially self-destructive position here, rather as in the case of telling people to be tolerant because no one is right? What we want is a reason for people to exercise restraint when confronted by beliefs contrary to their own; what we are actually given is a reason for declining to hold one's beliefs seriously.

Is there an escape-route in Gallie's argument? There is one, which, although only lightly stressed, may be vital to the coherence of the whole position. Noting the option of taking up 'an entirely uncommitted attitude', Gallie comments: 'But . . . in life this possibility is often precluded. The exigencies of living commonly demand that "he who is not for us is against us," or that he who hesitates to throw in his support or make his contribution on one side or the other is lost.'[26] So on this ground, Gallie continues, it may be rational to continue to prefer one restricted use, or to change one's use, of a concept. But consider an example: If someone says that 'Democracy means several things, such as participation, representation and equality, these things being stressed aggressively and defensively at different times in the history of the concept', and also 'Democracy really means maximum participation', he or she can be rescued from outright contradiction only if the word 'means' is used in two different ways. That is what Gallie's argument must imply, though he does not say it. When he introduces 'the exigencies of living', he implies that in addition to the discursive and non-restrictive meaning of historical description there is also the pragmatic and restrictive meaning of concrete application. *Here* and *now*, given *these* exigencies as *I* see them, these dangers, risks, opportunities, democracy means (implies, demands) maximally increased participation in all key social institutions: 'means' here is parallel to 'This means war!' as opposed to '*Felis* means "cat".' We have to apply our concepts, make judgements, accept restrictions and take sides. With all this one may certainly agree; but the grounds of the argument have shifted significantly.

What is *now* claimed is that there is an indeterminate space between believing and doing, and that people who hold the same beliefs may disagree vigorously about their application. But this is true whatever our view may be on the issue of discursive meaning. We could disagree in this way even if we were Rawlsians with our goods definitively ranked.[27] We could disagree in this way — *pace* Sir Isaiah Berlin — even if we 'never disagreed about the ends of life',[28] for to agree on ends in the sense of ultimate values or perspectives is not to eliminate conflict over ends in the sense of objectives with pragmatic content. Consensus over ultimate ends does not translate automatically into political harmony; nor, it might be added, does recognition of the diversity of ends translate automatically into approval of political dissent. There is no straightforward symmetry such as the moral pluralist theses assume.

The Limits of Moral Pluralism

The alternative argument, which makes choice depend upon diversity, is developed in a paper by Joseph Raz.[29] Stressing the central importance of autonomy among liberal values, Raz contends that autonomous choices can be made only where there are legitimate alternatives. There must be a choice other than between right and wrong, which is a dictated choice; autonomy thus depends upon moral pluralism, defined, as we have seen, as the belief that 'there are many worthwhile and valuable relationships, commitments and plans of life which are mutually incompatible, so that autonomous people can and should choose between them'.

It is necessary to this argument, it would seem, that the claims made by moral philosophers of 'generalisation' be abandoned or at any rate considerably weakened. The moral pluralist model, as Raz describes it, requires that I should understand that others are justified in doing one thing even though I am justified in adopting some incompatible value. This requirement appears to exclude the requirement that I should approve of the principles of my own and of others' actions on the same terms. What one person thinks it is right for him or her to do is not (always) what he or she would require everyone else to do as a condition of acting morally. Now there may well be good reasons for accepting this as a more realistic picture of moral life,[30] and certainly no objections will be offered here; but to abandon the generalisation argument is also to abandon the position that one's view of others' decisions has necessary consequences for one's view of one's own. If different people, differently situated, may validly make different moral decisions, that means that my recognition of the moral validity of others' decisions does not make a particular decision non-dictated for me. I may well recognise that you, being who you are and situated as you are, must do something that I, being who I am and situated as I am, must not do: but clearly that does not mean that *my* choice about what *I* should do is open. I may well believe that 'I must', or 'I can do no other', even if I accept that others may be obliged to do something quite different. Whether or not there are alternatives which would be legitimate if taken by someone else — whose decisions I would respect — is quite beside the point. The dictation or non-dictation of my choice, and my recognition or non-recognition of the moral legitimacy of rival choices, would seem, therefore, to be separable questions. Moral pluralism is not a sufficient condition, then, for autonomy, for the fact that it admits a diversity of right actions for people generally does not mean that it preserves a diversity of options for any given individual.

If we ask about necessity of condition, we run into a different question: that of *whose* approval of moral pluralism is necessary. Is the argument that moral pluralism is a necessary condition of approving of a liberal society, that is, a society in which choices are protected? Or is it that moral pluralism is a necessary condition of living in such a society and of respecting its institutions' legitimacy? Either of the possible answers is troublesome for the diversitarian thesis. Suppose the moral pluralism is the philosopher's: in the light of it, the philosopher approves of a regime which secures freedom of thought and expression, rights of association, and whatever else is necessary to foster plurality in moral belief; how can such structural provisions ensure that its subjects perceive moral choice as morally justified, as opposed to politically legitimate? Moral pluralism, taken as the justifying theory of a free society, cannot sanction only the freedom to be a moral pluralist; the freedom which it sanctions covers exclusive moral claims by people who believe that others' moral claims are false without qualification. The political availability of choices will not inherently make moral choices non-coercive for those who actually have to make them; they may all be true believers who hold other beliefs in contempt, and if they manage to restrain themselves in the ways that a liberal system requires there must — once again — be some other basis for their willingness to do so.

But if it is the chooser who has to be a moral pluralist — to be auto-nomous, his or her choice must be 'perceived to be one between morally acceptable options'[31] — one is simply left in doubt as to how this can be achieved. If any state at all can determine what kind of moral experi-ences people have, a liberal state is precluded even from trying to do so by liberal beliefs themselves. It can justifiably place limits upon what people do about their moral views, but it can neither dictate nor hope to predict what their views about morality can be. So it cannot rest on moral pluralism, because it cannot rest on any such thing.

As in the case of Gallie's argument, we are led to the conclusion that what is needed is a theory of what can be done politically about one's moral beliefs — not of what can be morally believed. What bears the weight is not the nature of the moral beliefs held by members of a liberal society but their sense of what difference it makes that moral beliefs (sometimes) occupy a political context: it is not moral monism, but political authoritarianism, that liberal theory excludes. The point rests partly on the logical consideration that a regime which values moral freedom cannot consistently require any particular moral beliefs to be held or expressed: but it also rests on the historical consideration that liberalism just is not defined by moral pluralist beliefs.

The classical writings on liberalism express or rely upon different moral positions and offer different theological or philosophical accounts of moral knowledge; pluralist accounts of moral knowledge, however, are not among them. Among several arguments for toleration offered by Locke, one rests — most provocatively, in this context — on the grounds of 'there being one truth'.[32] If there were indeed many truths, Locke in effect argues, there would be *less* strong a case against intoler-ance, for the chances of a ruler's finding one of these truths would be quite high, as would the chance, therefore, of his subjects' being 'led into' truth if required to conform to their ruler's beliefs. But since there is only *one* truth, there is no hope that 'more men would be led into it' if states maintained policies of religious conformity. Now to this it is likely to be objected that although Locke affirms the uniqueness of truth he also denies that it is knowable, which restores a situation of plurality to all intents and purposes. Here, however, we must take account of the still stronger claim that the use of coercion in matters of conscience is wrong for reasons that have nothing to do with the limits of knowledge: '*if it could be manifest* which of . . . two dissenting churches were in the right, there would not accrue thereby unto the orthodox any right of destroying the other. For churches have neither any jurisdiction in worldly matters, nor are fire and sword any proper

instruments wherewith to convince men's minds of error, and inform
them of the truth.'[33]

Similarly, Mill directly raises the question of the reasons for toleration in a context of certainty (which is not, as in Locke's case, a merely
hypothetical question). He entertains the possibility that 'after some
length of time and amount of experience, a moral or prudential truth
may be regarded as established', and thus that interference with personal
conduct which is inconsistent with it would be justified. And what he
(interestingly) calls 'the strongest of all the arguments against the interference of the public is that, when it does interfere, the odds are that
it interferes wrongly, and in the wrong place.' He continues: 'It is easy
for anyone to imagine an ideal public which leaves the freedom and
choice of all individuals in all uncertain matters undisturbed, and only
requires them to abstain from modes of conduct which universal experience has condemned. But where has there been seen a public which
sets any such limit to its censorship?'[34] As in Locke's case, what we are
offered is not a theory of the plurality of truth, but a theory of the unavailability of truth as a constitutional entity. We can take what view
we wish on the question of the philosophical unavailability of truth:
our answer to that question, as both Locke and Mill make clear, is not
decisive. What is decisive is the political reality that truth is not something that can be given constitutional expression. This is not to be
confused with the claim − false, as Raz is right to say[35] − that states
lack the power to 'promote ideals': while there are logical and empirical
limits to their power to do so, they can certainly promote (and demote)
ideals in significant ways; but the point at issue is that while a constitution can assign powers which are effective for ideal-promoting purposes,
it cannot prescribe the motives or intentions of those who exercise the
powers.

A constitution attaches powers to offices and distributes offices
according to set criteria. It defines offices and assigns powers to them
in the light of certain reasons; and the offices are valued to the extent
that these reasons are thought to be good. But we do not know what
reasons are entertained by those who will fill the offices at any given
time, for the reasons for which they act may differ from the reasons
for which we value their having the power to act. And here we are
brought back, by a different route, to the notion of distinctness: to
the understanding that each person acts for reasons that are compelling
to him or her and which are not subsumable under some role which
someone else may wish to assign. 'We may imagine' (in Mill's words)
some ideal holder of power who will adopt precisely the reasons that

we (the philosophers) happen to approve of — just such a projection is vital to the argument of the *Republic*;[36] but that is imagination, not politics, to the extent that we fail to take account of the difference between valuing the existence of a power and predicting the uses to which it may be put. Surely it is in this context, rather than that of the ontological status of individuals and wholes, that arguments such as Locke's or Mill's are committed to recognising distinctness, as a condition that governs any constitutional arrangement. And not only is distinctness thus understood not trivial, it provides the basis for a more cogent argument than diversity can do, as well as being more faithful to what liberals have actually said.

The Paradigm of Concourse

It is Plato's view, and also Comte's, that freedom is premised on uncertainty, and that unqualified truth licenses unqualified authority. Such an argument renders freedom so vulnerable that it is scarcely a surprise to find that it is favoured by authoritarians.[37] It *is* a surprise to find it or some version of it offered as nothing less than the foundation of liberalism. Generally speaking, liberals have had to make a case for freedom which could be grasped by rulers and publics who were not noticeably troubled by moral uncertainties, and it is surely implausible to suppose that they would have constructed a case of interest only to those who did not need to hear it. What has been suggested above is that the justification of liberal principles is fundamentally misguided if the issue is taken to be one of pluralism *versus* monism. Liberalism is rightly distinguished from traditions of thinking such as Plato and Comte originated; but what distinguishes it is not an issue in moral philosophy — on which liberals have held widely divergent views — but a view about the relationship between philosophy and life.

In a philosophical context, a model of unity is provided by discourse, through which differences are resolved and contradictions removed. This process has several distinctive features: rivalry is in principle between propositions and not persons; the victory of one proposition implicates everyone in its truth, though it may happen that some (through stupidity or prejudice) cannot see that they are implicated; and consent adds nothing to the validity of a proposition which has been shown to be true, validity being independent of which people or how many people happen to grasp it. It is plain that such a model of unity, translated into a political context, has illiberal implications. Consent ceases to be of importance for legitimacy, and merely has the consequence – for both Plato and Comte – of bringing into being a regime which can then dispense with it; it is not a constitutional ingredient of legitimacy, it merely licenses an order of things which thought has justified already. No representation of opinion is necessary, for it is a feature of truth that it implicates people regardless of their opinion. And since unity is imagined as something brought *to* a society rather than as something arising *out of* interrelations, it requires a privileged bearer – 'some authority which will hold to the same idea . . . that you had before you in framing the laws'.

To the model of discourse may be opposed a model – to borrow Tocqueville's term again – of concourse, which has the opposite features. Principally, it differs in denying that one person's experience is inclusive of or substitutable for another's, that one person's decision can implicate others; consent alone implicates. It also differs in making consent a component of legitimacy, so that who agrees and how many agree becomes important – the subject and number of verbs, so to speak, are relevant, while in the model of discourse they are not. It also differs in presenting unity, to the extent that it is achieved, as something arising out of many distinct efforts and tendencies, the pattern of which it reflects. In all these respects the model of concourse would sustain a political regime in which the fact of individual distinctness was given constitutional weight; in which individuals or their interests are not subsumed under others', in which each pursues interests or follows reasons or makes choices which are 'his own'. If discourse is in principle subjectless, in concourse subjectivity is stressed, in that society is conceived of as being experienced from multiple viewpoints which, whether diverse or not, are distinct.

To picture a society as a concourse of distinct agents is to set limits to the scope of deductive argument in politics. It is a feature of discourse that a chain of propositions can be constructed the coherence of which does not depend on the number of minds which happen to follow it through. To the extent that logical goodness is our concern, the plurality of minds is merely a contingent feature of the world, and the fiction of a single mind may perfectly well be assumed in connecting premises with conclusions. But politics does not lend itself to such a model. To the extent that political conclusions involve or imply predictions about what agents will do, their validity does rest upon the extent to which they come to be shared; the plurality of minds is a necessary and not a contingent feature of political thought. The sense in which 'plurality' is necessary, and the senses in which it is not, have been suggested above.

Notes

*I am grateful to S.V. LaSelva and members of his graduate seminar in 1983-84 for their assistance with this paper.

1. Richard Wollheim, 'Crime, Sin and Mr. Justice Devlin', *Encounter* 13 (November, 1959), p. 38.
2. Basil Mitchell, *Law, Morality and Religion in a Secular Society* (London, Oxford University Press, 1967), p. 90.
3. P.F. Strawson, 'Social Morality and Individual Ideal', *Philosophy* 36 (1961), p. 17.
4. John N. Gray, 'On the Contestability of Social and Political Concepts', *Political Theory* 5 (1977), p. 335. Gray offers this not as his position but as his version of what he takes one argument for liberalism to be.
5. Alasdair MacIntyre, *Secularization and Moral Change* (London, Oxford University Press, 1967), p. 45.
6. Joseph Raz, 'Liberalism, Autonomy and the Politics of Neutral Concern', in Peter A. French *et al.* (eds.), *Midwest Studies in Philosophy VII*.
7. Isaiah Berlin, *Four Essays on Liberty* (London, Oxford University Press, 1969), pp. 190-1.
8. Ralf Dahrendorf, *Life Chances* (Chicago; University of Chicago Press, 1979), p. 97.
9. For a fuller examination of this point, see Richard Vernon and Samuel V. LaSelva, 'Justifying Tolerance', *Canadian Journal of Political Science* 17 (1984), pp. 3-23.
10. See F.M. Barnard and Richard Vernon, 'Socialist Pluralism and Pluralist Socialism', *Political Studies* 25 (1977), pp. 474-90.
11. In effect Durkheim's theme in *The Division of Labour in Society*.
12. John Rawls, 'Constitutional Liberty and the Concept of Justice', in Carl J. Friedrich and John W. Chapman (eds.), *Justice* (New York, Atherton, 1963), p. 124.
13. John Dunn, *Western Political Theory in the Face of the Future* (Cambridge, Cambridge University Press, 1979), pp. 33, 43.
14. 'Concurrence' is given as a translation in J.P. Mayer (ed.), *Democracy in America* (Garden City, Doubleday, 1969), p. 94: this is quite reasonable, though the connotations of agreement could be misleading.
15. J.S. Mill, *On Liberty* (Harmondsworth, Penguin, 1974), pp. 133-4.
16. R.P. Wolff, *The Poverty of Liberalism* (Boston, Beacon Press, 1968), p. 19.
17. Richard J. Arneson, 'Mill versus Paternalism', *Ethics* 90 (1980), p. 479. See also Robert F. Ladenson, 'Mill's Conception of Individuality', *Social Theory and Practice* 4 (1977), pp. 167-82.
18. See the *Cours de philosophie positive* (Paris, Hermann, 1975), vol. II, p. 28.
19. See the 1822 essay republished in the Appendix to the *Système de politique positive* (Paris, Société Positiviste, 1929), p. 53.
20. *On Liberty*, pp. 106-7.
21. *Democracy in America*, p. 47.
22. Berlin, *Four Essays*, p. 192.
23. See G.J. Warnock, 'On Choosing Values', *Midwest Studies in Philosophy* III (1978), pp. 28-34.
24. W.B. Gallie, 'Essentially Contested Concepts', *Proceedings of the Aristotelian Society* 56 (1956), p. 167-98.
25. See the discussion by Gray, 'Contestability of Social and Political Concepts'. This discussion is critical of the attempt to derive liberal principles from

the idea of essential contestability, but does not appear to find the attempt itself to be incoherent.

26. 'Essentially Contested Concepts', p. 190.

27. As is forcefully explained by Benjamin Barber in 'Justifying Justice: Problems of Psychology, Politics and Measurement in Rawls' in Norman Daniels (ed.), *Reading Rawls* (Oxford, Blackwell, 1975), pp. 292-318.

28. *Four Essays*, p. 118.

29. See note 6 above.

30. See Peter Winch, 'The Universalizability of Moral Judgments', *The Monist* 49 (1965), pp. 196-214.

31. Raz, 'Liberalism', p. 115.

32. John Locke, *A Letter Concerning Toleration* (Indianapolis, Bobbs-Merrill, 1955), p. 19.

33. Ibid., p. 26 (emphasis added).

34. *On Liberty*, pp. 148-51.

35. Raz, 'Liberalism', p. 100.

36. See lines 497 c-d. Translations of this passage are interestingly varied: Cornford has 'our state must always contain some authority which will hold to the same idea of its constitution that you had before you in framing its laws'; *The Republic of Plato* (London, Oxford University Press, 1941), p. 206.

37. See also James Fitzjames Stephen, *Liberty, Equality, Fraternity* (Cambridge, Cambridge University Press, 1967), p. 108: 'If our notions of moral good and evil are substantially true . . . the object of causing people to believe in them is good, and . . . social intolerance on the behalf of those who do towards those who do not believe in them cannot be regarded as involving evils of any great importance.'

9 PLURALISM, COMMUNITY AND HUMAN NATURE

Caroline McCulloch and Geraint Parry

Ideals of community are often claimed not simply to rest on assumptions about human nature but — more seriously — to founder upon them. Critics have argued that communitarians entertain utopian notions about the possibility of communal co-operation and unity which render communitarian theory implausible and authoritarian if translated into political practice. Communitarians and anti-communitarians, therefore, take up a variety of positions on the relation of community to human nature. On the communitarian side one can distinguish support for the following:

(a) There is a communitarian instinct in human nature which, however, may be frustrated by certain economic and social institutions and structures.

(b) There are a number of human needs which political society assists in providing for, but there is a particular basic need for belonging or for a sense of identity with others which is reflected in community living.

(c) Community is a basic need and for the most part other human needs are not universal but shaped by community.

(d) Altruism is one disposition amongst other and contrary dispositions which may be harnessed to produce a substantially more co-operative and trusting society deserving the name community.

(e) Human nature is not fixed but may be moulded by choice so as to encourage the formation of co-operative groups which will either stimulate the development of a range of human capacities or by contrast will result in groupings of people with a specific pattern of life or culture.

Each of these positions faces in its own way a common problem of reconciling the exclusiveness associated with community with the universalist moral notions. For some, like Kropotkin, this is expressed in an internal tension within communitarianism itself. For liberal and socialist writers the tension is one between the particularism of community and the universal moral principles they normally profess. Traditional conservatives (and we may, somewhat provocatively, include Rousseau

162

among their number) do not face this problem since they are able to offer a moral defence of particularism *per se*, making few concessions to any principle of universalisability.[1]

Anti-communitarians argue variously that: (a) human beings (or at least post-lapsarian human beings) are by nature self-interested and that genuine community cannot, therefore, be a natural product or cannot occur in our world. Political order is artificial; (b) although communitarian instincts form part of human nature they are insufficient to sustain an extensive group of people; (c) the instinct toward community exists and is powerful but that it is also primitive and restrictive of human development and should be consciously suppressed.

In order to specify more closely the connection between the concepts of human nature and community it is necessary to recognise, however summarily, the multi-dimensional character of 'human nature' and the highly contested meaning of 'community'.

Taking first the notion of 'human nature' we can identify three distinct elements which are variously cited in communitarian theories: capacities, dispositions and needs. Capacities *enable* us to act – they make action possible. Their specification will be crucial for delimiting the range of social possibilities. Dispositions (and the notions of trait and instinct seem also to fall under this category) *prompt* us to act in particular ways. We act in these ways because of our natures rather than as a product of reflection or choice. Finally, needs refer to objects or behaviours which serve our ends, and while our dispositions must always reflect some capacity that we possess, our needs would seem to be distinct from – indeed, may even be at odds with – our dispositions and capacities.[2]

Communitarians and their commentators often fail adequately to distinguish between these different dimensions, sliding between them under the generic heading of human 'nature' or 'essence'. Yet not only are they clearly distinct, but the strength of the communitarian claim for human nature will crucially depend upon which of the three is being invoked.

Turning to the concept of community, we encounter rather more obstacles to clear specification. Michael Taylor is not alone in noting recently that 'The word is used in connection with an enormous variety of things.'[3] It is, however, possible to identify some core characteristic which, though rather formal, may nevertheless provide a working base from which to examine different formulations of the community – human nature relation. We can, for example, locate community along some dimension of sociability. Communitarians and their critics often start by asserting that human beings are 'naturally social': thus, Martin Miller writes, of Peter Kropotkin's view, 'It is inconceivable to speak of man as isolated from society.'[4] While this is a fairly minimal premise, it does have some importance and force — reminding us, for example, that Robinson Crusoe was at least *once* a member of human society, and that without such origins he would, like the wild boy of Aveyron, be unrecognisable as a human being. Further, the degree of mutual consideration and respect conveyed by the term 'social' is illuminated by the contrary notion of 'anti-social' behaviour. Yet if it is not entirely uninformative, 'social' is still a very general conception, encompassing a wide range of relationships. Miller continues: 'Man's essence is to co-operate with his fellows to secure his basic needs' — but this elaboration does not seem to take us much further forward. There is, for example, nothing in this statement to distinguish Peter Kropotkin from Adam Smith. While barter and exchange in the market place clearly are forms of co-operation (and, for Smith, a co-operation which promotes — albeit unintentionally — the general welfare as well as particular interests) it needs to be distinguished from what most writers understand as *communal* co-operation.

Tönnies' classic distinction between *Gesellschaft* and *Gemeinschaft* is pertinent here. Both are forms of social life, and both involve co-operation, but whereas the co-operation of *Gesellschaft* is of a self-interested, instrumental and essentially contractual nature — in which the needs and desires of the other are of no intrinsic concern — the co-operation of *Gemeinschaft* proceeds from a consciousness of common identity and common interest and expresses the felt primacy and unity of the group.

The difference, then, would seem to reside in the perceptions and attitudes of the co-operative actors — and, indeed, a recent theorist has defined community in precisely these terms: community, David Clark claims, consists essentially in a 'sense of solidarity and a sense of significance'.[5] Similarly, Alan Ritter defines the anarchist conception of community in terms of 'reciprocal awareness'.[6] It is this subjective awareness of group membership and the motivations that spring from it that distinguish communal co-operation from the behavioural co-operation manifested in the market place. Yet we cannot dispense entirely with the behavioural dimension; where people have a strong sense of mutual identification and responsibility but, nevertheless, behave in highly competitive and mutually destructive ways (even with regret — for reasons, say, beyond their control) we would not wish to characterise their relationships as altogether 'communal'.[7]

We may conclude, then, that community consists in a sense of common identity and mutual concern *which is expressed* in co-operative behaviour.

Having thus identified the conceptual structure and core of human nature and community respectively, we can turn to an examination of their relationship in a range of communitarian conceptions. The most direct relationship between the two concepts is that posited by the claim that community is itself immanent in human nature. Community, on this view, is the most 'natural' form of social organisation — the form that most closely corresponds to and expresses certain immutable features of the human character. A classic statement of this position is found in the work of Peter Kropotkin, but it has echoes in more recent writings. Glenn Tinder, for example, asserts that 'the longing for community expresses the essence of humanity' — community is an 'imperative of human nature'.[8] Such a view is supported by Maslow's contention that the sense of social membership afforded by communal relationships is one of a hierarchy of human needs, the satisfaction of which is essential to psychological well-being and development.

Yet a closer examination of these arguments reveals a number of distinct claims — corresponding both to different aspects of the communitarian relationship and to the different elements of human nature.

In Kropotkin, for example, community is understood as the social embodiment of the principle of *mutual aid*, which signifies the practices of reciprocal assistance and co-operation that spring from a sense of solidarity with one's fellows. There are two distinct levels on which the principle of mutual aid operates (though Kropotkin presents them as simply different points along a single continuum): first, in relations with immediate and specific others — members of one's clan, tribe, guild, village, neighbourhood and so on; and second, in relations with strangers, where mutual aid operates as a kind of generalised altruism, born of a wider *human* identification and concern.

The most fundamental and relatively uncontroversial claim in Kropotkin's *Mutual Aid* is that human beings have the *capacity* for localised communal relationships; that is, the kind of co-operative relationships characteristic of small, face-to-face groups. Thus, in refutation of the Hobbesian claim that the natural human condition is one of competition and conflict, Kropotkin demonstrates that human beings are eminently capable of living together in peaceable collaboration and have, indeed, done so from the earliest point in their history.

Yet the historical precedents for community are taken by Kropotkin to imply much more than that community is *possible*. Rather, he argues that they reflect an instinct, which has been evolved in response to the imperatives of survival. Kropotkin wishes, then, to root communal behaviour in genetic traits which human beings share with animals and which are functional for both individual and species.

To the extent that mutual aid is rooted in the need for survival, one might characterise it as self-interested and instrumental in a very fundamental sense. However, this would be to confuse two distinct levels of analysis. While the explanation for the existence of a disposition to mutual aid is made in terms of individual and species self-interest, the disposition itself is, at the level of experience and expression, a *non-self-interested* one — by definition.

This instinct of mutual aid explains the ubiquity of co-operative institutions and practices throughout history, and is the basis for Kropotkin's faith in both the possibility and inevitability of anarcho-communism. Human beings (like animals) are 'disposed toward communal existence'[9] — in the absence of artificial institutions (particularly, government and private property) people will *spontaneously develop and sustain* communal practices.

We can identify three sets of problems arising from this conception of a communitarian human nature. The first relates to the elasticity of communal identification and sentiment. Kropotkin sees a continuity between localised reciprocity on the one hand, and generalised altruism on the other. There would, however, seem to be a qualitative difference between the two and a recurring controversy in communitarian theory is precisely whether the sense of community with one's face-to-face fellows *can* be extended to wider social groupings — and, particularly, to humanity at large. Much of Kropotkin's argument and evidence pertain to the reciprocal practices of localised mutual aid, which — though important in themselves — leave open the question of extendability. Further, isolated instances of extended and genuinely disinterested altruism (as, for example, the voluntary lifeboat association) — though similarly telling against the Hobbesian view of human nature — cannot carry the full weight of the claim that there is an altruistic disposition sufficient to generate and sustain a peaceful and communal world order.

Secondly, despite his assertion of a 'unity in nature', Kropotkin does not (and perhaps cannot) apply consistent criteria to animals and humans in his characterisation of mutual aid and his discussion of its functionality. Even if we accept that animals who co-operate fare better in the struggle for survival than do those who compete, it is far from clear that such co-operation qualifies as 'mutual aid', which, in its application to humans, seems crucially to require a motivational dimension.

Further, it is difficult to sustain the direct link between mutual aid and survival when discussing human existence. While human survival may require some form of co-operation, it clearly does not require that specific form represented by mutual aid. Kropotkin thus shifts the criterion of functionality from 'survival' to 'progress', claiming that *communal* co-operation is the necessary condition for individual and species development and achievement. As David Miller puts it, Kropotkin 'believed that all advances in science, technology and art could be attributed to the mutual aid current . . .'[10] Yet, whatever its merits, this is (as Miller points out) a normative claim, and it can lend no support to the argument that mutual aid is an instinct developed through evolution in response to natural imperatives.

A final set of problems for this notion of a communal instinct arises from the need to explain why intrinsically communal persons have consistently developed anti-communal forms. In part, Kropotkin attributes anti-communitarian sentiment and behaviour to the corrupting socialising effects of 'artificial' political and economic institutions: 'Man' he notes 'is a result of both his inherited instincts and his education.'[11] Communal institutions generate fellowship and common concern; commercial activity and the extension of political authority nurture egoism and indifference to others. Thus, Kropotkin describes at length the destructive effects of state power on the communal feeling and motivation of the population at large. He needs, however, to explain not only the persistence but also the origin of these anti-communal institutions, and he sometimes suggests that the desire to dominate – to obtain and extend power over others – is not simply a *capacity* but is itself a *disposition*, which is expressed in, as well as fostered by, anti-communal institutions. Mutual aid, he acknowledges, is only one factor in evolution – and it is in constant struggle with the other factor of self-assertion.

> The desire to dominate others and impose one's own will upon them; the desire to seize upon the products of the labor of a neighbouring tribe; the desire to surround oneself with comforts without producing anything, while slaves provide their master with means of procuring every sort of pleasure and luxury – these selfish, personal desires *give rise to* another current of habits and customs.[12]

Yet, if this is the case, it is not clear why the institutions arising from one disposition should be called 'natural' while those arising from the other disposition are designated 'artificial'. David Miller, in his book *Social Justice*,[13] suggests that part of what Kropotkin *means* by 'natural' in this context is 'functional', but if this is the case, it would seem to be an illegitimate and thoroughly misleading use of the term. As we have seen, Kropotkin's claim for the function of mutual aid in human society is that it best promoted cultural development and progress and — as Miller acknowledges elsewhere[14] — this is a normative claim for the *desirability* of mutual aid, distinct from any claim about its 'naturalness'.

In order to acknowledge an instinct of self-assertion which is destructive of community and avoid total reliance on the normative conclusion that community is nevertheless *better*, Kropotkin seems to claim that the communal instinct is *dominant* and will, therefore, ultimately triumph. Yet the evidence in *Mutual Aid* provides little support for this — indeed, it is difficult to imagine what would constitute evidence for such a case. Kropotkin seems to be left, then, with an unsupported assertion about the dominance of the communal instinct or with a normative conclusion that community is the more progressive instinct.

Thus far the discussion has focused upon the strongest communitarian claim — that human beings are innately disposed toward communal existence. An alternative formulation of the direct link between community and human nature is that community expresses a fundamental human need. Here the focus of the conception of community shifts from the co-operative quality of communal relationships to the underlying sense of communal attachment and solidarity. The 'need', then, is not so much for the expression of an intrinsically co-operative disposition but rather for a source of distinctive social identity. This notion of a *need* for community as the basis of psychological 'health' and/or individual development has found its way into contemporary criticism of the anomie and alienation of modern social life. Erich Fromm, for example, cites 'the need for relatedness, rootedness, the need for a sense of identity and the need for a frame of orientation and devotion'.[15] These arguments have found psychological support in the work of A.H. Maslow.

In the first place, Maslow links the concept of need to that of disposition or instinct. Needs, he claims, are 'instinctoid' — they are the basis of dispositions to act in particular ways. Yet human beings differ crucially from animals in that there is no simple one-to-one correlation between instinct and behaviour; rather, a whole set of social and cultural factors intervene to mediate or even deflect the expression of our instincts. Thus, unlike cats, dogs and birds — whose 'impulse voices are loud, clear and unmistakeable',[16] ours may be lost or distorted through the din of cultural socialisation, such that we may need help (for example through psychoanalysis, or social change) to recover our self-awareness and become healthy, fulfilled human beings.

This conception of needs as 'weak instincts'[17] dilutes the determinism usually associated with instinct theories and introduces the explicitly normative dimension into the theory. Need fulfillment is essential for psychological (and therefore − by extension − social) well-being yet weakly instinctive needs can not be assured of satisfaction. They require, then, a 'beneficent culture for their appearance, expression and gratification and are easily blasted by bad cultural conditions'.[18]

Community enters into Maslow's theory at two points: in direct response to a basic human need and as a prerequisite for the fulfillment of *other* needs. Maslow posits five basic human needs: physiological; safety; belongingness and love; esteem; and self-actualisation. These are ranked such that the satisfaction of higher needs requires the prior satisfaction of the lower needs. It is the third need in the hierarchy which is clearly of most direct relevance to the present discussion. Maslow contends that, once hunger and insecurity have been overcome, individuals will strive for the sense of belonging that derives from social membership. The link between need and disposition here is evident in his observation of our 'deeply animal tendency to herd, to flock, to join, to belong'.[19] Whilst the family is the most immediate source of need gratification in this context, Maslow also argues for the importance of wider social identifications:

> We still underplay the importance of neighbourhood, of one's territory, of one's clan, of one's own 'kind', one's gang, one's familiar working colleagues.[20]

This belongingness need, then, would seem to underpin a range of social attachments of widely varying scope − from family through to country. That the communal sentiment is not, however, infinitely elastic, is revealed by Maslow's 'strong impression' that

> some proportion of youth rebellion groups . . . is motivated by the profound hunger for groupiness, for contact, for real togetherness in the face of a common enemy, *any* enemy that can serve to form an amity group simply by posing an external threat.[21]

In our earlier discussion of Kropotkin we noted that it was a subject of some controversy whether, as a matter of empirical possibility, communal sentiment could transcend fairly localised boundaries. Yet Maslow's formulation suggests that such transcendence may be logically precluded, since the existence of clear boundaries and counter-groups is essential to and even partly definitive of communal attachments. This clearly limits the potential inclusiveness of community and suggests that Kropotkin was guilty of some serious fudging in positing a continuity between local and universal community. This point has been made most acutely by David Miller, who notes that communal solidarity may involve

> a sense of the common humanity of all men as such . . . or it may mean a sense of unity with your own sectional group, into which the existence of other potentially hostile groups enters as a necessary ingredient. Clearly it will not do to present instances of the latter as partial realisations of the former, since it is essential to group solidarity that it is non-universal.[22]

Maslow's theory provides a systematic formulation of the view that the kind of social relationships characteristic of community correspond to some fundamental human needs. This view assumes that underpinning cultural diversity there is an 'essential biologically based inner nature' which can be specified in terms of a set of basic needs, which in turn provides objective criteria for the evaluation of different social forms. If true, Maslow's classification would provide the basis for a 'scientific ethics, a natural value system, a court of ultimate appeal for the determination of good and bad, right and wrong'.[23] The issue has been addressed more recently by Raymond Plant,[24] who also acknowledges a set of basic needs which have to be satisfied for any individual to act in pursuit of any conception of the good. However, at another level he recognises that conceptions of needs are extremely diverse and necessarily dependent on the community context. Recently Michael Walzer has argued along somewhat similar lines.[25] He rejects the instrumental view (usually associated with a contractarian mode of thought) according to which a political association or a community is a means to satisfying supposedly universal needs. Community is, for Walzer, itself a fundamental need but in that it plays an architectonic role in shaping conceptions of needs. According to him 'the primary good that we distribute to one another is membership in some human community'.[26] A contractual notion of society is acceptable as long as it is appreciated that 'one of our needs is community itself'.[27] The contract is not to be seen as simply an arrangement between people to promote mutual assistance since that is something which they may owe to others as human beings.

It is a means by which a set of human beings mark themselves off from others in order to pursue a particular way of life. Two consequences of this position then become apparent — that partners in a community may determine who will be members and that what will be regarded as a human need will henceforth be largely shaped by the community.

According to Walzer states are a mixture of a club and a family. They are 'the political expression of a common life and (most often) of a national family'.[28] Like clubs they must have the rights of admission and exclusion.

> Without them, there could not be *communities of character*, historic-ally stable, ongoing associations of men and women with some special commitment to one another and some special sense of their common life.[29]

A theory which, by contrast to Walzer's, was grounded in notions of universal needs, as much individualist liberalism is, necessarily has difficulties with such notions as communities, memberships and bound-aries.[30] Common humanity might seem to demand universal principles of redistribution which, as Walzer puts it, 'would tend over time to annul the historical particularity of the national clubs and families'.[31] In fact, Walzer himself recognises that there is some claim of absolute need which would prevail over the right of a community to preserve its way of life over territory and which could be used to relieve the neces-sity of outsiders. However, Walzer cannot admit this principle so far as to accept that humanity itself establishes a claim to equal territory or resources. Short of that point (but how short remains unclear), the community has the right to reassert its way of life, which, as in Walzer's instance of Australia, may include the love of open spaces, and restrict new members.

Similarly Walzer argues that the idea of universal human needs can-not take one far in discussions of distributive justice which must, in his view, begin with an account of community membership. It is inappro-priate to commence with assumptions about rational human beings, in a form of the state of nature, who are invited to choose between goods behind a veil of ignorance. The starting point is, rather, with persons who are members of a particular community and share certain views about priorities. As in the case of membership, Walzer is prepared to admit that absolute need, such as famine, has to be met by any com-munity.[32] Beyond this, again undefined but minimal, realm of necessity, need is understood collectively. 'Needs' may be understood by reference to the religion of the community, to the wish to cultivate a civic spirit, or to the modern idea that all are entitled to relief from unemployment and ill health. The manner in which needs are interpreted, the extent of provision and the priorities allotted are all the result of the interpretation of the meaning of the way of life of the community.

It might seem that Walzer is committed to an almost completely relativist communitarianism. However, like other liberal and socialist theorists of community, he is unable to accept that certain collectivities can be described as communities other than in a descriptive sense. For Raymond Plant, by contrast, community is itself a contestable concept. One should resist any temptation to suppose that there is a neutral, non-ideological and purely descriptive core to the notion of community. Walzer, however, feels that, *prima facie* at least, a collectivity which distributed resources so as to favour a ruling class or elite would not fully engage 'the wisdom of the community'.[33] If the population in general supported this biased distribution, there might be grounds for suspecting that the bias was mobilised through some political formula or ideology. If by contrast the population at large is convinced of the legitimacy of an unequal distribution then the justice of the arrangement lies in its conformity to the 'shared understandings' of the community members.[34] One of democracy's several virtues is that it provides opportunities for citizens at large to use their political judgements to mould this shared understanding.

Such a unity does not imply the uniformity which some still fear would be produced by a democratic majority. Walzer holds that community is entirely compatible with plurality. A plural society is one in which the variety of human activities flourishes and where each is governed according to appropriate principles of justice. In such a setting success or failure in one sphere would not be translated into another thereby increasing the likelihood of diversity in the leading roles and minimising monopoly. Yet it is here that one central problem of communitarianism recurs which Walzer for all his ingenuity perhaps does not solve. Is the recognition of this diversity of human interests and potential fully compatible with a communal way of life which would permeate all the spheres of justice and inform the relations between the spheres? Or is the tolerance of such diversity the distinctive achievement of that very thin-blooded collectivity which Oakeshott terms the 'civil association' in which persons and groups are united only by a common recognition of a jurisdiction and the rule of law?[35] When Walzer says that 'a decent state . . . will act to maintain the integrity of its various institutional settings',[36] he seems to be arguing for a limited government which might reduce the very possibility of the community employing political power to encourage and to constrain activities so as to shape a distinctive culture.

A rather more substantive conception of community emerges from the work of R.H. Tawney. Tawney's socialist theory was based upon a commitment to the moral values of community – in particular, to the value of 'fellowship'. He developed an explicitly normative case for community which relied neither upon excessively optimistic claims about human nature nor upon the potential of socio-economic transformation to effect a parallel transformation in human character and behaviour. If Tawney's Christianity convinced him of the moral necessity of community, his observation of human conduct convinced him both of its possibility and of the need for political action to achieve it.

Tawney acknowledged both negative and positive aspects of the human character. He recognised a human capacity for evil and for good, for selfishness and for altruism, for sin and for salvation. He seemed also to make the stronger claim that these are contrary *dispositions*, since he suggested that no social system will be able to eradicate or entirely suppress competitive and acquisitive inclinations. His argument, however, was that the social order need not and should not be founded upon such dispositions – as he believed capitalism to be. Rather, Tawney claimed that there is also an inherent moral sense and conscience which could be mobilised to develop and support a communal social and economic order. Whilst not making any large claim about the transformative potency of institutional change – 'no change of system or machinery can avert those causes of social malaise which consist in the egotism, greed or quarrelsomeness of human nature'[37] – he did believe that such dispositions could be banished to the periphery of social and economic life. Further, he drew on evidence from contemporary society – from human behaviour as it is *now* – to demonstrate the feasibility of a more communitarian order. He supported, for example, the call for the professionalisation of industry by citing the widespread acceptance of a professional ethic in the fields of medicine and teaching. This did not require any transformation in the characters of medical practitioners and teachers, but merely an appeal to conscience and reason that, whatever their personal inclinations, their work activities should be regulated by certain standards of service.

To understand the role of institutional change in creating a communal society, we need to distinguish between two conceptions of fellowship in Tawney's writing. There is, in the first place, a clear regard for and admiration of the close, solidaristic fellowship characteristic of working-class movements and the war-time experience of soldiers at the front – and which is typically associated with communitarianism. However, institutional change cannot, in Tawney's view, play a *direct* role in the creation of such relationships. It is a more diluted conception of fellowship that lies within the sphere of political direction, a conception derived from his Christian premise of equal moral worth of all persons, and their common identity as children of God. From this premise, Tawney developed a theory not of rights but of duties; equality implies social obligation – the recognition that the needs and claims of others are of equal status to one's own. These are the principal ingredients of Tawney's conception of *moral* fellowship; a sense of common *human* identity, a mutual respect based upon an acknowledgement of equal worth, and a social awareness and sense of obligation to one's fellows. This conception is expressed in the ethic of 'service' which Tawney wished to see institutionalised in the sphere of industrial organisation. It is, clearly, a fairly minimal notion of fellowship – indeed, it might be better described as the moral raw material of fellowship itself, since the latter usually conveys more social and psychological substance. For Tawney, the more positively *communal* relationships, captured in notions of fraternity and solidarity, may develop with the framework set by institutionalised 'right relationships'; they consist, in effect, of a heightened awareness and mobilisation of moral fellowship in the creation of a more intimate and active reciprocity. Both levels of fellowship are, in Tawney's view, within human potential, but only the minimal level is within the direct reach of political change. Politics can institutionalise social responsibility and encourage people to behave toward one another with moral consideration. It cannot, however, institutionalise that positive social feeling or sense of comradeship that communitarians typically desire. Political and economic change can create a sufficiently egalitarian environment that people will be 'within reach of each other'[38] – it cannot actually unite them in communal togetherness. Tawney's political theory of community, then, seeks to permit and facilitate the development of more intense communal sentiments – it neither relies upon them, nor does it seek to manufacture or enforce them.

Tawney's moral concern led him to concentrate upon the removal of those inegalitarian and atomising social and economic structures which encourage people to focus upon their differences rather than to recognise their essential moral sameness – that is, the removal of obstacles to moral fellowship. His conception of fellowship is thus implicitly universal in character, and this led him to regard localism or particularism of any kind with some degree of concern and suspicion.

Despite a certain romantic appreciation of cultural diversity, Tawney
held to a Christian conception of morality in which his notion of fellowship was rooted and which he believed to be above any particular cultural predilection:

> The conception of Natural Law is not now in fashion but the truth
> once expressed by it — the truth that there is a political morality
> which is in the character of man as a rational being — is not one to
> be discarded. To suppose that the existence of a score of sovereign
> states is the sole reality which counts, as though facts of human life
> and the principles of human condition changed with every change
> in the uniform of customs officers is something worse than mere
> exaggeration. It is mental perversity and moral obtuseness.[39]

However, part of the distinctive force of communitarianism as a critique
of 'ecumenical liberalism'[40] is that it seems to offer some account and
consideration of what is significant in social relationships — in particular, the issue of distinctive social membership and identification. While
Tawney recognised the pull of particular community attachments —
and, indeed, their basis in human characteristics and needs — he seemed
to regard such attachments as retrogressive. Of his proposals for greater
European political and economic integration, for example, he acknowledged regretfully that 'Reason is on its side: but the natural human
egotisms of interest and emotion, of locality, class and occupation, or
regional loyalties and national pride, will rally to resist it.'[41] Tawney
thus wished to embrace some aspects of the communitarian ideal but
not others. His communitarianism sought to provide a moral alternative
to liberalism which was, nevertheless, equally ecumenical.

The problems faced by liberalism in reconciling its universal ideals
with the particularism of community can be well illustrated by J.S. Mill.
He shares some of the ideals associated with communitarians but is
strenuously opposed to others. At the same time, he launched a brilliant
onslaught on the uses of the term 'nature' in philosophy.[42] Nevertheless,
Mill illustrates one important approach to the issue.

Mill asserts that all that is valuable in natural man are his capacities.
Virtue has not been attained by obedience to instinct but by 'victory
over instinct'.[43] Mill insists that one's character is not entirely formed
for one but can be formed by the individual. Character is shaped by
circumstances but amongst those circumstances is the individual's desire
to shape his or her character.[44] The feeling of moral freedom consists
of the feeling that one can mould one's character if one wishes or, at

the least, that when one's character and one's wishes come into conflict in a particular instance it will be possible for one's wishes to prevail.[45] A virtuous person will be one who cultivates his or her character by amending nature rather than following it.[46]

One of the prime concerns Mill then had for political institutions was to examine what type of organisation would most effectively promote self-culture. This was not to be understood in individualistic terms since for Mill an essential aspect of the formation of character was familiarisation with the aspirations and interests of other human beings in all their diversity. For this there were few substitutes for experience acquired through participation in political processes and organisations. Decentralisation of government permitted more citizens to engage in responsible decision-making. At the local level, persons were more likely to be knowledgeable and to gain a clearer understanding of the interests of others. A centralised system would minimise the opportunities for political education through experience.[47]

So far Mill shares the widespread preference for smaller political units with communitarians. In another crucial respect, however, Mill resisted communitarian ideals. Whilst he believed that participation would help to integrate the citizen into the political system, he was averse to any tendency to produce a tightly-knit community to which the individual would be mentally subordinate. Mill saw the value of co-operating in a common enterprise as training responsibility and as developing the wide range of qualities of which human beings were capable. He recognised that nationality was a factor integrating both countries and minorities but like many liberals, he appears uneasy with any suggestion that community might rightly cultivate distinct and exclusive characteristics. It is better for a member of a minority such as a Breton, a Basque, a Welshman or a Scottish Highlander to benefit through his integration into French or British citizenship than:

> to sulk on his own rocks, the half-savage relic of past times, revolving in his own little mental orbit, without participation or interest in the general movement of the world.[48]

For Mill, therefore, community is not a value in itself but instrumental in establishing the circumstances in which human character may be formed in the diversity of which it is capable. By contrast, Rousseau with a somewhat similar notion of participation as an educative process regards a closely-knit community as an educative factor in itself, moulding the general will. The virtuous person may superficially be like Mill's characterful individual in 'thinking his own thoughts' but these thoughts will have themselves received the impression of the habits and customs of the community.

Each of the views of the relationship between human nature and community just discussed assumes them to be basically compatible, though each differs about the manner and ease with which they are reconciled. There are, however, very significant critics of the aspiration to community who challenge the essential claim to compatibility. Community may be perhaps a laudable goal but it is one that runs counter to fundamental tendencies in human nature. Human beings are not by nature communal animals. Association must instead arise from some voluntary act or through process of invention.

Stronger and weaker versions of this view may be detected. The strongest holds that mankind is by nature sinful. The sins of pride and envy throw human beings into contention with one another. The major source of this theme in western thought is St Augustine. God created man good but also created him with free will. The will was free to turn either toward or away from God. Evil is, therefore, contrary to nature in the sense that it is a misdirection of the will. It is also part of human nature in the sense that the will is itself a creation of God.[49] The conflict amongst men engendered by the misdirection of the will can be attenuated by earthly cities which can provide a degree of order. To the extent that this order conforms to the universal order laid down for men by God, a state will possess also an element of justice. It cannot, however, achieve true justice. Equally, the state cannot offer full society or fellowship. Genuine fellowship occurs only where a people is united by a common agreement as to what is right and just. This is in the City of God where not only do all citizens share a common love of God as their ruler but where there is also, through God, a bond of community amongst themselves.[50] The peace of the City of God arises from a union of the hearts of all its citizens in a common object:

There shall be peace made pure in the sons of God, since God shall be all in all. We shall have God as our common object of vision, God as our common possession, God as our common peace.[51]

Community in a real sense, therefore, is possible only for those, drawn from all nations and speaking all languages, who by the gift of grace can become citizens of the City of God.

Although Hobbes has been described as a secular Augustine he appears to offer still less prospect for community. The competitive elements in human nature, as Hobbes hypothesises it, are simply that. They are not to be regarded as particularly sinful but as features of humanity which must be taken into account by the philosopher and the statesman. In the Will and Artifice tradition order has to be created out of chaos by voluntary act. According to the opening sentence of *Leviathan* the creation by man of the state, the political universe, is modelled on the creation of the world by God.

> Nature, the art whereby God hath made and governs the world, is by the *art* of man, as in many things, so in this also imitated, that it can make an artificial animal.[52]

An almost fatal mixture of pride, fear, equality and limited resources ensures that no sense of trust and community can develop naturally: '. . . men have no pleasure, but on the contrary a great deal of grief, in keeping company . . .'[53] Instead of a natural tendency to mutual support each will seek to extract from others the evaluation that he sets on his own status and power.

Hobbes anticipates the objections of those who believe that man is by nature both a social and a political animal. 'It may seem strange to some man, that has not well weighed these things, that nature should thus dissociate . . .'[54]

Those who are not convinced by the arguments Hobbes has mounted on the basis of his hypotheses concerning nature are offered the evidence of experience. Men who lock their doors and chests and protect themselves when on journeys are thereby admitting the continuing existence of anti-social man who will emerge once the conditions of an extraneous civilised existence are stripped away. The only unity an aggregation of individuals can possess is as a result of the decision to combine in a commonwealth under a sovereign respresentative. A commonwealth does not have a natural unity but one arising from the status of the sovereign's will as representing the will of individuals. The virtues expected of subjects in their dealings with one another such as equity or the avoidance of pride and arrogance may be those a communitarian would also advocate. But although enjoined by natural law it is within the confines of the artificially established political world that they can be put into practice. They are the modes of behaviour which rational self-preferring persons would come to adopt once the conditions for their pursuit are instituted. The artificial chains of law[55] hold them together as long as sanctions exist to deter them from the easy and tempting act of breaking the chains. The qualities of community are not necessary to such ordered and mutually beneficial relationships. The benefits of companionship only flourish in the ordered artificial world. Communities exist as, and are defined as, lawful assemblies with authority over their communicants to include or to excommunicate to the extent that the sovereign permits.[56] Only in this limited sense which equates community with association can a commonwealth be described as a community. Hobbes might be regarded as the converse of Kropotkin in that artifice harnesses certain natural propensities, such as fear, in order to remedy the dissociating effects of nature.

For a weaker version of the view that man is not a communal animal we may turn to Hume. In the conclusion of Book I of the *Treatise* Hume declared that 'Human Nature is the only science of man; and yet has been hitherto the most neglected.'[57] Hume was, famously, a companionable man and one who had no time for the solitary and monkish virtues. However, much as he admired an open disposition, Hume did not believe that a natural fellow-feeling could extend far amongst human beings. Mankind was characterised by 'selfishness and confin'd generosity'.[58]

The generosity extended to friends and above all to family, where the distinctions of mine and thine so central to society disappear. The self-centredness of Hobbesian man is remote from reality but so is the community-mindedness of Plato's guardians. Partiality to self and to friends and relations coincides with the scarcity of resources and the ease by which they can be transferred from one person to another. Human beings are naturally tempted to favour themselves in any distribution or redistribution of resources. This is something which cannot be rectified in or by nature.[59] Human nature cannot be changed. The remedy is 'not to be deriv'd from nature, but from artifice' whereby a group of persons — a government — is instituted with the duty and the interest to establish rules of justice amongst those who have come together to ensure the stability of possessions and their transfer.

As with Hobbes, no community exists in nature. Hume does suggest that a sense of community may be cultivated. There is a quality of sympathy amongst human beings which may be encouraged by contiguity and frequency of interaction. Regularity of communication between people tends to result in shared opinions. The force of opinion (which plays such a major part in the writings of eighteenth-century philosophers from Locke onward) exerts its pressure on those who are concerned to earn a good reputation amongst their fellows. It is this, rather than Montesquieu's climatic factors, which leads to the formation of a stable national character where 'even the proudest and most surly take a tincture from their countrymen and acquaintance'.[60] The regularity and uniformity with which different social situations produce differences of sentiments (or even differences in physique in the case of the day-labourer and the 'man of quality') indicates that they proceed from necessary and uniform principles of human nature.[61]

It is for these reasons that a science of politics was in principle possible. The social situations themselves, including the formation of national character, will very largely be the outcome of artifice, ranging from the invention of government itself to the impact of laws and political institutions on habits and opinion. Although the rules of justice are artificial rather than natural this is not to say, in another sense of the term, that they are unnatural. They are invented, but the invention is necessary and in that sense natural.[62] Community is not necessary to the existence of human society whilst the rules of justice, civil association, are. Moreover, there is nothing to indicate that Hume believed that a more tightly-knit society with a distinctive national character was in itself something to be admired. Some were to be admired, particularly for certain republican virtues, others to be condemned. Nor could one character be more in accord with human nature than another. Each was to be explained by a complex of causal chains which linked human nature to such factors as the example of leaders, the economic circumstances of the society, the provision of manufactures, or the institution of social ranks. In Hume's science of politics 'natural and moral evidence cement together'.[63]

Community for Augustine is a Christian's hope for the future. For Hobbes it is either a sad fantasy or else is reduced to so attenuated a legal form as to drain it of much of its moral force and its emotional appeal. Even for the clubbable Hume it is not a necessary feature of human life but one which may develop in certain conditions either for good or ill. To find an uninhibited attack on community one needs to turn to that great admirer of Hume, Hayek. He rejects the distinction between natural and artificial as it comes down from the Greeks whilst praising Hume for recognising that the category of phenomena which should concern the social sciences was that which was the result of human action but not of human design and, therefore, partook of both the natural and the artificial.[64] Two kinds of order may exist in human affairs. An arranged order presupposes an agreed set of goals and an organisation to achieve them — a hierarchy, a relation of command and obedience. A spontaneous order is a structure of relationships which grows up between persons who have individual purposes most of which are unknown to one another. The order emerges 'naturally' from the unhampered choices (artifices) of individuals. A spontaneous order is in essence a free order. It does require some positive action, however, to maintain such an order. The rules of a spontaneous order must be independent of the purposes of individuals or classes but equally and impartially facilitate the achievement of those purposes.

Hayek's profound conviction is that the possibility that human beings could live in peace and prosperity according to the rules of a spontaneous order was 'perhaps the greatest discovery mankind ever made'.[65] Since the rules must apply to the unknown purposes of unknown individuals they are in principle universal or tending to universality. Hayek regards these abstract rules as incompatible with the demands of lesser groups, such as communities are often conceived, which have concrete purposes. The recognition of abstract rules is a moral and intellectual achievement freeing human beings from the repressive effects of shared, and usually enforced, purposes. The decline of the small group with its personal ties, shared sentiments and sense of coherence is the price that has to be paid for the Great Society. The Rousseauesque nostalgia for that community is variously described as wallowing 'in the emotion inherited from the tribal society', as a failure of intellectual and moral maturity, as based on 'unreflected "natural" emotions deeply grounded on milennia of life in the small horde', as 'the altruistic craving for visible common purposes'.[66] The Great Society cannot be grounded on such sentiments as love which are the highest virtue of the small group. The efforts to reconcile plurality and individual liberty with the unity and cohesion of community which have, as we have seen, exercised communitarian writers are dismissed by Hayek as misguided. Universality and community cannot be combined. There is no agreed hierarchy of values, even though the idea that it would be a good thing is 'deeply founded in the history of the human race'. Such an idea is the greatest obstacle to the achievement of the unknown and unknowable variety of human objectives.

> A Great Society has nothing to do with, and is in fact irreconcilable with 'solidarity' in the true sense of unitedness in the pursuit of known common goals.[67]

Clearly Hayek would not assert that community was incompatible with human nature. One might even say that anything which human beings have done must be consistent with their nature. Indeed, Hayek goes further and recognises that there is a deep instinct in people to wish for the warmth and certainty of community. But it is an instinct which must be resisted however difficult it may be to set aside the effects of 'hundreds of thousands of years'. The abstract rules of conduct which underpin the Open Society, i.e. market society, are difficult to grasp and require intellectual effort. Yet they also reflect a view of humanity – that human beings are equal and that the obligation to treat them impartially applies to 'not only the members of our tribe but persons of ever wider circles and ultimately all men'.[68] The principle of universalisability is one which is gradually learned and its acquisition is the badge of civilisation.

Whilst J.S. Mill's position is uneasily balanced between his communitarian sympathies and his belief in universal liberal principles, Hayek is driven in one clear direction by what he regards as the logic of the liberal case. The force of Hayek's attack on communitarian thought lies partly in its insistence that values which some communitarians wish to uphold, such as impartiality, equality and individual autonomy are incompatible with the exclusivity and prior commitment to fellow members which are, arguably, part of the definition of community. One response to such criticisms is to argue against the conception of human beings Hayek puts forward. Persons who strip away all the vestiges of community to step forward as 'man' are, it is alleged, unrecognisable as part of the human species. Such a person lacks any identity. Alasdair MacIntyre has recently proposed that the self is united 'by a narrative which links birth to life to death'.[69] Attempts, such as by Sartre, to separate the individual and his or her roles destroys the possibility of understanding the unity of a person's life and also prevents one from recognising the authentic self displayed in a variety of roles. The integrity of the self consists, instead, only in denying the authenticity of social roles.

For MacIntyre, the self is not prior to roles but is shaped by roles. The self is to be understood in its settings, by which MacIntyre means not only such roles as being a doctor or wife or mother but the wider community in which such a person shares her life. People live their lives 'in the light of certain conceptions of a possible shared future'.[70] In MacIntyre's teleological philosophy present actions are informed by images of future goals which are never entirely particular to oneself but are grounded in concrete settings.

> I belong to this clan, that tribe, this nation. Hence what is good for me has to be the good for one who inhabits these roles. As such, I inherit from the past of my family, my city, my tribe, my nation, a

variety of debts, inheritance, rightful expectations and obligations. These constitute the given of my life, my moral starting point. This is in part what gives my life its own moral particularity.[71]

This means that one cannot simply choose what one is to be.[72] MacIntyre connects the idea of the self to the idea of community in a manner not entirely dissimilar to that of Walzer: '. . . the story of my life is always embedded in the story of those communities from which I derive my identity . . .'[73]

It is not, however, clear how strong a sense of community is being invoked. Nor is it certain that some individualistic thinkers could not accommodate MacIntyre's argument without excessive discomfort.[74] MacIntyre does not have in mind a community which might exercise a hegemonic domination over the individual self such that the member totally identifies with its values. A Rousseauean community would ideally have educated its citizens so thoroughly in its customs and manners that their very choices would have been moulded in such a way as to reinforce community identity.[75] MacIntyre's community is more of a home base from which the individual self will set out.

> . . . the fact that the self has to find its moral identity in and through its membership in communities such as those of the family, the neighbourhood, the city and the tribe does not entail that the self has to accept the moral *limitations* of the particularity of those forms of community.[76]

Whilst MacIntyre certainly wishes to insist that those who seek to guide themselves entirely by universalisable maxims deny some essential aspect of their individuality, it is far less certain how positive a role community plays in the formation of personal identity or, indeed, whether it is a genuine notion of community that he is employing. Is he saying anything more than that people 'take a tincture from their countrymen', as even Hume insisted? MacIntyre specifically contrasts his own community-embedded account of personal identity with those of Locke and Hume which are couched in terms of the continuity of psychological states.

Yet even Locke insisted that human beings could not be totally abstracted from the moral relations that are established in their society, nor should they ignore the debt which they owe to those who have built up the stock of human knowledge. However much men should strive to express their individuality, personality will still bear an imprint or 'tincture' (as Locke also says) of society. A person who lacked such an imprint would be either a God or a beast.

It seems that a number of difficulties beset attempts to root community in human nature. Perhaps the only views which emerge as relatively uncontentious are the rather weak claims (a) that human beings have the *capacity* for the closeness and co-operation characteristic of the most communal form of social life; or (b) that they have a need for some form of common life in and through which they may develop and fulfil other socially derived and defined needs. The first of the formulations retains a fairly strong conception of community but reduces the 'naturalistic' claim to the trivial one that anything human beings have done at some stage of their history must have been something they were capable of doing. Or, as Mill puts it: 'Nature, then, in its simplest acceptation, is a collective name for all facts, actual and possible.'[77] Not only is this trivial, but it implies that community has a status no different from anti-communitarian social forms which people have also shown themselves eminently capable of developing. The second formulation makes a stronger claim for human nature, but at the cost of draining community of any positive *communal* content. At the same time, Mill, Tawney and Hayek remind us, albeit in very different ways, that to say that something is natural is not necessarily to say either that it is good or that it is impervious to human modification. Thus, Tawney claims that we have communal dispositions and that they *should* be expressed in and cultivated through institutional social and political forms. Hayek, on the other hand, whilst recognising some communal instinct, argues for its suppression — or, perhaps, transcendence — in the greater cause of liberty.

Finally, even those who agree on the basic human propensity or need for communal attachment have very different conceptions of its desirable social expression. They differ on the appropriate level and intensity of communal commitment. There are few who believe that the intense warmth of fellowship attaches in fact to humanity as such, and some who suggest that it never can do except in the most unusual circumstances of isolation when one is least at home and at ease in one's surroundings. As David Hume put it.

We love company in general; but 'tis as we love any other amusement. An *Englishman* in *Italy* is a friend: A *European* in China; and perhaps a man wou'd be belov'd as such, were we to meet him in the moon.[78]

Notes

1. See Geraint Parry, 'Tradition, Community and Self-Determination', *British Journal of Political Science*, vol. 12 (1982), pp. 399-419. See also the discussion of Rousseau by Barnard and Vernon, 'Pluralism, Participation, Politics', *Political Theory*, May 1975, pp. 180-97.

2. That the link between need on the one hand and capacity and disposition on the other is a contingent one is most clearly illuminated by Glenn Tinder's recent analysis of community. Tinder proceeds from the observation that community has been a strikingly persistent social ideal, with an appeal that crosses all ideological boundaries: 'Every major historical period has responded to the lure of community by creating a simulation and myth of community.' In offering the promise of an authentic and non-alienated social existence, community answers to a fundamental human 'longing'. Yet if the communal ideal is 'an imperative of human nature' it is also precluded by it: 'Man is not capable of community.' The need for community, then, exists in direct opposition to human capacities; community, Tinder concludes, is a 'tragic ideal'.

3. Michael Taylor, *Community, Anarchy and Liberty* (Cambridge, Cambridge University Press, 1982), p. 25.

4. Martin Miller, *Kropotkin* (Chicago, University of Chicago Press, 1976), p. 182.

5. D.B. Clark, 'The Concept of Community: A Re-examination', *Sociological Review*, 21 (1973), pp. 403-4.

6. Alan Ritter, *Anarchism: A Theoretical Analysis* (Cambridge, Cambridge University Press, 1980), p. 27.

7. See Raymond Plant, 'Community: Concept, Conception and Ideology', *Politics and Society*, vol. 8, no. 1 (1978), pp. 79-107 and C. McCulloch, 'The Problem of Fellowship in Communitarian Theory: William Morris and Peter Kropotkin', *Political Studies* XXXII, 3 Sept., 1984, pp. 437-50.

8. Glenn Tinder, *Community: Reflections on a Tragic Ideal* (Baton Rouge, Louisiana State University Press, 1980), p. 5.

9. Ritter, *Anarchism*, p. 30.

10. David Miller, 'Kropotkin', *Government and Opposition*, vol. 18 (1973), p. 334.

11. Peter Kropotkin, 'Law and Authority' in R.N. Baldwin (ed.), *Kropotkin's Revolutionary Pamphlets* (New York, Dover Publications, 1970), p. 203.

12. Ibid (emphasis added).

13. David Miller, *Social Justice* (Oxford, Oxford University Press, 1978), p. 231.

14. Miller, 'Kropotkin', *Government and Opposition*, vol. 18, p. 334.

15. Erich Fromm, *The Sane Society* (London, Routledge and Kegan Paul, 1955), p. 19.

16. A.H. Maslow, *Motivation and Personality* (New York, Harper and Row, 1970) (2nd edn.), p. 83.

17. Ibid., p. 82.

18. Ibid., p. 85.

19. Ibid., p. 44.

20. Ibid., pp. 43-4.

21. Ibid., p. 44.

22. Miller, *Social Justice*, p. 236. For a further discussion of this issue, see C. McCulloch, 'The Problem of Fellowship in Communitarian Theory: William Morris and Peter Kropotkin', *Political Studies* XXXII.

23. A.H. Maslow, *Toward a Psychology of Being* (Princeton, N.J., D. Van Nostrand Co. Inc., 1968) (2nd edn.), p. 4.

24. Raymond Plant, *Community and Ideology* (London, Routledge and Kegan Paul, 1974), pp. 79-84. R. Plant *et al.*, *Political Philosophy and Social Welfare* (London, Routledge and Kegan Paul, 1980), ch. 10.

25. Michael Walzer, *Spheres of Justice* (Oxford, Martin Robertson, 1983), p. 31.

26. Ibid., p. 31.

27. Ibid., p. 65.

28. Ibid., p. 42.

29. Ibid., p. 62.

30. See Geraint Parry, 'Tradition, Community and Self-Determination', *British Journal of Political Science*, vol. 12 (1982). The implications of boundaries and membership have surfaced again in a world which has seen both the continued growth of the international economy and a resurgence of nationalism and ethnicity and displacement of populations as a result of civil unrest. See Bruce Ackerman, *Social Justice in the Liberal State* (New Haven, Yale University Press, 1980), ch. 3; P. Brown and J. Shue (eds.), *Boundaries: National Autonomy and Its Limits* (Totowa, N.J., Rowman and Littlefield, 1981).

31. Walzer, *Spheres of Justice*, p. 48.

32. Ibid., pp. 8, 26, 79.

33. Ibid., p. 83. See also R. Plant, 'Community: Concept, Conception and Ideology', *Politics and Society*, vol. 8. no. 1 (1978).

34. Ibid., pp. 312-4.

35. M. Oakeshott, *On Human Conduct* (Oxford, Oxford University Press, 1975), chs. II and III.

36. Walzer, *Spheres of Justice*, p. 290.

37. R.M. Tawney, *The Acquisitive Society* (London, Bell and Sons, 1945), p. 222.

38. R. Terrill, *R H. Tawney and His Times* (Cambridge, Massachusetts, Harvard University Press, 1973), p. 218.

39. R.H. Tawney, *The Western Political Tradition*, Burge Memorial Trust Lecture (SCM Press, 1949), p. 12.

40. Ibid., p. 23.

41. Ibid., p. 24.

42. J.S. Mill, 'Nature' originally published in 1874. Citations to reprint in M. Lerner (ed.), *Essential Works of J.S. Mill* (New York, Bantam Books, 1969).

43. Ibid., p. 390.

44. J.S. Mill, *A System of Logic*, Eighth edition (London, Longmans, 1906), Book VI, ch. II. para. 3, pp. 550 1.

45. Ibid.

46. Mill, 'Nature' in Lerner, *Essential Works*, p. 395.

47. See the discussion by R.J. Halliday, *John Stuart Mill* (London, Allen and Unwin, 1976), ch. IV.

48. J.S. Mill, *Representative Government* (London, Everyman, 1972), pp. 363-4.

49. St. Augustine, *City of God*, Book XIV, ch. II.

50. Ibid., Book XIX, chs. 17, 23, 24.

51. *Enarrationes in Psalmos*, LXXXIV, 10; *Corpus Christianorum* Series Latina, XXXIX, p. 1170, cited by H. Deane, *The Political and Social Ideas of St Augustine* (New York, Columbia University Press, 1963), p. 99.

52. Hobbes, *Leviathan*, Introduction (Oakeshott, ed.) (Oxford, Blackwell), p. 5.

53. Ibid., ch. 13, p. 81.

54. Ibid., p. 82.

55. Ibid., ch. 21, p. 138.

56. Ibid., ch. 42, p. 335.

57. *A Treatise of Human Nature*, Book I, pt. IV, sect. VII, (Selby-Bigge ed.) (Oxford, Oxford University Press, 1888), p. 273.

58. Ibid., Book III, pt. II, sect. II, pp. 498-9.

59. Ibid., p. 488.

60. Ibid., Book II, pt. I, sect. XI, p. 317.

61. Ibid., Book II, pt. III, sect. I, pp. 481-2.

62. Ibid., Book III, pt. II, sect. I, p. 484.

63. Ibid., Book II, pt. III, sect. I, p. 406.

64. F.A. Hayek, *Law, Legislation and Liberty*, vol. I (London, Routledge, 1973), pp. 20-1.

65. Ibid., vol. 2 (London, Routledge, 1976), p. 136.

66. Ibid., pp. 146-50.

67. Ibid., p. 111.

68. Ibid., p. 146.

69. Alasdair MacIntyre, *After Virtue* (London, Duckworth, 1981), p. 191.

70. Ibid., p. 200.

71. Ibid., pp. 204-5.

72. Ibid., p. 206.

73. Ibid., p. 205.

74. See on this general point, but without reference to MacIntyre, S.I. Benn, 'Individuality, Autonomy and Community' in E. Kamenka (ed.), *Community as a Social Ideal* (London, Arnold, 1982), pp. 43-62, especially p. 50.

75. See Parry, 'Tradition, Community and Self-Determination', *British Journal of Political Science*, vol. 12 (1982).

76. MacIntyre, *After Virtue*, p. 205.

77. Mill, Nature', p. 369.

78. David Hume, *A Treatise of Human Nature*, Book III, pt. II, sect. I, p. 482.

10 FREDERICK M. BARNARD: A BIBLIOGRAPHY

Janet Menard

Explanatory Note

Books, articles, review articles and chapters in books are listed chronologically according to the year of publication. Book reviews are arranged alphabetically according to the name of the author of the book. Review articles are listed twice, in the section dealing with articles and as book reviews under the name of the author of the book. In the latter instance, the title of the review article directly follows the title of the book.

Books

Zwischen Aufklärung und Politischer Romantik (Berlin, Erich Schmidt Verlag, 1964), p. 218.

Herder's Social and Political Thought (Oxford, Oxford University Press, 1965) p. xv, p. 177.

Second edition with revisions (Oxford, Oxford University Press, 1967), p. xv, p. 211.

Herder on Social and Political Culture (Cambridge, Cambridge University Press, 1969), p. xii, p. 342.

Excerpts included in:

Baumer, Franklin Le Van *Main Currents of Western Thought*. (rev. edn. New York, Knopf, 1978).

Hesse, Marta Gudrun *Approaches to Teaching Foreign Languages* (Amsterdam, North Holland Pub. Co., 1975).

Richardson, Robert D. *The Rise of Modern Mythology*, 1680-1860 (Bloomington, Indiana University Press, 1972)

Socialism with a Human Face: Slogan and Substance (Saskatoon, University of Saskatchewan Press for Public Lecture Series, 1973), p. 15.

Articles, Review Articles and Chapters in Books

'The Hebrews and Herder's Political Creed', *Modern Language Review*, LIV, 1959, pp. 533-46

'Education for Management Conceived as a Study of Industrial Ecology', *Vocational Aspect*, LVI, 1963, pp. 22-6

'Herder's Treatment of Causation and Continuity in History', *Journal of the History of Ideas*, XXIV, 1963, pp. 197-212.

'Christian Thomasius: Enlightenment and Bureaucracy', *American Political Science Review*, LIX, 1965, pp. 430-8.

'Herder and Israel', *Jewish Social Studies*, XXVIII, 1966, pp. 25-33.

'Metaphors, Laments, and the Organic Community', *Canadian Journal of Economics and Political Science*, XXXII, 1966, pp. 281-301.

'Bachofen', *Encyclopedia of Philosophy* (New York, 1967).

'Morgan', *Encyclopedia of Philosophy* (New York, 1967).

'Reinhold', *Encyclopedia of Philosophy* (New York, 1967).

'Spinozism', *Encyclopedia of Philosophy* (New York, 1967).

'Sumner', *Encyclopedia of Philosophy* (New York, 1967).

'Weber', *Encyclopedia of Philosophy* (New York, 1967).

'Culture and Political Development', *American Political Science Review*, LXIII, 1969, pp. 379-97.

'The Practical Philosophy of Christian Thomasius', *Journal of the History of Ideas*, XXXII, 1971, pp. 221-46.

'Between Opposition and Political Opposition', *Canadian Journal of Political Science*, V, 1972, pp. 533-51.

'Culture and Civilization in Modern Times', *Dictionary of the History of Ideas* (New York, 1973).

'Pluralism, Participation, and Politics', (with Richard Vernon) *Political Theory*, III, 1975, pp. 180-97.

'Sensibility, Self-Understanding and Self-Redemption', *Canadian Journal of Political and Social Theory*, I, 1977, pp. 109-19.

'Infinity and Finality: Hannah Arendt on Politics and Truth', *Canadian Journal of Political and Social Theory*, I, 1977, pp. 29-57.

'Socialist Pluralism and Pluralist Socialism', (with Richard Vernon) *Political Studies*, XXV, 1977, pp. 474-90.

'The Prague Spring and Masaryk's Humanism', *East Central Europe*, V, 1978, pp. 215-31.

'Marriage for Socialism: Emotions and Notions', *Canadian Journal of Political and Social Theory*, III, 1979, pp. 130-9.

'Natural Growth and Purposive Development: Vico and Herder', *History and Theory*, XVIII, 1979, pp. 16-36.

'Evaluation of Revolutions' in Harold Johnson (ed.), *Revolutions, Systems, and Theories* (Dordrecht, D. Reidel Publishing Co., 1979), pp. 11-19.

'Nationality, Humanity, and the Hebraic Spirit: Heine and Herder', in Raymond Immerwahr and Hanna Spencer (eds.), *Heinrich Heine: Dimensionen seines Wirkens* (Bonn, Bouvier, 1979), pp. 56-67.

'Particularity, Universality, and the Hebraic Spirit', *Jewish Social Studies*, XLIII, 1981, pp. 121-36.

'Accounting for Actions: Causality and Teleology', *History and Theory*, XX, 1981, pp. 291-312.

'T.G. Masaryk in Retrospect: From Thought to Actuality', *East Central Europe*, IX, 1982, pp. 162-7.

'National Culture and Political Legitimacy: Herder and Rousseau', in Toivo Miljan (ed.), *Culture and Legitimacy* (Waterloo, Wilfred Laurier University Printing Services for the Fifth Annual Southwest Ontario Comparative Politics Conference, 1982), pp. 1-41.

'Electoral Confrontation under Socialism', I, *Kosmas, Journal of Czechoslovak and Central European Studies*, I, 1982, pp. 35-47.

'Electoral Confrontation under Socialism', II, *Kosmas, Journal of Czechoslovak and Central European Studies*, I, 1982, pp. 15-26.

'Electoral Confrontation under Socialism', III, *Kosmas, Journal of Czechoslovak and Central European Studies*, II, 1983, pp. 15-31.

'Thomasius, Kant and Herder', *Deutsche Vierteljahrs Schrift für Literaturwissenschaft und Geistesgeschichte*, LVII, 1983 pp. 278-97.

'Self-Direction: Thomasius, Kant and Herder', *Political Theory*, XI, 1983, pp. 343-68.

'Recovering Politics for Socialism: Two Responses to the Language of Community' (with Richard Vernon), *Canadian Journal of Political Science*, XVI, 1983, pp. 717-37.

'National Culture and Political Legitimacy: Herder and Rousseau', *Journal of the History of Ideas*, XLIV, 1983, pp. 231-53.

'Patriotism and Citizenship in Rousseau', *The Review of Politics*, XLVI, 1984, pp. 244-65.

'Actions, Reasons and Political Ideology', in J.M. Porter (ed.), *Sophia and Praxis: The Boundaries of Politics*, (Chatham, Chatham House, 1984), pp. 35-64.

'Will and Political Rationality in Rousseau', *Political Studies*, XXXII, 1984, pp. 369-84.

'Socialism, Politics and Citizenship: Reflections on a Czech Thought-Experiment', *East Central Europe*, in press.

Book Reviews

Bell, D.V.J., *Power, Influence, and Authority: An Essay in Political Linguistics* (*Canadian Journal of Political Science*, IX, 1976).

Berlin, I., *Vico and Herder* ('Sensibility, Self-Understanding, and Self-Redemption', *Canadian Journal of Political and Social Theory*, I, 1977).

Čapek, M. and Hrubý, K. (eds.), *T.G. Masaryk in Perspective: Comments and Criticisms* ('T.G. Masaryk in Retrospect: From Thought to Actuality', *East Central Europe*, IX, 1982).

Cooper, B., *Merleau-Ponty and Marxism: From Terror to Reform* (*Canadian Journal of Political Science*, XIII, 1980).

Fishkin, J.S., *Tyranny and Legitimacy: A Critique of Political Theories* (*Canadian Journal of Political Science*, XIV, 1981).

Funda, O.A., *Thomas Garrigue Masaryk, Sein philosophisches, religiöses und politisches Denken* (*East Central Europe*, VIII, 1981).

Gildin, H., *Rousseau's Social Contract: the Design of the Argument* (*Canadian Journal of Political Science*, XVII, 1984).

Gillespie, M.A., *Hegel and Heidigger on the Ground of History* (*Canadian Journal of Political Science*, in press).

Goodin, R.T., *Manipulatory Politics* (*Philosophy of the Social Sciences*, XIII, 1983).

Hall, C.M., *The Sociology of Pierre-Joseph Proudhon 1809-1865* (*Canadian Journal of Political Science*, V, 1972).

Hajek, H.J., *T.G. Masaryk Revisited: A Critical Assessment*, (*The Slavic Review*, XLIII, 1984).

Laslett, P. and Fishkin, J. (eds.), *Philosophy, Politics and Society: Fifth Series* (*Canadian of Political Science*, XIV, 1981).

Mackenzie, N. (ed.), *The Letters of Sidney and Beatrice Webb* ('Marriage for Socialism: Emotions and Notions', *Canadian Journal of Political and Social Theory*, III, 1979).

Misch, J., *Die politische Philosophie Ludwig Woltmanns. Im Spannungsfeld von Kantianismus* (*Journal of the History of Philosophy*, XVI, 1978).

Nauen, F.G. *Revolution, Idealism and Human Freedom: Schelling, Hölderlin and Hegel and the Crisis of Early German Idealism* (*Canadian Journal of History*, VIII, 1973).

Pelczynski, Z.A. (ed.), *Hegel's Political Philosophy: Problems and Perspectives* (*Canadian Journal of Political Science*, VI, 1973).

Pupi, A., *La formazione della filosofia de K.L. Reinhold 1784-94* (*Journal of the History of Philosophy*, VIII, 1970).

Regin, D., *Freedom and Dignity: the Historical and Philosophical Thought of Schiller* (*Canadian Journal of History*, I, 1966).

Saner, S., *Kant's Political Thought: Its Origins and Development* (*Canadian Journal of Political Science*, VII, 1974).

Schorske, C.E., *Fin-de-Siècle Vienna. Politics and Culture East Central Europe*, VII, 1980).

Shillinglaw, D.B. (ed.), *The Lectures of Professor T.G. Masaryk at the University of Chicago, Summer 1902* (*East Central Europe*, VII, 1980).

Szporluk, R., *The Political Thought of Thomas G. Masaryk* ('T.G. Masaryk in Retrospect: From Thought to Actuality', *East Central Europe*, IX, 1982).

Tinder, G., *Tolerance: Toward a New Civility* (*Canadian Journal of Political Science*, X, 1977).

White, H., *Metahistory: The Historical Imagination in Nineteenth Century Europe*, (*Canadian Journal of Political Science*, IX, 1976).

INDEX

DATE DUE
